SELECTED WRITINGS

T.E. HULME was born in Staffordshire in 1883, and educated at high school in Newcastle-under-Lyme and at St John's College, Cambridge. After working in Canada as a labourer and teaching English in Brussels, in 1908 Hulme joined the 'Poets' Club', a discussion group, for which he wrote 'A Lecture on Modern Poetry' in 1908. Of the six poems Hulme published in his lifetime, four appeared in Poets' Club anthologies in 1909. In 1909 he left the Poets' Club and formed a group of poets that included Ezra Pound, which he called the 'Secession Club'. He began lecturing on the French philosopher Henri Bergson at this time, going on to write around twenty articles on his work. Between 1912 and 1913 Hulme lived in Berlin, becoming increasingly involved with art criticism after his return to England. On the outbreak of war in 1914, he enlisted as a private. He continued to write and publish on art, politics and philosophy, arguing against pacificism. He was killed in Flanders in 1917.

PATRICK MCGUINNESS is a Fellow of St Anne's College, Oxford, where he lectures in French. In 1998 he won an Eric Gregory award for poetry from the Society of Authors, and his poems and translations have appeared in *The Independent*, the *London Review of Books*, *Picador New Writing*, *Poèsie 2002*, *PN Review*, *Poetry Wales* and *Leviathan*. A selection of his poetry appears in *New Poetries II* (Carcanet, 1999). His books include *Maurice Maeterlinck and the Making of Modern Theatre* (OUP, 2000), *Symbolism, Decadence and the fin de siècle*, an edition of Laura Riding and Robert Graves, *A Survey of Modernist Poetry* (Carcanet, 2002) and an anthology of Symbolist poetry (Les Belles Lettres, 2001). He is the translator of Mallarmé's *For Anatole's Tomb* in the Fyfield*Books* series.

Fyfield*Books* aim to make available some of the great classics of British and European literature in clear, affordable formats, and to restore often neglected writers to their place in literary tradition.

Fyfield*Books* take their name from the Fyfield elm in Matthew Arnold's 'Scholar Gypsy' and 'Thyrsis'. The tree stood not far from the village where the series was originally devised in 1971.

> *Roam on! The light we sought is shining still.*
> *Dost thou ask proof? Our tree yet crowns the hill,*
> *Our Scholar travels yet the loved hill-side*

from 'Thyrsis'

T.E. HULME

Selected Writings

Edited with an introduction by
PATRICK McGUINNESS

Fyfield*Books*

CARCANET

First published in Great Britain in 1998 by
Carcanet Press Limited
Alliance House
Cross Street
Manchester M2 7AQ

This impression 2003

A CIP catalogue record for this book is available from the British Library
ISBN 1 85754 722 5

The publisher acknowledges financial assistance from Arts Council England

Printed and bound in England by SRP Ltd, Exeter

Contents

Plates (following p. 148):
The Rock Drill, by Jacob Epstein (*The New Age*, 25 December 1913)
Chinnereth, by David Bomberg (*The New Age*, 2 April 1914)
Study, by William Roberts (*The New Age*, 16 April 1914)
The Chauffeur, by C.R.W. Nevinson (*The New Age*, 30 April 1914)
The Farmyard, by Edward Wadsworth (*The New Age*, 30 April 1914)

Introduction

I

It is seeing real clay, that men in agony worked with, that gives plea-
sure. To read a book which is *real clay* moulded by fingers that had
to mould something, or they would clutch the throat of their
maddened author. *No* flowing on of words, but tightly clutched
tense fingers leaving marks in the clay. These are the only books
that matter – and where are they to be found?
                    – T.E. Hulme, 'Notes on Language and Style'

Between 1909 and his death in battle in 1917, T.E. Hulme published
on a wide variety of issues germane to the artistic, cultural and political
movements of the early twentieth century in Europe. The range of
subjects Hulme compressed into this short writing life is impressive,
and the list, even partial, reads like a breathless but purposeful trek
through the period. He wrote poems described by T.S. Eliot as among
the 'most beautiful short poems in the English language';[1] he wrote
and lectured on poetry and poetic theory; he composed, in fragmented
but clear-edged form, a 'Sketch for a New Weltanschauung' and
'Notes on Language and Style'; he championed the French philoso-
pher Henri Bergson, before switching allegiance to Bergson's detrac-
tors; he argued for 'Classicism' and the 'Religious Attitude' against
'Romanticism' and 'Humanism', sending those arguments hurtling
out of the literary and into the political – the *practical* political – realm;
he plucked, too, from the theological, buttressing his arguments with
talk of 'Original Sin'; he translated and explained the work of the
French Syndicalist Georges Sorel, and, finding in Pierre Lasserre and
Charles Maurras a fusion of literary philosophy with political action,
supported the activities of the reactionary group Action française. He
engaged with the philosophy of Husserl, G.E. Moore and Bertrand
Russell (among many), with the aesthetic theories of Worringer, Riegl
and Lipps (to name a few), and promoted the painting and sculpture of
Wyndham Lewis, Henri Gaudier-Brzeska and Jacob Epstein (again, a
selection). He wrote chronicles and reviews of modern French and
German poetry, and was often to be found reading German political
literature in his trench. He argued with Bertrand Russell about paci-

fism, upholding the necessity of a war he had no illusions about, which killed him, and in whose urgent idiocy 'great and useless sacrifices [...] are as negative, barren, and as *necessary* as the work of those who repair sea-walls'.

So much said and written and done, so fast, in so short a time: but Hulme did not hold, and hold *to*, all of these opinions simultaneously. The fact that he moved so rapidly makes it especially important to understand that he moved *to* and *from* various points. Faced with a writing career that spans less than a decade but covers so much, it is crucial not to be misled into thinking of it as an explosive blur, a Modernist blunderbuss, wide-angled but unwieldy. Misdating of his writings, and some critical work based on misdating, have made it seem as if Hulme were constantly contradicting himself, or holding several mutually exclusive positions at once.[2] Between 'Cinders' and 'A Notebook' (formerly called 'Humanism and the Religious Attitude'), much ground has been covered, many bridges burned and ladders kicked away, though the mind they reveal, its characteristic processes, and some of its central preoccupations, are still there.[3]

Hulme has been assigned many roles in the various histories of what we (should carefully) call Modernism: 'prodigal father' (of Imagism, for instance); mediating explicator (of, say, Bergsonism); prophetic anti-romantic (who influenced Eliot's 'classicism') and muscular anti-humanist; prophet and explicator (of geometrical art and its theories); champion of radical new artists (Lewis, Gaudier-Brzeska, Epstein); intellectual mixer and matcher (of socialist, anarchist and reactionary political philosophies). He has had his ardent supporters, as well as his ardent detractors. Depending on where one derives one's information, depending on whose narrative of Modernism one is reading, and on which Modernism(s) are being written about, the image of Hulme – the *idea* of Hulme – shuttles back and forth along the same line, between the same points: was he modernism's back-seat driver, or its noisiest passenger? This line, and all the stops along it, tend to confine the terms of our engagement with him. One of the least productive, most restricting, manifestations of this mode of thinking – one that detracts from Hulme's interest by tunnelling vision down to one brief phase of his writing life – has been the debate about Imagism. Ezra Pound, publishing Hulme's 'Complete Poetical Works' in *Ripostes* in 1912, referred to his 'forgotten school of 1909' as the progenitors of

'*Les Imagistes*'. 'I refrain from publishing my own *Historical Memoir* of their forerunners', concludes Pound, 'because Mr Hulme has threatened to print the original propaganda'. Already, on the crest of the Imagiste moment, the 'good fellowship' is splintered by issues of seniority and genealogy which have remained tiresomely alive in Modernist literary histories.

In 1915, F.S. Flint, Hulme's friend and member first of the 'forgotten school', then of Pound's 'Imagistes', and subsequently of Amy Lowell's 'Imagists' (Pound, by now a 'Vorticist' called them 'Amygists'), wrote a 'History of Imagism' for *The Egoist* giving Hulme pride of place, with Pound coming later, and Edward Storer and F.W. Tancred making up the background. According to Flint, recalling the group's meetings, 'there was a lot of talk and practice among us, Storer leading it chiefly, of what we called the Image', and he goes on:

> In all this Hulme was ringleader. He insisted too on absolutely accurate presentation and no verbiage; and he and F.W. Tancred [...] used to spend hours each day in search for the right phrase.[4]

The 'Imagism' issue of *The Egoist*, in addition to revealing disagreements of precedence between the movement's members, provoked both condemnation and mockery from outside Imagist circles. One of the most interesting examples of this is a satirical poem (there were many parodies of Imagist verse in circulation at the time) by Allen Upward entitled 'A Discarded Imagist', which appeared on the 'Correspondence' page of the following issue of *The Egoist*. Upward, perhaps the greyest of Modernist *éminences grises*, and clearly believing that his own work had anticipated the 'School of Images', seems to have been stung into satirical action by Flint's 'History':

> And now I have read in a history of Imagism
> That the movement was started in nineteen hundred and eight
> By Edward Storer and T.E. Hulme.
> (Poetry the crystal of language,
> Passion frozen by art,
> Fallen in love with its likeness.)[5]

In 1938 Pound attempted to settle the question by writing 'This Hulme Business' for *The Townsman*, in which he claimed that Ford Madox Ford rather than Hulme had been the motivating force behind his own Imagist enterprise (and by implication therefore, behind Imagism).[6]

The Imagism debate is symptomatic of Hulme's posthumous treatment by his contemporaries and by the critics who have aligned themselves with them. On the one hand, Pound and Poundians might seek to elide Hulme from the history of Imagism; on the other, those who follow Flint might seek to give him pre-eminence in the movement.[7] But in neither position are we likely to get at Hulme's particular significance, his particular achievement, because in both cases the need to 'place' him – whether to remove him from contention or to establish his 'copyright' – comes at considerable cost. This has to do with the processes by which Modernist literary histories are written. Such figures as Pound, Yeats, Eliot, Joyce are, as it were, *allowed* not to 'fit in', they are given leeway to escape 'placing', largely because theirs have been the terms by which the 'fitting in' has been conducted. The so-called 'minor figures', however, need to be steadied (where they are not ignored), so that the 'great Modernists' can spin their multifarious and exciting courses around them. Thus we lose, for instance, John Rodker, Ford Madox Ford, Isaac Rosenberg, F.S. Flint, Richard Aldington. This is particularly true of the English Modernists. We 'lose' them, and we do so by 'placing' them; we do not see them as forces in dynamic forward movement, but frozen in the retrospective glare of a story of Modernism which has already made up its mind about how that story ends. We refine them away.

It is partly a question of remembering that things, and the motivating – perhaps unrecorded – energies behind them, looked very different in 1909 or 1912, 1914 or 1917, from the way they did when the Pound–Joyce–Eliot constellation first took literary-historical shape. It is also partly a case of remembering that 'Modernism' was a much more knotted, dynamic, pluralistic movement then, and that the knottedness, dynamism and plurality are largely due to the fact that 'placing' and 'fitting in' were not – as they can never be *in medias res* – issues.[8] There is a passage by another *éminence grise* of Modernism, Ernest Fenollosa, which provides a not-too-fanciful analogy for the 'placing' process outlined above. It occurs in *The Chinese Written Character as a Medium for Poetry*, and is about the process of abstraction in language (something Hulme too was concerned with), and the way we build 'pyramids':

At the base of the pyramid lie *things*, but stunned as it were. They can never know themselves for things until they pass up and down among the layers of the pyramids. The way of passing up and down the pyramid may be exemplified as follows: We take a concept of lower attenuation, such as 'cherry'; we see that it is contained under one higher, such as 'redness'. [9]

'It is evident that this process of abstraction can go on indefinitely', writes Fenollosa, and his method, applicable to 'all sorts of material', he says, provides a model of Modernist literary history. At the base of the pyramid lie our so-called 'minor' Modernists, 'stunned'; at the apex, their 'major' contemporaries. In the intervening stages – or levels – of the pyramid, a process of 'refinement' or 'abstraction' has been working its way upwards by what Fenollosa characterises as the *contained under* method. The words 'contained' and 'under' hold the clues. But the pyramid did not always exist, because the notion of base and apex did not always exist. We could try another approach: lay the pyramid horizontally and we have a beam of torchlight; the light gets fainter as its angle widens, but what it takes in still depends on the focal intensity of its source, a focal intensity which shapes and governs all of the beam's subsequent illuminations. It determines not just how we see but what we see. The pyramid, the beam of light, are literary history; the apex and the light source, we could say, Pound, Eliot, Yeats.

II

A melancholy spirit, the mind like a great desert lifeless, and the sound of march music in the street, passes like a wave over the desert, unifies it, but then goes.

– T.E. Hulme, 'Cinders'

Thomas Ernest Hulme was born in Staffordshire on 16 September 1883, the son of a gentleman-farmer. He attended High School in Newcastle-under-Lyme, from which he gained an exhibition in Mathematics to St John's College, Cambridge. Lazy, rebellious and generally rowdy, he was 'sent down' in 1906 after a riot in a theatre.

This was the first of two attempts to study at Cambridge. He briefly attended the University of London, before sailing to Canada, where he supported himself by working as a labourer. This visit to Canada was a formative experience, and it was around this time that Hulme began 'Cinders', a jagged series of meditations on philosophy, language, truth and knowledge, announced as nothing less than 'a sketch for a new weltanschauung' (a new 'world-view'). The trip also spurred him into writing poetry: 'the first time I ever felt the necessity or inevitableness of verse, was in the desire to reproduce the peculiar quality of feeling which is induced by the flat spaces and wide horizons of the virgin prairie of western Canada' ('A Lecture on Modern Poetry').

In mid-1907, Hulme returned briefly to England, before leaving for Brussels, where he taught English. 'Notes on Language and Style' date from this period, and like 'Cinders' take the form of fragmented jottings. 'Notes' reflect broadly the same 'new weltanschauung' as 'Cinders', but here the enquiry is aimed more specifically at issues arising out of poetry and poetic language. In 1908 Hulme joined a poetry discussion group called 'The Poets' Club'. The club was mostly a gathering of amateurs, very different from the company Hulme was to keep in the coming years, founded and presided over by a banker, Henry Simpson. It was a far cry from the noise and controversy of Hulme's later associations with the likes of Pound and Wyndham Lewis, but he brought his own characteristic muscle to the enterprise. 'A Lecture On Modern Poetry', given to the Poets' Club in late 1908, begins by dismissing, as an example of 'the kind of statement that I utterly detest', some remarks about poetry and religion made by the club's president, and proceeds to castigate the 'bluff' and 'hocus-pocus' of poetic discussions. The lecture was a call for a new and liberated form of poetry, based on trenchant observation but at the same time reflective of the radical diffidence he sees as characteristic of the modern spirit. He argues, in a markedly aggressive tone, for a 'tentative and half-shy' poetry. The club produced two anthologies, *For Christmas MDCCCCVIII* and *The Book of the Poets' Club* in January and December 1909. Of the six poems Hulme published in his lifetime, 'A City Sunset' and 'Autumn' appeared in the first book, and 'The Embankment' and 'Conversion' in the second. In January 1912 *The New Age* published 'The Complete Poetical Works of T.E.

Hulme' ('Autumn', 'Mana Aboda', 'Conversion', 'Above the Dock' and 'Embankment'). These were published again in October in Ezra Pound's *Ripostes*. In early 1909, Hulme left the Poets' Club, and gathered another group of poets around him which included Flint, Edward Storer, Florence Farr and Francis Tancred. Ezra Pound, a recent arrival in London, was introduced to the group in April. This gathering, in which Flint recalls sustained discussions and experimentation with 'what we called the image', was what Pound meant by 'the forgotten school of 1909'. Hulme himself called it the 'Secession Club'.

Hulme's writings hereafter increasingly reflect his absorption in politics, philosophy and aesthetics. This is not to say that he stops thinking about poetry, but rather that it becomes inseparable from deeper-reaching issues. He began lecturing and writing on the French philosopher Henri Bergson in 1909, though he had been familiar with his work since 1907. Already 'Cinders' and 'Notes', when not Bergsonian in outlook, certainly display a mind ripe for productive engagement with Bergson's ideas. Bergson's reputation nowadays is such that it is not easy to conceive of his extraordinary pre-eminence in the late nineteenth and early twentieth centuries, and his profound impact not only on philosophy and aesthetics but on literary and political theory. Hulme's work between 1909 and 1911, and subsequently in a more antagonistic way, reflects this; his translation of Bergson's *Introduction à la métaphysique* appeared in 1912. Bergsonism penetrated one of the first histories of the Symbolist movement, Tancrède de Visan's *L'Attitude du lyrisme contemporain*, which Hulme reviewed in August 1911, as well as the political theory of another of his guiding lights, the French Syndicalist Georges Sorel. Hulme wrote some twenty articles on Bergson and lectured on his philosophy in London and Cambridge, becoming one of the clearest public exponents of an important movement in early twentieth-century thought.

But Hulme was dissenting from Bergson even as he devoted himself to explaining his philosophy. As his political consciousness developed, Hulme became increasingly attracted to the reactionary French group Action Française. The movement's luminaries were the literary critic Pierre Lasserre and the politician Charles Maurras. The prospect of a literary politics which was both *literary* and *political*, that came equipped with a literary philosophy and a programme of political

action, profoundly impressed Hulme. The movement's principal
tenets were Royalism, political ultra-conservatism, and anti-
Romanticism; its sub-tenets took the form of anti-Semitism (the group
was founded in the wake of the Dreyfus affair), nationalism, and a
respect for the church and its institutions (though not necessarily
belief in God). T.S. Eliot and Irving Babbit were among Hulme's pro-
Action Française contemporaries. Like Hulme himself, Action
Française was an idiosyncratic assembly of ideas: among the figures to
whom they paid homage, and whose work they respected, were the
French anarchist Pierre-Joseph Proudhon and the revolutionary
Syndicalist Georges Sorel, whose *Reflections on Violence* Hulme trans-
lated and prefaced in 1915. Reactionary, politically legitimist, reli-
giously orthodox, nationalist in the extreme and unflinchingly
classical, Action Française does two things of interest in early twen-
tieth century cultural and practical politics: deriving impetus from
radical anarchists and socialists, it also shows the double-edged nature
of revolutionary thought, its adaptibility to the needs of the political
right. In this respect too, Hulme captures the convolutions of his
times: an English conservative, translating the political theory of a
French socialist, and prefacing his translation with a quotation from a
French anarchist. Hulme was discomfited enough by Lasserre's claim
that Bergson was merely a cunningly disguised Romantic to go and
meet him in 1911. He recounts their meeting in his article 'Balfour,
Bergson, and Politics' in *The New Age* of 9 November 1911. In July
1912 Hulme delivered a lecture at Clifford's Inn Hall on 'The New
Philosophy of Art as Illustrated in Poetry'. It later became
'Romanticism and Classicism', and refers approvingly to the disrup-
tion of lectures in Paris by the activist wing of Action Française in
autumn 1910. In this lecture on poetry and poetic theory, politics and
political theory, Hulme discusses Bergsonism, Action Française,
conservatism, original sin and anti-Romanticism: a foretaste of the
extraordinary sweep and aggressive confidence of his later work. The
'sloppiness' and excess of 'Romantic' verse is characterised not simply
as an isolated literary phenomenon, but as one symptom of a post-
Rousseau attitude of mind whose greater manifestations embrace
political philosophy (democracy), history (a belief in 'Progress' and
human perfectibility) and religion (man as 'innately good'). He was by
now extending his notion of classicism and anti-Romanticism into a

more all-embracing anti-humanism: it was not just the 'spilt religion' of Romanticism he attacked, but its roots in 'Renascence' humanism.

Bergson wrote in support of Hulme's second – equally ill-fated – attempt to study at his old Cambridge college in early 1912:

> Je me fais un plaisir de certifier que je considère Mr T.E. Hulme comme un esprit d'une grande valeur. Il apporte, à l'étude des questions philosophiques, de rares qualités de finesse, de vigueur, et de pénétration. Ou je me trompe beaucoup, ou il est destiné à produire des oeuvres intéressantes et importantes dans le domaine de la philosophie en général, et plus particulièrement peut-être, dans celui de la philosophie de l'art.[10]

Bergson's reference uncannily predicts Hulme's imminent role in the Modernist art movements of Wyndham Lewis, Jacob Epstein and David Bomberg, as well as his enthusiasm for the aesthetic theories of Wilhelm Worringer. Bergson was not to know, however, that Hulme's 'philosophie de l'art' was preparing to position itself – at least in terms of political anti-Romanticism – against his own work. Nor was he to know that within a few months, his protégé would once again have to leave Cambridge, this time for writing unsuitable ('obscene') letters to a Roedean schoolgirl.[11] Pursued by the angry father's solicitors, Hulme went abroad once more, spending several months in Berlin between late 1912 and early 1913.

In Berlin Hulme met Rupert Brooke, attended the 'Berlin Aesthetic Congress', where he heard lectures by Wilhelm Worringer, and wrote 'German Chronicle' for *Poetry and Drama*. 'German Chronicle' is one of the earliest pieces of open-minded and informed criticism of Expressionist and post-Expressionist poetry in Germany, and ranks with Flint's longer essay, 'Modern French Poetry', as a key text in Modernist reception of European literatures. On his return, Hulme moved on to art criticism, and from December 1913 to July 1914 was publishing and lecturing on modern art. Worringer's 1908 book *Abstraktion und Einfühlung* (*Abstraction and Empathy*), provided a means of relating the art of the English 'avant-garde' to the pre-Renaissance 'geometrical' art of Egyptian and Byzantine civilisations. Though Hulme emphasised that 'primitive' and 'modern' art were *not* the same, he claimed to discover certain temperamental similarities between them. These lay in the anti-vitalist and anti-humanist spirit he discerned as common to both periods, what he later called, in opposition to 'humanism', the 'religious attitude'. Worringer enabled him to draw the work of Lewis, Bomberg and Epstein into his developing argument, to see art not in isolation but as a definite expression of a spiritual climate: the period's 'attitude of mind'. This phase of Hulme's activity takes in Cubism, Vorticism and Futurism, as well as the predecessors against which they rebelled. His art writings, both theoretical ('Modern Art and Its Philosophy') and reviews (of Epstein, Bomberg, Lewis *et al.*) provide detailed, on-the-spot accounts of the English 'avant-garde', along with an examination of its European dimensions, and a (perhaps wishful) tracing of its precedents. Hulme's gift for apposite and clear-sighted syntheses, combined with his own incisive polemics, make his articles valuable documents in the development of Modernist art.[12]

By 1914 he had been involved with a range of literary, political, philosophical and artistic movements at home and abroad. He had constructed, appropriated and applied theories that examined everything from individual lines of poetry to sweeping historico-philosophical lines of thought. Hulme's energy and personal argumentativeness ensured that he moved among, but remained independent of, a wide variety of friends and acquaintances. He had contacts with Bergson, Lasserre, Jules de Gaultier and Worringer; his circle of friends included such seemingly irreconcilable figures as Ezra Pound and Rupert Brooke, Edward Marsh and Wyndham Lewis. He is found, in diverse accounts of the period, talking, arguing, fighting, always on the peripheries of self-styled movements, but always at the centre of contemporary debate. Whether holding forth in his London rooms about 'Original Sin', enjoying riots in Paris or beating up Wyndham Lewis in a conflagration over a woman (Lewis ended up being suspended upside-down by his turn-ups from the railings of Great Ormond Street), Hulme is remembered as an energetic and irrepressible character.[13]

When the war broke out in August 1914, Hulme enlisted as a private and was sent to the trenches. For a writer who thought always by analogy and illustration, the trenches must have appeared as concrete representations of the 'cinders' he describes in his early writings. If, as he wrote of his visit to Canada, 'travel is an education in cinders', then in life in the trenches, and trench warfare, Hulme was able to experience the 'cinders' not simply as an extended metaphor for the underlying disunity of the world, but as a concretisation of that metaphor, as something *lived*. 'Diary from the Trenches' is a series of letters to his family about life at the front, and was first published in 1955. The parallels between it and Hulme's 'Sketch for a new Weltanschauung' ('The cosmos is only *organised* in parts; the rest is cinders') are striking. In the 'Diary' he records:

> It's curious to think of the ground between the trenches, a bank which is practically never seen by anyone in the daylight, and it is only safe to move through it at dark. It's full of dead things, dead animals here & there, dead unburied animals, skeletons of horses destroyed by shell fire. It's curious to think of it later on in the war, when it will again be seen in the daylight. [14]

The trenches, lines of order and strategy cut through the mud and mess, and the no man's land between them, correspond, as a kind of nightmare literalisation, to the lines of organised thought cut through the 'cinders', to the 'floating heroic world [...] and the cindery reality' he evoked in 'Cinders': 'This plurality consists in the nature of an ash-heap. In this ash-pit of cinders, certain ordered routes have been made, thus constituting whatever unity there may be – a kind of chess-board laid on a cinder-heap.' Hulme's letters from the front are characteristically clear-headed and unemotive. 'In reality there is nothing picturesque about it', he wrote, 'It's the most miserable existence you can conceive of'. They also reveal that the gift for intense observation and fractured lyricism of his poetry remained with him:

> The only thing that makes you feel nervous is when the shells go off & you stand out revealed quite clearly as in daylight. You have then the most wonderful feeling as if you were suddenly naked in the street and didn't like it. [...] It's really like a kind of nightmare, in which you are in the middle of an enormous saucer of mud with explosions & shots going off all round the edge, a sort of fringe of palm trees made of fireworks all round it.

In April 1915 Hulme was wounded and sent back to England. Pound, who included the poem 'Trenches St. Eloi' ('abbreviated from the conversation of Mr. T.E.H.') in his *Catholic Anthology*, describes Hulme's recuperation in a Wimbledon hospital in *Canto XVI*:

And ole T.E.H. he went to it,
With a lot of books from the library,
London Library, and a shell buried 'em in a dug-out,
And the Library expressed its annoyance.
        And a bullet hit him in the elbow
... gone through the fellow in front of him,
And he read Kant and Hegel in the Hospital, in Wimbledon,
in the original,
And the hospital staff didn't like it.[15]

Between November 1915 and March 1916, Hulme published 'War Notes' for *The New Age* and *The Cambridge Magazine*.[16] Writing under the *nom de plume* 'North Staffs', he took up cudgels against the pacifists. With such provocative titles as 'The Kind of Rubbish We Oppose' and 'Why We Are in Favour of This War: The Case Against "Another Cucumber Sandwich"', Hulme's articles chiefly target Bertrand Russell, one of the principal pacifists of the day. Hulme's defence of the war is entirely free of jingoism, idealism or rhetorical heroism. His 'position' on the war – war both as mass-slaughter and as moral dilemma – is disconcertingly comfortless: 'So it comes about that we are unable to name any great *positive* "good" for which we can be said to be fighting. But it is not necessary that we should; there is no harmony in the nature of things.' This was the war about which Pound wrote in *Hugh Selwyn Mauberley*, 'There died a myriad [...] for an old bitch gone in the teeth, For a botched civilization'.

At this time, Hulme began his final work. 'A Notebook' ('Humanism and the Religious Attitude') was published in *The New Age* in seven instalments between December 1915 and February 1916. These articles are the summation of Hulme's thinking; they mark out the stages of its evolution while arriving at its most complete articulation. 'A Notebook' is Hulme's most wide-ranging work, drawing on Bergson, Dilthey, Nietzsche, Husserl and G.E. Moore, 'Original Sin', medieval and 'Renascence' civilisations, poetry, modern and ancient art, war and contemporary politics. The greater this scope, the narrower the margin for negotiation, the more brutal the assertions, and the less probing and intimidated the style. A passage from 'A Notebook' exemplifies this, as well as resuming one of Hulme's favourite claims, that edifices of rational argument and balanced thought are built around convictions so embedded as to be rationally irreducible:

> I remember one occasion, when [...] I let myself drift aimlessly through the controversies of three years. When the last ounce of solidity seemed thus to melt away in the universal deliquescence, the thing became a horror, and I had to rescue myself. I drew up a list of antitheses, of perpetual subjects of dispute, on each of which I had convictions, based on a *brutal* act of assertion, which no argument could touch. These were solid rock, whatever might be the extent of the flux elsewhere.

In March 1916 Hulme received his commission in the Royal Marines Artillery. He was killed in an unexpected burst of shelling on 28 September 1917, at Nieuport. An officer who encountered him while he was serving with his battery remembered: 'What a man! He'd argue a dog's hind leg off.'

III

> When Hulme was killed in Flanders in 1917, he was known to a few people as a brilliant talker, a brilliant amateur of metaphysics, and the author of two or three of the most beautiful poems in the English language. In this volume he appears as the forerunner of a new attitude of mind, which should be the twentieth-century mind, if the twentieth century is to have a mind of its own.
> – T.S. Eliot, *The Criterion*, 1924

For the reader coming to Hulme for the first time, it is necessary to provide some means of approach to a writer who, though frequently discussed, still largely occupies Modernism's grey area. It is to the substance of his thought and the style of its exposition that we must turn if we are to read him rewardingly and without preconceptions.

'The covers of a book are responsible for much error', writes Hulme in 'Cinders'. 'They set a limit round certain convenient groups of ideas, when there are really no limits.' From his earliest work, Hulme is concerned to expose the artificiality and expediency of systems, to emphasise their source and motivation in human need rather than in any stable 'Truths' proposed by 'capital lettrists'. These unifying systems ('amplifications of man's appetites') are absolutely necessary to sane and healthy existence. In the same way, Hulme argues, a railway line built through a desert is necessary for getting from A to B across unpredictable and dangerous terrain. The problems arise when the railway is treated as a 'given', rather than a 'made' necessity, and when the cindery desert is deemed incidental rather than integral. Hulme – and this is one of his most unmistakable characteristics – is a relentlessly analogical thinker (discussing analogical processes in poetry and language), and the governing analogy of flimsy systematic order imposed upon fundamental chaos turns up in many guises throughout his writings: language (one of many sense-making systems) is a 'chessboard', a 'gossamer web [...] woven between real things'; words and phrases are 'counters' moved according to artificial rules with abstract propositional cargoes; philosophy is a 'Room' sheltered from the cinders, where 'certain groups of ideas [are] as huts for men to live in'; ideas about 'Good' are 'like oases in the desert [...] cheerful houses in the storm'. For Hulme, 'All heroes, all great men, go to the outside, away from the Room, and wrestle with cinders.'

'Cinders' and 'Notes on Language and Style' take these ideas as fundamental premises of a 'world-view', just as his later works take it as something to move beyond, to work in spite of. These texts are also the basis of Hulme's theories of poetry and poetic language, and are themselves in appropriately fragmented form. 'Unity is made in the world by drawing squares over it', avers Hulme. 'The unity of Nature is an extremely artificial and fragile bridge, a garden net.' The aim of all thought is 'to reduce the complex and inevitably disconnected world of grit and cinders to a few ideal counters'. Language – the 'language disease', as he calls language that has forgotten its source in needy artifice – is one aspect of the 'manufactured chess-board laid on a cinder-heap'. We note the *geometrical* thinking in Hulme's analogies: squares, lines, imposed shapes all help him to visualise our meagre impositions on the flux. They convey the necessary illusion of order, and – this feeds into the aggressive formalism of his later art theory – celebrate the *imposition* of order, of *form*. These geometrical forms, at this stage, are symptomatic of our needs; later, when he confronts vorticism and cubism, they become expressions of a muscular and anti-vitalist grappling with the flux. The same rules, or rather the same psychology of rules, governs Hulme's thinking on language, politics, progress, civilisation: just as language is recalcitrant matter needing to be shaped into precise expression, so man is intrinsically limited and bad, and only with rules can something good be got out of him (though he does not posit this as a politics yet).

Analogy itself is a means of understanding one thing through the workings of another, and analogy is crucial to Hulme. His *analogical imagination*, a direct response to lack of 'unity', consists in something like this procedure: there is no unity, and permanent comprehension is impossible; it thus becomes necessary not to look for absolutes, but to thread items of knowledge together by means of correspondences, analogically. He insists, however, that this is not to think relativistically. To think in terms of analogies, we could say, is to work horizontally: gathering parallels which mutually confirm each other's validity, moving probingly, step-by-step. To think in terms of absolutes is to think vertically: checking our ideas against a 'higher' set of truths. Alternatively, since no panoramic view is possible, we can only compose our perspective by recognising a few landmarks: the key is not to mistake our *join-the-dots* caricature for panoramic vision. A third *caveat* subsists: the only reason we aspire to panoramic vision, or believe such a thing exists, is because of the 'eagle's eye' fallacy, whereby we think that 'the further [we fly] the "purer" [our] knowledge becomes'. Not so: 'the eye is in the mud, the eye *is* mud'. Analogies are not linguistic tics or literary-stylistic trademarks, but part of the fabric of Hulme's thought. This needs emphasising, because it is so integral to all Hulme's writing, his ideas and his style – *style* as the expression of a writer's mental and emotional operations, as well as his 'turn of phrase'.

There is nothing particularly new in the substance of Hulme's vision: it certainly lends itself to Bergsonism, and his tone has an almost Schopenhauerian exuberance. Hulme claimed that the real interest of Bergson's philosophy lay not in its conclusions, but in the ways they were reached, in the *methods* rather than the *results*. This holds true for Hulme's own early philosophy, and in particular for the style of its exposition: a nightmare journey through flux and fragmentation, groping at analogies for navigation. Hulme describes the 'process of invention' as 'that of gradually making solid the castles in air', and notes the 'extraordinary difficulty of shaping any material': language, communication, knowledge, fugitive impressions or fictive

certainties, all grapple with expression, strain towards communication
and communicability in the face of shattering odds. 'The idea is
nothing: it is the holding on to the idea [...] The holding on through
waves': 'Cinders' and 'Notes' both enact and describe this. They are
not simply intellectual ruminations, but dark and intense fantasies
(with a protagonist, Aphra) on language and knowledge. A modern
reader might find them evocative of Beckett (the Beckett of *Proust*,
for instance) in their intensity and spaciousness, their visionary
frustration and their pithy and ragged quotability. They are also
funny.

Along with 'A Lecture on Modern Poetry', 'Romanticism and
Classicism', and the poems and fragments, these texts also contain
Hulme's literary ideas. As in another contemporary text, also
published posthumously, Fenollosa's *The Chinese Written Character as
a Medium for Poetry*, Hulme focuses on poetry and poetic language in
ways that illuminate the intellectual climate of early Modernism. Both
Hulme and Fenollosa have been the subject of disputes among the
influence-hunters: Fenollosa's *Chinese Written Character* was written
before 1908, but published by Pound in 1918.[17] We do not know the
precise range of its influence, because, although an important docu-
ment in Modernist poetic theory, much of what it was *seen* to argue for
had already been achieved. Similarly, though less traceably, Hulme's
thoughts on poetry were not published until after the moment of their
direct or instigatory relevance. 'Cinders' and 'Notes' appeared after
his death, 'A Lecture' was unpublished, and only a handful of poems
had appeared. Moreover, as Flint and others attest, Hulme's influence
on poetry would largely have taken the shape of discussion – conversa-
tions, lectures, arguments, monologues – to which a variety of people
were privy. His ideas were 'in the air', and no amount of periodical-
ransacking and stake-claiming can get at the generative atmosphere of
such discussions.[18] Part of the problem arises from trying to harness
Hulme to this or that 'school' or *ism*, rather than addressing his
thought face-on.

Language, and by extension poetic language, is inseparable from
the vision of the world as conceived in 'Cinders':

There is a kind of gossamer web, woven between the real things,
and by this means the animals communicate. For purposes of

communication they invent a symbolic language. Afterwards this language, used to excess, becomes a disease, and we get the curious phenomena of men explaining themselves by means of the gossamer web that connects them. Language becomes a disease in the hands of the counter-word mongers. It must constantly be remembered that it is an invention for the convenience of men [...] Symbols are picked out and believed to be realities.

In an article for *The New Age* published on 19 August 1909, 'Searchers After Reality: Haldane', Hulme elaborates:

Men for the purposes of communication have joined themselves together by an abstract mechanism, a web of language, of universals and concepts. I picture this by thinking of a number of telegraph poles connected by a network of wires, the poles being concrete men, the wires being the abstract, thin concepts of the intellect, the forms in which we think and communicate [...] The success of this mechanism leads us on to think that it alone is real [...] Surely this is the greatest comedy in history, that men should come to think themselves as made up of one of their own tools.

Central to Hulme's literary preoccupations are images, analogies, metaphors and similes. These 'shock' the mind out of the comforting pseudo-efficiency of language, and, when employed in poetry, have the capacity to combat the 'telegraph wire' fallacy, by disrupting its mechanical automatism. This should be remembered when entering the controversy of 'Imagism': for Hulme, 'the Image' is part of a general interest in figurative language as a whole. It does not confine itself, as Imagist 'doctrine' does, to theorising exclusively about the individual image or 'image-complex'. It is looser and more elastic, and Hulme's 'Image' can mean any form of figurative language that employs an image, however overt or submerged, direct or indirect. His poetry, for instance, frequently uses similes, drawing attention to the rhetorical process at work in the verse, something explicitly disallowed by the likes of Pound. We might compare Pound's definition of metaphor as 'the swift perception of relations' with the altogether more rhetorically-advertised 'imposition' of relations effected by the simile, and the consequences the two methods have on the 'simultaneity' of perceived relations.

Briefly (and very broadly) stated, Hulme makes a quasi-formalist distinction between prose and poetry with a characteristically clean-edged analogy: 'Verse is pedestrian, taking you over the ground, prose – a train which delivers you at a destination'. 'Pedestrian' is the opposite of 'mundane': poetry takes you over the difficult terrain, stopping at unexpected disjunctions, stumbling upon unexpected correspondences. This he calls a 'difference of intention'. In 'Romanticism and Classicism', he writes:

> In prose as in algebra concrete things are embodied in signs or counters which are moved about according to rules, without being visualised at all in the process. [...] One only changes the X's and Y's back into physical things at the end of the process. Poetry, in one aspect at any rate, may be considered as an effort to avoid this characteristic of prose. It is not a counter language, but a visual concrete one. It is a compromise for a language of intuition which would hand over sensations bodily. It always endeavours to arrest you, and to make you continuously see a physical thing, to prevent you gliding through an abstract process. It chooses fresh epithets and fresh metaphors, not so much because they are new and we are tired of the old, but because the old cease to convey a physical thing and become abstract counters. [...] Images in verse are not mere decoration, but the very essence of an intuitive language.

Hulme emphasises that poetry, however different in 'intention' from prose, is still a compromise for something. Mental operations and physical sensations can only be approximated, however direct, precise or innovative their linguistic expression. Poetry is language at its highest pitch because it strains against fully-felt limitations by forging 'fresh epithets and fresh metaphors' in an each-time-renewed fight against vagueness, obsolescence and automatism. We could call this Hulme's 'lifespan theory' of language.

According to the 'lifespan theory', metaphors or similes, images or analogies, are first used in poetry, where they are alive and unfamiliar, disruptive and strange, then descend into prose, where they become figures of speech passed over unnoticed. Prose is a 'museum', a 'graveyard', for once-fresh, once-living, expressions. In the article on Haldane, Hulme writes, using terms which we find again in his 'Lecture on Modern Poetry':

Nowadays, when one says the hill is 'clothed' with trees, the word suggests no physical comparison. To get the original visual effect one would have to say 'ruffed', or use some new metaphor. A poet says the ship 'coursed the seas' to get a physical image, instead of the counter word 'sailed'. Visual meanings can only be transferred by the new bowl of metaphor: prose is an old pot that lets them leak out. Prose is in fact the museum where the dead images of verse are preserved.

In 'Notes', prose is 'a museum where all the old weapons of poetry kept': 'Poetry always the advance guard in language. The progress of language is the absorption of new analogies.' Fenollosa, though arguing from a fundamentally different perspective, wrote that 'Metaphor was piled upon metaphor in quasi-geological strata'. For Hulme, analogies have brief explosive lives before 'dying' and becoming 'counters' (for Fenollosa they are sleeping and in need of recharging). The most ordinary linguistic usages are themselves figurative (*'clothed'* with trees'), but the shock of their novelty has been absorbed. According to the 'lifespan theory', the relation between the poetic 'birth' of an image or an analogy and its absorption into everyday prose as a 'counter' is similar to the relation between the fossil and the living animal: the outline remains, but the body is gone, the dimensionality lost. In 'A Lecture', the passage from expressive virility to expressionless stasis is figured thus: 'images are born in poetry. They are used in prose, and finally die a long and lingering death in journalists' English.' In this respect, Hulme is tackling many of the preoccupations that are soon to characterise the work of the Russian and Czech Formalists. Victor Shklovski, writing in 1914, draws upon the same analogy of lifespans and graveyards to markedly similar effect: 'The most ancient poetic creation of man was the creation of words. Now words are dead, and language is like a graveyard, but an image was once alive in the newly-born word.'[19] And Shklovski further notes that 'when you get through to the image which is now lost and effaced, but once embedded at the basis of the word, you are struck by its beauty – by a beauty which existed once and is now gone'.[20] Shklovski and the Formalists develop the notion of *ostranenije* (of 'strangeness' or 'estrangement' in the sense of 'defamiliarisation' or 'de-automatisation') to account for poetry's capacity to break

through the 'glass armour of familiarity'. This is equally important to
Hulme, who in 'Notes' likens the poetic use of language to 'staging' or
'framing': 'They [words or ideas] must appear separate and far from all
dirt and laughter at their low and common relations.' With Hulme we
have a clear desire to *renew* by defamiliarising, and the terms he uses to
express this – 'isolating', 'framing', 'staging' – are the same as those
employed by the Formalists. We may note in passing that these itin-
erant theatrical metaphors are soon to return to their literal home in
the drama and dramatic theory of Brecht, not to mention in the area of
theatre semiotics as developed from Formalism by the likes of
Bogatyrev, Veltrusky or Honzl. Yet there is in Hulme a countervail-
ingly strong insistence on the need for a constant and unresting
process of new-minting (whether of images, analogies or metaphors)
that lays more emphasis on their dying than on their revival. Though
he often entertains both notions simultaneously – that of 'raising' the
dead and that of leaving them in their 'graveyard' – the angle from
which he approaches the issue is perceptibly slanted towards *replace-
ment* rather than *recovery*. Forward-movement for Hulme implies loss
at least as much as it implies gain, it depletes rather than enriches, and
he constantly challenges the optimistic clichés about 'progress',
'novelty' and the unquestionable 'good' of change: the 'birth-rate' of
new analogies or images struggles to keep pace with the swelling
graveyards of language. This is the dark side of progress, the sinister
aspect of change, that Hulme relentlessly foregrounds.

    In this respect, a further point might be suggested: the early twen-
tieth century abounds in schemes for the renovation of poetic
language, and Hulme, like the Formalists, was only one among the
many who explored them. Whatever their differences, Shklovski and
Fenollosa have one point of contact which Hulme does not explore in
any depth: etymology. For Fenollosa, etymology is where the dormant
dynamics of our static nouns and automatic adjectives exist in *verbs*,
that is, in *movement*. For Shklovski, 'the etymology of words returns us
to the reality from which over time they have become estranged'.[21]
Etymology is the science that buttresses the dream of recuperability,
revealing, adding volume to, gathering energy for, and all the while
cleansing, the word. It renovates by going backwards. On this impor-
tant point, it is not so much a different angle that Hulme approaches
from, as a diametrically opposed current: his notion of movement is

defined by movement forward, whether for good or ill, whether it implies gain or loss. Most often it is the latter: death is final, the grave-yard is permanent and not mere *limbo*. A lot hinges on etymology, and whether its absence in Hulme's rhetoric of language-renewal (which, as we have seen, depends greatly on following through the model of its *extinction*) is explicable by a simple lack of interest in the 'academic' side of the question (he was no linguistician, so this might simply be a 'blind-spot'), or whether it can be put down to a more coherent refusal to cast backwards for solutions, it is a comfort Hulme seems prepared to do without. If, in the domain of poetic language, Fenollosa and Shklovski show that 'going backwards' is by no means 'backward-looking' – that it is, in fact, enriching and life-enhancing – then Hulme's example shows the extent to which 'going forwards' can be debasing, stultifying, life-denying. (This is an idea which certainly fits with his refusal, in the political and cultural spheres, to accept 'progress' as synonymous with 'improvement'.) Hulme, of course, *is* aware of the initial effect of an image, and in fact several times points out that its first appearance was explosive and shocking. But he does no more than point it out: it is finished. Fenollosa and Shklovski, from their different perspectives, would reveal the original semantic and associative eco-system that brought it about and might once again sustain it. Hulme runs counter-current to them on this most signifi-cant of issues. There is no reason why he should not, given that both currents were variously being followed by numerous writers and critics, throughout Europe, in the early twentieth century. What makes Hulme's individual contribution interesting is that his prose of this period, in 'Notes', 'Cinders', 'A Lecture' and 'Romanticism and Classicism', offers the spectacle of someone trying – perhaps without knowing it – to fit both currents into the same stream, to run opposite ideas in parallel rather than at loggerheads.

'Cinders' and 'Notes' contain fantasies of a language that is *not* a compromise, and under the heading '*Transfer physical to language*' Hulme writes, in 'Notes': 'Dome of Brompton in the mist. [...] And the words moved until they became a dome, a solid, separate world, a dome in a mist [...] Aphra took the words, and they grew into a round smooth pillar...'. Fantasies of solidity and precision jostle with fantasies of a language adequate to capturing the transitory and the fugitive, one that reflects the intuitive process, pre- or non-intellectual perceptions, flashes and insights. On the one hand, therefore, Hulme argues for precision and exactness, for a poetry that can convey the 'solid', the 'physical', the 'visual' (these are slippery terms, and he often uses them crudely); on the other, he is fascinated with capturing the 'blur', the transitory, the fleeting. Language is brute and recalcitrant *matter*, and Hulme's analogies reflect this: sculpture, modelling, planing, carving. He discusses poetry and language analogically, but also places analogy at the centre of poetic activity: analogy is both a means of comprehending the process of writing (and the process of comprehension itself) and poetry's primary resource. Writing is hand-blistering work, a fight against the 'resistance' of the material; language is a 'Large clumsy instrument' that does 'not naturally come with meaning'. Hulme exemplifies a general Modernist tendency to process writing through metaphors of the plastic arts, implying an entire discourse of violence and force against rather than with the medium. Hulme's view of poetry assumes 'a terrific struggle with language, whether it be with words or the technique of the other arts', and in 'Romanticism and Classicism' he expresses this struggle with some deft analogy-hopping:

> the fundamental process at the back of all the arts might be represented by the following metaphor. You know what I call architect's curves – flat pieces of wood with all different kinds of curvature. [...] I shall here have to change my metaphor a little to get the process in his mind. Suppose that instead of your curved pieces of wood you have a springy piece of steel [...] the state of tension or concentration of the mind, if he is doing anything really good in this struggle against the ingrained habit of the technique, may be represented by a man employing all his fingers to bend the steel out of its own curve and into the exact curve which you want. Something different to what it would assume naturally.

Beneath the heading '*Example of the Plastic Imagination*' he writes in 'Notes': 'The two tarts walking along Picadilly on tiptoe, going home, with hat on back of head. Worry until could find exact model analogy that will reproduce the extraordinary effect they produce. Could be done at once by artist in a blur.' Between 'reproduce' and 'produce' Hulme locates the entirety of the struggle. Here it is not 'solid' things but 'blur'. As with Bergson, and the post-Symbolists who take

Bergson as the philosopher of modern poetry, poetic language need not present the direct and precise, but the indirectness and imprecision of intuitive perception. That deflating afterthought – 'could be done by artist in a blur' – is a reminder of the fundamental intransigence and inefficiency of the chosen medium, words, as against an idealised notion of effects obtainable through other art forms. As in Pound, these metaphorical forays into other arts are symptomatic of a Modernist hunger for a new poetic language. Such passages as these, and it should be noted also that Hulme is an intense observer of the bustling transformations of the modern cityscape, call to mind Baudelaire's *Painter of Modern Life*. Where are we to seek modernity, asks Baudelaire, and how are we to capture it? For Baudelaire, discussing the painter Constantin Guys, modernity is 'the transitory, the fugitive, the contingent', it is to be found in everything from cities to women's fashions. Hulme looks at both of these. The metropolis, crawling with traffic and crowds, rush-hours, prostitutes, shops and lights, is life in flux, something always in transit, in mid-movement, an unresting web of energies. The fleeting, fugitive impressions left by clothes, factory smoke, strangers seen in passing, all are material for Hulme's poetry. They also represent, in their unfixability, the shock or intuitive apprehensions of daily life:

> The flounced edge of a skirt
>> recoiling like waves off a cliff.

Hulme's small poem is a masterpiece of economy, getting the idea of one movement across by means of another kind of movement. It pivots on a simile, so reads like a more cumbersome version of Herrick's 'tempestuous petticoat', of which Hulme is revealingly fond. But another poem,

> Old houses were scaffolding once
>> and workmen whistling[.]

does something more ambitious, and more gracefully. Major time-shifts are communicated by a sense of thriving temporariness, tracing the story of a building in reverse: from present solidity to erstwhile virtuality. 'Could be done by artist in a blur' – a brushstroke might capture the movement (of a skirt, say, or of a house taking shape beneath a welter of forgotten shapes and sounds). Language has more trouble: a blur, something not so much seen as apprehended in transit, traceable from the marks it leaves on air in a sequential vision of the multitude of tiny movements that make up the swish of its passing. Hulme's notion of the image is, in this respect, inflected by Bergson's thinking, and particularly by the idea of 'images successives' as it occurs in *Introduction à la métaphysique* and Tancrède de Visan's *L'Attitude du lyrisme contemporain*.

Expression consists of 'the simultaneous presentation to the mind of two different images', operates upon a 'deliberate choosing and working up of analogies': 'Thought is the joining together of new analogies, and so inspiration is a matter of accidentally seen analogy or unlooked-for resemblance' ('Notes'). Here too analogical thinking is integral not just to the poem, but to the way the mind intuits, rather than intellects, the world it experiences. Hulme has no time for pseudo-mystical discourse about poetic 'Inspiration': poetry is a 'keeping hold' of small epiphanies. It is *propelled intuition*:

> Say the poet is moved by a certain landscape, he selects from that certain images which put into juxtaposition in separate lines serve to suggest and to evoke the state he feels. To this piling-up and juxtaposition of distinct images in different lines, one can find a fanciful analogy in music. A great revolution in music when for the melody that is one-dimensional music was substituted harmony which moves in two. Two visual images unite to form what one may call a visual chord. They unite to suggest an image which is different to both. ('A Lecture')

Bergson's *images successives* are designed to prevent the mind from resting in a state of abstraction or fixity, and Hulme's 'analogies', designed to prevent it 'gliding through an abstract process'. Juxtaposition of two images produces a third substance, a kind of energetic by-product which Hulme describes as akin to 'fire struck between stones'. Successive images, taken from different orders, colliding and unfolding, argues Bergson, 'will, by the convergence of their action, direct consciousness to the precise point where there is an intuition to be seized'. By choosing images as disparate as possible, 'we may prevent any individual image from usurping the place of the intuition it is attempting to call forth'. This, suggests Bergson, enables consciousness to 'appear to itself unveiled'. The Bergsonian 'mission'

is to liberate the mind from the shackles of intellect and abstraction. It
is Hulme's, too. This adds a further instalment of the difference – not
so much in substance as 'intention' – between Hulme and the later
'Imagists'. Hulme's 'Image' addresses questions that only *begin* in
poetry, but are pursued to every level of language, consciousness,
perception and knowledge. As in Bergson, images – successive or
juxtaposed – do not simply *convey* the writer's precise or fuzzy impres-
sions, but *provoke* new and different ones in the reader. Successive
images are coterminous with intuition: they *induce* intuitive acts,
disrupt ordinary, lazy habits of thought. Hulme knows that, poetry
being an approximate art, precise expression (or even precise expres-
sion of an imprecise impression) is impossible. Analogies can prompt
an *analogous* or approximate feeling of disruption in the reader, by
preventing the mind from standing still, although what the writer sets
out to express and what the reader intuits from it may not (often *will
not*) be the same. Despite the force and clarity of his style, Hulme
grapples with all sorts of slippages: between experience and language,
intellect and intuition, reader and writer, *im*pression and *ex*pression,
flux and fixity. He deals with approximations and inefficiencies as
clearly and efficiently as possible, but without denying their existence.
Precision, when it is most needed, is always leaking out; imprecision,
when it is most sought, always freezing over into 'counters'. 'The
artist', writes Hulme in 'Romanticism and Classicism, 'I take to be the
man who simply can't bear the idea of that "approximately".' The
intolerable and deadening 'approximately' built into all communica-
tion is what Hulme always struggles to overcome.

'A Lecture on Modern Poetry' and 'Romanticism and Classicism'
are his most anthologised and widely-known pieces, and have formed
the basis of much critical 'placing' of Hulme (especially his relations
with Eliot, Pound and Imagism, and *vers libre*). In 'A Lecture' Hulme
reaches a new impatience with the ubiquitous *approximately* he diag-
noses in his earlier writings, arguing for precision in both poetic
language and critical discourse about poetry. The piece also contains
the germ of the practical and cultural politics of 'A Notebook' and 'A
Tory Philosophy'. The *lifespan theory* extends to take in not just items
of poetic expression but swathes of poetic tradition and their accom-
panying 'attitudes of mind': 'verse forms, like manners, and like indi-
viduals, develop and die. They evolve from their initial freedom to

decay and finally to virtuosity.' 'A Lecture' is full of references to death, decay, putrefaction, obsolescence and redundancy, as Hulme attempts to clear away the accumulated detritus of poetic tradition. The poet is in a different position from the actor or the dancer, who work in arts 'of which no record can be kept, and which must be repeated for each generation'. Permanence kills, immortality is death:

> The actor has not to feel the competition of the dead as the poet has. Personally I am in favour of the complete destruction of all verse more than twenty years old. [...] Meanwhile it is necessary to realise that as poetry is immortal, it is differentiated from those arts which must be repeated. [...] it is only those arts whose expression is repeated every generation that have an immutable technique.

We cannot imagine Pound or Eliot advocating the destruction of poetry more than twenty years old, and this side of Hulme approaches the museum-razing discourse of Artaud (whose writings crawl with images of putrefying cultural preservation). If death and decomposition are paradoxically aligned with preservation, then freshness and virility are aligned with the renewable freedoms of cultural amnesia:

> The latter stages in the decay of an art form are very interesting and worth study because they are particularly applicable to the state of poetry at the present day. They resemble the latter stages in the decay of religion when the spirit has gone and there is a meaningless reverence for formality and ritual. The carcass is dead, and the flies are upon it. Imitative poetry springs up like weeds, and women whimper and whine of you and I alas, and roses, roses all the way.

Modern poetry should learn from French *vers libre*: 'the length of the line is long and short, oscillating with the images used by the poet; it follows the contours of his thought and is free rather than regular'. Poetry should not imitate *vers libre*, but recognise its emancipatory potential, less as a refreshing new technique of verse (novelty *per se* is something Hulme is deeply suspicious of) than as an expression of a distinctly new 'attitude of mind'. Pretensions to permanence – whether of poetic expression or metaphysical systems – are no longer valid, because we 'no longer believe in perfection, either in verse or in thought'. 'The ancients', as Hulme calls them, built with a view to permanence because they were aware of the flux and fluidity of the world: their art, their monuments, their epic scales, were attempts to build things that 'would stand fast in the universal flux which frightened them'. Geometry and stylisation are viewed not as lack of 'know-how' but as expressions of a spiritual need to shape order from disorder. The 'modern spirit' retreats from pretensions to absolute truth, order or immortality. This brings adjustments of ambition, a lowering of sights:

> Instead of these minute perfections of phrases and words, the tendency will be rather towards the production of a general effect [...] We are no longer concerned that stanzas shall be shaped and polished like gems, but rather that some vague mood shall be communicated. In all the arts, we seek for the maximum of individual and personal expression, rather than for the attainment of any absolute beauty.

It is not merely a question of poetic form (what metre to use, whether to rhyme), but of substantially different things to express. 'What is this new spirit, which finds itself unable to express itself in the old metre?' asks Hulme. 'Are the things that a poet wishes to say now in any way different to the things that former poets say?':

> I believe that they are. The old poetry dealt essentially with big things [...] But the modern is the exact opposite of this [...] it has become definitely and finally introspective and deals with expression and communication of momentary phrases in the poet's mind.

Hulme's ideas here can be examined in the light of a number of contemporary Modernist trends, notably Ford Madox Ford's 'Impressionism', though it is not our purpose to enter upon a comparison. What is important to note is how Hulme's idea of lowered sights and diminished ambitions being characteristic of the modern spirit lays the emphasis on freedom and individuality of expression, on breaking 'rules' in order to express individual rather than general or 'universal' themes. The new verse, for instance, is meant to be 'read in the study' rather than solemnly 'chanted'. Where old rhythms were meant to conjure assenting quasi-hypnotic trances, the new are meant to 'arrest' attention, 'so much so that the succession of visual images should exhaust one'. Modernity is characterised by a 'tentative and half-shy manner of looking at things', but also by a diffident restlessness. To put this temperament into fixed verse forms is like 'putting a child into armour'. Hulme's lecture is a strikingly *un*tentative and extroverted argument for shy-ness, and the discrepancy between his tone and his message is instructive. If what is said conveys a point, the way it is said conveys something of the mental background from which that point springs: 'modernity' is not *just* half-shy and tentative, but also fully understanding of the wider implications of that diminishment of scope (so, not 'Romantic'). Individualism is not a kind of sneaky 'back-door' Romanticism with a secret retinue of words like 'infinite' and 'universal', but a version of individuality as confinement and boundedness. Hulme is quite adamant about this, and whenever he feels he is applauding 'vagueness' and 'subjectivity' his reflex is to justify it:

> Monsieur de Visan's book is a reasoned attempt to prove that the spirit which finds expression in the Symboliste movement [...] is the same as that represented by Bergson in philosophy. They are both reactions against the definite and the clear, not for any preference for the vague as such, not for any mere preference for sentiment, but because both feel, one by a kind of instinctive, unconscious process and the other as the result of reasoning, that the clear conceptions of the intellect are a definite distortion of reality. (Review of *L'Attitude du lyrisme contemporain*)

To say that Hulme's ideas are contradictory in such passages displays the same kind of reductiveness that would see Pound's 'Direct treatment of the thing, whether subjective or objective' as contradictory: 'thing' and 'treatment' belong to different orders. Individualism, even at this stage of Hulme's thinking, is a response to limitation, an affirmation of that limitation, not an attempt to exalt the individual: originality is something we are *forced* to.

If we were schematically to phrase the gist of Hulme's argument here, we could say that it is motivated by, and insists on, a breaking of established rules in order to achieve the individual *expression* of an individual's *impression*. Is there a contradiction between this and the assertion, in 'Romanticism and Classicism', that 'Man is an extraordinarily fixed and limited animal [...] It is only by tradition and organisation that anything decent can be got out of him'? Not really, although 'A Lecture' can be read as an individualist's manifesto, and

'Romanticism' as an individual's attack on individualism, which becomes Hulme's guiding principle. It is true that this shift in Hulme's thinking points up a general Modernist shift from individualism to authoritarianism, and it is not hard to see a politics taking shape. Hulme would certainly distinguish between his 'Bergsonism', with its faith in the individual, impressionism, intuition and general rule-breaking, and the Action Française argument that Bergson was a closet Romantic. But, at the risk of making sweeping statements, we might suggest that there need not be such incompatibility between arguing for rule-breaking from an individualist point of view and arguing for rule-observing from an anti-individualist perspective. Both camps – individualists and anti-individualists – have a passionate and principled faith in final authority, a faith that is prone to what William Carlos Williams called (in a completely different context) *easy lateral sliding*. Both, in their different ways, have a hierarchical model of *authority* that transcends differences about where authority is to be located.

The debate about whether or not Bergsonism is 'back-door' Romanticism is in many ways misleading, but needs addressing for reasons that go beyond Hulme and open onto Modernist politics generally. Though Hulme never abjures the findings of Bergsonian thought (which are also his own), he changes his mind about how to proceed from them. Bergson's is one of the most convincing arguments for the boundedness and limitation of the subjective, the individual, and it is but a small step from Bergson's ideas about flux, lack of unity, intuitive as opposed to intellectual apprehension (all of which are, after all, diagnoses, however liberating, and not solutions), to the desire to respect or impose laws to live by in spite of them. Indeed, it is likely that Bergsonism gave a new urgency to political authoritarianism *for these very reasons*: not because one denied his findings but because one found them too convincingly dangerous to live by. A respect for the church that does not shake one's atheism or make it hypocritical (which was Maurras's position) is an example of just this kind of thinking. In Eliot we find a brand of pseudo-altruistic cageyness, an exemplary and self-abnegating individuality parading as model citizenship, that bears useful comparison.

In 'Romanticism and Classicism', Hulme's cultural politics harden. Taking and extending Coleridge's distinction between Imagination and Fancy, Hulme stage-manages a fight between two persuasions, the Romantic and the Classical. Briefly stated, the modern 'Classical' spirit employs Fancy, while the outmoded (though lingeringly influential) Romantic still clings to 'Imagination'. To the Romantic, 'man's nature is like a well', to the Classical, it is 'like a bucket'. The lecture, which Hulme probably delivered in July 1912, explores several of the ideas observed so far: modern verse and its attitude of mind; 'counter' prose, images and analogies in poetry; overt (rather than implied) politics behind literary tastes (he refers to Action Française); the difficulty of 'shaping' language to expression. Whereas Romantic verse 'seems to crystallize [...] round metaphors of flight', the classical temperament 'always remembers that he is mixed up with earth': 'even in the most imaginative flights there is always a holding back, a reservation. [...] He may jump, but he always returns back; he never flies away into circumambient gas.' Hulme emphasises that this 'Classicism' is not to be equated with 'a return to Pope'; indeed he suggests that 'when it does come we may not even recognise it as classical'. Though Hulme marshals a set of specific targets – Hugo, Swinburne, Ruskin – 'Romanticism' is also a repository of things he dislikes, and which were in dire disrepute among the Anglo-American modernists generally: Victoriana, Pre-Raphaelitism, dilettante criticism and general self-indulgence ('emotions [...] grouped round the word infinite'). To these standards, by which 'poetry that isn't damp isn't poetry at all', he opposes the 'dry hardness' of the Classical, for whom there is no attainable 'beyond', no visitable 'infinite'. It is an unequal contest. His Classicism is nimble, swift-witted, a supple and lithe antagonist for a slow and punch-drunk Romanticism. At roughly the same time as 'Romanticism and Classicism', Hulme is still involved in Bergsonism. Two Bergson articles are particularly relevant, both as background to Hulme's ideas and as explanations of powerfully influential aesthetic philosophies of the early twentieth century. 'The Philosophy of Intensive Manifolds' (originally a lecture series) and 'Bergson's Theory of Art' (published in *The New Age* in 1922 as 'The Note-Books of T.E. Hulme'). These, though not included in this selection, show how Bergsonism, for a while at least, is not only tenable alongside his anti-Romanticism, but indeed compels him to it.

'A Tory Philosophy', which appeared in instalments in 1912, elaborates what are hitherto literary notions with political undertones (one can tell someone's politics from their literary tastes) into an examination of profoundly entrenched political attitudes. It is the 'romanticism in politics' that Hulme denounces. 'Always "escaping", that is it!', he gleefully announces, attacking the feeble politics of attainable perfection, progress, freedom ('the amount of freedom in man is greatly exaggerated'), all of which 'betrays itself in the epithet NEW'. We are becoming used, by now, to a certain hard schematicism in Hulme's arguments, which, if we are not careful, threatens to mask the 'cinderiness' of the 'world-view' he is starting from. The less definite, analysable and comprehensible his subject, the harder, clearer and more seemingly confident the writing. The two are inextricable; the one is a response to the other.

Hulme is, in the frankest sense, assertive. In his political writings – in their sweep rather than their local details – we find his rhetoric of control, order-imposition, stress and violence applied not to language or planes of steel or wood, but to the individual human being. The artist, we recall, struggles against the natural, the ingrained habits of the material (language, steel, wood, clay). So, now, it is against the natural and ingrained tendencies of a flawed human nature that politics should fight. They must do so by making rules and laws that act both as practical guides to living and as concrete reminders of more abstract limitations. In Sorel, Hulme finds an exemplarily problematic figure: a revolutionary Syndicalist who believes in the boundedness and limitation of man, a reactionary who advocates class war but denies 'progress' and is disillusioned with democracy. It is dangerous to speculate about how Hulme's politics would have looked had he survived the war, but one footnote to *Reflections on Violence* deserves highlighting, so assuredly is it stated:

> Some of these [attacks on democratic ideology] are merely dilettante, having little sense of reality, while others are really vicious, in that they play with the idea of inequality. No theory that is not fully moved by the conception of justice asserting the equality of all men, and which cannot offer something to all men, deserves or is likely to have any future.

Also in a footnote to Sorel, Hulme alludes to 'Humanism' as the 'germs of the disease' that eventually becomes Romanticism, and to art. In championing the work of the English avant-garde, Hulme shows himself equally capable of producing highly-charged polemical reviews and more generally theoretical writings. His first such review was perhaps the most controversial. In December 1913, *The New Age* published Hulme's appreciation of Jacob Epstein's exhibition, which Epstein remembered as 'the sanest article written about me'. Hulme dismisses Epstein's detractors, but with such vitriolic personal attacks on a particular critic that it spawned a series of shocked letters to *The New Age*. The victim, Anthony Ludovici, is called 'a charlatan', a 'little Cockney intellect', 'stupid and childish'. 'The most appropriate means of dealing with him would be a little personal violence', writes Hulme. It is more than an off-the-cuff remark, capturing the atmosphere of aggression and violence that permeates English avant-garde discourse (especially that of Wyndham Lewis, who took Hulme's side in the controversy). Hulme is fond of claiming that the strength of a belief is measurable by the extent to which one is prepared to fight for it. When, for instance, Action Française disrupted a lecture in Paris, he opines: 'That is what I call a real vital interest in literature.' For poetry to be 'real', he claims, 'it has to affect the body.' Such instances may be found throughout his writings: if all spheres of intellectual and artistic endeavour are linked, so too are the mental and physical apparatus. It is as if debate in print were a page-bound metaphor for a physical fight, and physical fighting were a concretisation of verbal argument. They are *analogous*, the same operations performed by different orders.

Discovering Worringer and other continental art theorists, Hulme proceeds to extend his enquiries to modern and ancient art (among his papers were plans for a book on art and a monograph on Epstein). Worringer gives Hulme a means of assessing the implications of modern sculpture and painting. His *Abstraction and Empathy* attempted to analyse the 'attitudes of mind' that lie behind 'vital' and 'geometrical' art. Art, stated Worringer, was symptomatic of a race's or a period's sense of its place in the world. Bound up with this sense of place, whether harmony and unity or disharmony and flux, comes an art which expresses the period's spiritual needs. It was fallacious to see ancient stylisation as a sign of lack of skill gradually progressing, through the Renaissance, towards ever greater know-how. This is all grist to Hulme's mill, though he is keenly aware of the differences between the various arts. In 'A Notebook' he suggests that modern and pre-'Renascence' art share a certain 'religious attitude' which can be gauged by 'a feeling for certain absolute values that are independent of vital things':

> Renascence art we may call a 'vital' art in that it depends on plea- sure in the reproduction of human and natural forms. Byzantine art is the exact contrary of this. There is nothing vital in it; the emotion you get from it is not a pleasure in the reproduction of natural or human life. The disgust with the trivial and accidental characteris- tics of living shapes, the searching after an austerity, a *perfection* and rigidity that human things can never have, leads here to the use of forms which can almost be called geometrical.

The attitude behind both the modern and the ancient arts is this: 'Man is subordinate to certain absolute values: there is no delight in the human form, leading to its *natural* reproduction; it is always distorted to fit into the more abstract forms which convey an intense religious emotion.'

In 'Modern Art and Its Philosophy' he discusses a range of artists, from Cézanne to Brancusi, in order to explain the 'new geometrical art' he sees emerging, 'different in kind from the art which preceded it, being much more akin to the geometrical arts of the past': 'It seems to me beyond doubt that this, whether you like it or not, is the character of the art that is coming [...] I believe it to be the precursor of a much wider change in philosophy and general outlook on the world.' Hulme has been busily prophesying – new poetry, new painting, new sculp- ture, new *Weltanschauungen* – and he has been following an ever- widening range of concerns. By now, he has moved from literary romanticism to what he calls, observing the root cause of degeneration in the Renaissance, 'Humanism'. He is, to twist Fenollosa's phrase, *feeling back along the ancient lines of retreat.*

In 'A Notebook' Hulme attains the fullest application of his thought. The 'religious attitude', which does not imply religion itself, premises Original Sin, while 'humanism' premises the perfectibility of man, placing the 'divine' on the human plane. He had argued that Romanticism was 'spilt religion', religion as humanist self-celebration, rather than a stark and limiting absolute. Romanticism in literature, Relativism in ethics, Idealism in philosophy and Modernism in reli- gion are all 'mixed or bastard phenomena'; placing Perfection in *humanity* gives rise to 'that bastard thing Personality, and all the bunkum that follows from it'. Humanity does not 'progress', it merely shifts between possible attitudes of mind, misconstruing these changes as forward motion. Just as modern 'Classicism' is not a return to Pope, so the related 'religious attitude' is not a new 'mediaevalism'. Each new attitude of mind is inflected by the preceding ones: modern Classicism will be different because it has been through Romanticism; the modern religious attitude will be different because it has been through a period of 'spilt religion'; modern geometrical art will be different because it has been through a period of 'vital' art. There are no idealised returns in Hulme, no nostalgia, and despite his talk of religious attitudes, religion *per se*, and the church as an institution, are of little importance: 'I am not [...] concerned so much with religion, as with the attitude, the 'way of thinking', the categories, from which a religion springs, and which often survive it.' It is *dogma*, 'doctrines felt as facts', Hulme claims, that characterise the modern temperament – 'chatter' about 'secondary notions' like 'God, Freedom, and Immortality' are a distraction. It was Baudelaire who asserted that 'Were God not to exist, Religion would remain holy and *Divine*', and Eliot, in his introduction to Christopher Isherwood's translation of Baudelaire's *Intimate Journals*, makes the unlikely – but once made, sustainable – parallel between Hulme and Baudelaire on religion, Original Sin and human imperfectibility.[22]

'A Notebook', like much of Hulme's work, is more (or perhaps less) than analysis or argument; it is assertion. He calls for a 'new attitude' at the same time as diagnosing it, a 'disposition of mind which can look at a *gap* or chasm without shuddering'. Humanism, as he depicts it, is unconsciously based on taken-for-granted principles of continuity, but there are unbridgeable chasms between the three 'regions of reality': the inorganic world (mathematical and physical science), the organic world ('dealt with by biology, psychology and history'), and the 'world of ethical and religious values'. The middle zone, the one in which we predominantly move, is 'covered with some confused muddy substance', while the outer zones 'have an *absolute* character', and thus 'the perfection of geometrical figures'. We are so submerged in the 'muddy mixed zone', that we cannot see beyond it. Romanticism, humanism or whatever it is masquerading as, takes a further pernicious step: it is so immersed that it sees everything *through* the mud ('the eye is in the mud, the eye *is* mud'). Philosophers such as Bergson and Nietzsche, Hulme argues, were useful inasmuch as they recognised the chasm between the organic and the inorganic, but no post-Renaissance thinker had recognised the chasm between the organic and the 'ethical' or 'religious'. This is still humanism, forgetting that 'man is in no sense perfect, but a wretched creature, who can yet apprehend perfection'. 'Original Sin' is thus the necessary dogma, the doctrine that must be *felt as fact*.

Classical and Romantic, humanist and anti-humanist, vital and geometrical: to what extent are these terms related, to what extent are they different? Is the new 'classicism' he predicted simply a different name for the 'anti-humanism' he advocated at the end of his brief writing life? Critics disagree, though there is enough continuity between the two for us confidently to locate the differences between the two terms not so much in their premises as in the extent of their application. They are close enough to be matched up, but not to be interchangeable. As Hulme writes, the categories he writes about widen, swallowing up centuries of thought as voraciously as the arts or the politics they refer to. To the Classical temperament, he opposes the Romantic. But when he sets the 'religious attitude' against 'humanism', he reaches further back, through the Renaissance, through mediaevalism, through ancient civilisations. Hulme moves relentlessly sideways, acquiring examples from all spheres of contemporary art and politics. He also moves backwards, tracing lineages and pedigrees. The man who once advocated the destruction of all verse more than twenty years old finishes up by claiming that humanity, if it is to escape the pernicious myth of progress and perfectibility, ought 'always to carry with it a library of a thousand years as a balancing pole'.

Hulme's thought undoubtedly develops, but the links between 'A Notebook' and the early writings (particularly those, like 'Cinders' and 'Notes on Language and Style', which set out a 'world view') are important: an insistence on the discontinuities and 'gaps' between the world and our perception of it; the fragility and temporary validity of systems; the absence of 'unity' and our means of imposing unity; the issue of 'rules' (poetic, linguistic, moral, political, philosophical); and the struggles of an aggressive, comfortless 'modern spirit' to come to terms with this. These links apart, Hulme's attitude has undergone considerable shifts. These shifts have less to do with the basis – the 'cindery' basis – of his findings, than with the conclusions he draws from them, or rather with their application to the various areas of thought with which he engages. If the 'diagnosis' remains relatively steady, the possible 'remedies' have been in constant development. 'Cinders' sets out on a wide-ranging but raw and fragmented journey through several areas of knowledge; 'A Notebook' retains and expands that range, but fills it out confidently and with a disabused clarity of purpose. In the intervening years his explorations have taken Hulme over the necessary examination of particulars. Always widening his scope, Hulme cannot engage with any one area of thought without seeing its reverberations in, and attachments to, a multiplicity of other branches of enquiry. For Hulme, an attitude to poetry is determined by an (often unexamined) way of seeing the world; this implies a cast of mind, a temperament, which implies a politics, which in turn reflects a taste in art. These lines – whether a philosophy which tapers down to a line of poetry, or a line of poetry that marks the vanishing-point of a philosophical attitude – are themselves determined by other things: from a shared national or cultural history to particular biographical arrangements.

The course of Hulme's multiple preoccupations – their shifts as well as their continuities – represents developments in several aspects of the Modernist sensibility. Hulme touches on many of the artistic, political and philosophical movements of a formatively turbulent time, always close enough to the moment to convey the urgency of controversy, always detached enough to deploy informative, though hardly impartial, analyses. Hulme is also an instigator, a *provocateur*, he challenges and questions as much as he explains and clarifies. Poet and literary theorist, philosopher and aesthetician, political theorist and avant-garde art critic, his work illuminates the period, as well as restoring a powerful individual presence to our too-limited gallery of Modernists. '*Always I desire the great canvas for my lines and gestures*', wrote Hulme in the 'Fragments' that appeared after his death, and his short writing career is one of the most ambitious and comprehensive of his times.

PATRICK MCGUINNESS

Notes

1 T.S. Eliot, 'A Commentary', *The Criterion*, II, 7 (April 1924), p. 231. Eliot goes on to call Hulme 'the forerunner of a new attitude of mind, which should be the twentieth-century mind', and to claim that Bertrand Russell and his circle are representative of a 'dead present', to which Hulme is the clear alternative. Though Eliot frequently returns to Hulme in his writing, most notably in his cultural criticism, he is also intent on maintaining Hulme's originality as a poet. In his 1917 essay 'Reflections on *vers libre*' Eliot had quoted Hulme's poem 'The Embankment' as an example of 'the skilful evasion of iambic pentameter' (*To Criticize the Critic and Other Writings*, London: Faber and Faber, 1978, pp. 185–6). In a 1919 letter to Mary Hutchinson, Eliot wrote: 'I am not sure whether you thought that Hulme is a really great poet, as I do, or not? I can't think of anything as good as two of his poems since Blake' (T.S. Eliot, *Selected Letters. Volume One: 1898–1922*, ed. Valerie Eliot, London: Faber and Faber, 1988, p. 311). See also C.K. Stead's fine chapter on 'Eliot and the Revolutionary Right', in *Pound, Yeats, Eliot and the Modernist Movement* (Basingstoke: MacMillan, 1986).

2 Frank Kermode, in *Romantic Image* (London: Routledge and Kegan Paul, 1957), is the clearest and most convincing exponent of the theory of Hulme's 'self-contradictions'. For a full bibliography of the considerable range of writings about Hulme between 1909 and 1984, see K.E. Csengeri, 'T.E. Hulme: An Annotated Bibliography of Writings about Him', in *English Literature in Transition*, 29/4 (1986), pp. 388–428.

3 Among the critics who have stressed the developing nature of Hulme's thought, two in particular should be signalled. Michael Levenson, who devotes two chapters to Hulme in his excellent study *A Genealogy of Modernism: A Study of English Literary Doctrine 1908–1922* (Cambridge: Cambridge University Press, 1984), charts Hulme's progress and maps it onto more general trends in Modernist cultural politics. Karen Csengeri provides a useful introduction to her edition of *The Collected Writings of T.E. Hulme* (Oxford: Oxford University Press, 1994). Csengeri's edition scrupulously dates Hulme's writings, and provides a valuable free-standing corrective to the misunderstandings created by the confused ordering of his writings in earlier studies and selections. See also Patrick McGuinness, 'Essentials: T.E. Hulme' (review of *The Collected Writings of T.E. Hulme*, *PN Review*, 106 (1995).

4 F.S. Flint, *The Egoist*, 2 (1 May, 1915), pp. 70-1. This is the 'Imagism' issue of *The Egoist*, where Aldington reviews Pound, Flint reviews H.D., Olivia Shakespear reviews D.H. Lawrence, in which Harold Monro contributes 'The Imagists Discussed' and new poems appear by Marianne Moore, Flint, Aldington, Amy Lowell and Lawrence.

5 Allen Upward, 'A Discarded Imagist', *The Egoist* (1 June 1915), p. 98. See also F.W. Tancred's poem 'To T.E. Hulme', *Poetry Review*, I, 2 (December, 1912), p. 537.

6 'The critical LIGHT during the years immediately pre-war in London shone not from Hulme but from Ford Madox Ford', avers Pound in *The Townsman*, 2 (January 1939).

7 The disagreements between Pound and Flint over the matter of Imagism's 'history', and issues of 'copyright', were never fully resolved. See, in this context, Christopher Middleton, 'Documents on Imagism from the papers of F.S. Flint', *The Review*, 15 (April 1965), pp. 36–51. Among the many studies of Imagism, written from numerous perspectives, see: John T. Gage, *In The Arresting Eye: The Rhetoric of Imagism* (Baton Rouge: Louisiana State University Press, 1981); Stanley Coffman, *Imagism: A Chapter in*

the History of Modern Poetry (New York: Octagon, 1972); J.B. Harmer, *Victory in Limbo: Imagism 1908–1917* (London: Secker and Warburg, 1975).

8   It is true that the Modernists – Eliot and Pound especially – are acutely conscious of issues of 'fitting in', both as followers of a tradition and as creators of it. Their 'place' in literature, as well as their 'placing' of other writers, are projects they invest in very early in their literary enterprises and are high on their critical agendas. The point here, however, is that literary history tends to have endorsed Pound's and Eliot's value-systems, along with their estimations of their contemporaries, in a way that obscures other aspects of the literary field of the period .

9   *The Chinese Written Character as a Medium for Poetry*, edited by Ezra Pound (San Francisco: City Lights Books, 1936), p. 26.

10 Reference in St John's College, Cambridge. It is quoted by kind permission of the Master, Fellows and Scholars of St John's College, Cambridge.

11 The relevant documents, along with letters, university reports and sundry material relating to Hulme's attempts to study at Cambridge, are kept in the archive of St John's College, Cambridge. They tell a tale of unpaid bills, academic laziness, and irrepressible troublemaking.

12 See Richard Cork, *Vorticism and Abstract Art in the First Machine Age* (London: Gordon Fraser, 1976). Cork's excellent work devotes considerable space to Hulme, and assesses his contribution to English avant-garde art.

13 Wyndham Lewis, Jacob Epstein, Ezra Pound and David Bomberg are among those who have written about him in memoirs or elsewhere, while Michael Roberts, in *T.E. Hulme* (London: Faber and Faber, 1938; Manchester: Carcanet, 1982) , and Alun Jones, in *The Life and Opinions of T.E. Hulme* (London: Gollancz, 1960), provide fuller and more impartial accounts of his life.

14 'Diary from the Trenches', so-called by Samuel Hynes in his edition of *Further Speculations* (Minneapolis: University of Minnesota Press, 1955), is a series of letters written in 1914–15 by Hulme to members of his family.

15 Ezra Pound, *The Cantos* (London: Faber and Faber, 1986), p. 71.

16 Hulme became associated with *The New Age*, edited by A.R. Orage, in 1909, and continued to write for it until his death. See Wallace Martin's *The New Age Under Orage* (Manchester: Manchester University Press, 1967).

17 For discussions of Hulme and Fenollosa, see Donald Davie, *Articulate Energy: An Inquiry into the Syntax of English Poetry* (London: Routledge & Kegan Paul, 1955). See also *Purity of Diction in English Verse and Articulate Energy* (Harmondsworth: Penguin, 1992).

18 Such figures as Eliot, Lewis, Flint and others attest to Hulme's having played an active part in the London avant-garde scene, and that, contrary to the Poundian line that he was marginal and flitting, Hulme was very much in evidence. A 1915 letter from Eliot to Mrs Jack Gardner speaks of him in such a way as to situate him at the centre both of the art and ideas of the period, and of a 'group': 'One of the most interesting of the radicals – Gaudier Brzeska – do you know of him? – is in the trenches, (as is the interesting T.E. Hulme); cubism is still represented by Wyndham Lewis, by Jacob Epstein, and a man whose work I like exceedingly, Edward Wadsworth.' *Selected Letters*, p. 94.

19 Shklovski, 'The Resurrection of the Word' (1914), translated by Richard Sherwood, in

Russian Formalism: A Collection of Articles and Texts in Translation (Edinburgh: Scottish Academic Press, 1973), p. 41. See also Michael Grant, 'Pater, Leavis and the Truths of Style', *PN Review*, 105 (1995).
20 Shklovski, 'The Resurrection of the Word', p. 41.
21 Ibid.
22 *Charles Baudelaire. Intimate Journals*, translated by Christopher Isherwood (London: Blackmore Press, 1930), p. 25.

Select Bibliography of Hulme's Writings

Speculations, ed. Herbert Read. London: Routledge and Kegan Paul, 1924.

Notes on Language and Style, ed. Herbert Read, *Criterion*, 3 (July 1925), 485–97.

Notes on Language and Style, ed. Herbert Read. University of Washington Chapbook, Seattle, no. 25, 1925.

Michael Roberts, *T.E. Hulme*. London: Faber and Faber, 1938. Reprinted with an introduction by Anthony Quinton, Carcanet Press: Manchester, 1982.

Further Speculations, ed. Samuel Hynes. Minneapolis: University of Minnesota Press, 1955.

Alun R. Jones, *The Life and Opinions of T.E. Hulme*. London: Gollancz, 1960.

The Collected Writings of T.E. Hulme, ed. K.E. Csengeri. Oxford: Oxford University Press, 1992.

Note on the Text

Hulme is often inconsistent in matters of punctuation, spelling, capitalisation and hyphenation. These inconsistencies have been left as they originally appeared. However when obvious errors occur, notably in his French and German, these have been silently corrected.

Acknowledgements

I am grateful to the following for permission to reproduce extracts from Hulme's writings: Routledge, for the texts of 'Cinders', 'Romanticism and Classicism', and 'Modern Art and its Philosophy' from Herbert Read's *Speculations*; Carcanet Press, for 'Notes on Language and Style' and 'A Lecture on Modern Poetry' from Michael Roberts's *T.E. Hulme*; and Gollancz for poems from *The Life and Opinions of T.E. Hulme* by Alun R. Jones. Our attempts to trace the copyright holder to Hulme's poetry were unsuccessful. Thanks go to The Master, Fellows and Scholars of St John's College, Cambridge, and to Malcolm Underwood, the Archivist, for letting me consult material relating to Hulme's attempts to remain an undergraduate. The university libraries of Hull and Keele allowed me to see manuscripts and letters by and relating to Hulme, including original typescripts and handwritten letters and poems. The Bodleian Library in Oxford provided photographs of the *New Age* pages of Hulme's 'Contemporary Drawings' series, and Richard Cork kindly let me have the photograph of Hulme reproduced on the cover of this book.

As a reader and editor of Hulme, I am indebted to previous scholars and commentators who have kept his work available: Herbert Read, Michael Roberts, Alun R. Jones, Samuel Hynes, and, most recently, Karen Csengeri. Their works are noted in the introduction and bibliography.

I owe a great deal to Paul Morris and Vivien Bowyer for help with scanning and typing the source texts, using technology that would have had even the Futurists thinking twice about welcoming the age of machines, and to Robyn Marsack for her astute editing. I benefited greatly from the conversations, advice and practical help of the following: Scott Ashley, Paul Bishop, Richard Cork, David Cowling, Ian Firla, Graham Glass, Robert Jones, Charles Mundye, Patrick Quinn, Alan Raitt, Michael Schmidt, Richard Sheppard, Evelyn Silber, Janis Spurlock and Clive Wilmer. Angharad Price translated the German poems of 'German Chronicle', and helped and encouraged me in many ways. The book is for my parents and for my sister.

Poems and Fragments[1]

A City Sunset

Alluring, Earth seducing, with high conceits
is the sunset that reigns
at the end of westward streets...
A sudden flaring sky
troubling strangely the passer by
with visions, alien to long streets, of Cytherea
or the smooth flesh of Lady Castlemaine...
A frolic of crimson
is the spreading glory of the sky,
heaven's jocund maid
flaunting a trailed red robe
along the fretted city roofs
about the time of homeward going crowds
– a vain maid, lingering, loth to go...

Autumn

A touch of cold in the Autumn night
I walked abroad,
And saw the ruddy moon lean over a hedge
Like a red-faced farmer.
I did not stop to speak, but nodded;
And round about were the wistful stars
With white faces like town children.

Mana Aboda

Beauty is the marking-time, the stationary vibration, the feigned ecstasy of any arrested impulse unable to reach its natural end.

Mana Aboda, whose bent form
The sky in archèd circle is,
Seems ever for an unknown grief to mourn.
Yet on a day I heard her cry:
'I weary of the roses and the singing poets –
Josephs all, not tall enough to try.'

Above the Dock

Above the quiet dock in midnight,
Tangled in the tall mast's corded height,
Hangs the moon. What seemed so far away
Is but a child's balloon, forgotten after play.

The Embankment
(The fantasia of a fallen gentleman on a cold, bitter night)

Once, in finesse of fiddles found I ecstasy,
In a flash of gold heels on the hard pavement.
Now see I
That warmth's the very stuff of poesy.
Oh, God, make small
The old star-eaten blanket of the sky,
That I may fold it round me and in comfort lie.

Conversion

Light-hearted I walked into the valley wood
In the time of hyacinths,
Till beauty like a scented cloth
Cast over, stifled me, I was bound
Motionless and faint of breath
By loveliness that is her own eunuch.
Now pass I to the final river
Ignominiously, in a sack, without sound,
As any peeping Turk to the Bosphorus.

The Man in the Crow's Nest
(Look-out Man)

Strange to me, sounds the wind that blows
By the masthead, in the lonely night
Maybe 'tis the sea whistling – feigning joy
To hide its fright
Like a village boy
That trembling past the churchyard goes.

Susan Ann and Immortality

Her head hung down
Gazed at earth, fixedly keen,
As the rabbit at the stoat
Till the earth was sky,
Sky that was green,
And brown clouds past,
Like chestnut leaves arching the ground.

The Poet

Over a large table, smooth, he leaned in ecstasies,
In a dream.
He had been to woods, and talked and walked with trees.
Had left the world
And brought back round globes and stone images,
Of gems, colours, hard and definite.
With these he played, in a dream,
On the smooth table.

A Tall Woman

Solid and peaceful is Horton town,
Known is all friendship and steady.
In fixed roads walks every man.

A tall woman is come to Horton town…
In the midst of all men, secretly she presses my hand.
When all are looking, she seems to promise.
There is a secret garden
And a cool stream…
Thus at all men she looks.
The same promise to many eyes.
Yet when she forward leans, in a room,
And by seeming accident her breasts brush against me,
Then is the axle of the world twisted.

A Sudden Secret

A sudden secret cove by Budley
Waveless water, cliff enclosed.
A still boudoir of the sea, which
In the noon-heat lolls in to sleep.

Velvet sand, smooth as the rounded thigh
Of the Lady of Avé, as asleep she lay.
Vibrant noon-heat, trembling at the view.
Oh eager page! Oh velvet sand!
Tremulous faint-hearted waves creep up
Diffident – ah, how wondering!
Trembling and drawing back.

Be hold – the Abbé blesses – 'tis only feignéd sleep.
Oh smooth round thigh!...

A rough wind rises, dark cliffs stare down.
Sour-faced Calvin – art thou whining still?

In the Quiet Land

In the quiet land
There is a secret unknown fire.
Suddenly rocks shall melt
And the old roads mislead.

Across the familiar road
There is a deep cleft. I must stand and draw back.
In the cool land
There is a secret fire.

At Night!

At night!
All the terror's in that.
Branches of the dead tree
Silhouetted on the hill's edge.
Dark veins diseased,
On the dead white body of the sky.
The tearing iron hook
Of pitiless Mara.
Handling soft clouds in insurrection.
Brand of the obscene gods
On their flying cattle,
Roaming the sky prairie.

Town Sky-line

On a summer day, in Town,
Where chimneys fret the cumuli,
Flora passing in disdain
Lifts her flounced blue gown, the sky.
So I see her white cloud petticoat,
Clear Valenciennes, meshed by twisted cowls,
Rent by tall chimneys, torn lace, frayed and fissured.

In the City Square

In the city square at night, the meeting of the torches.
The start of the great march,
The cries, the cheers, the parting.
Marching in an order
Through the familiar streets,
Through friends for the last time seen.
Marching with torches.

Over the hill summit,
The moon and the moor,
And we marching alone.
The torches are out.

On the cold hill,
The cheers of the warrior dead
(For the first time re-seen)
Marching in an order
To where?

Madman

As I walk by the river
Those who have not yet withdrawn pass me
I see past them, touch them.
And in the distance, over the water,
Far from the lights,
I see Night, that dark savage,
But I will not fear him.
Four walls are round me.
I can touch them.
If I die, I can float by.
Moan and hum and remember the sea
In heaven, Oh my spirit,
Remember the sea and its moaning.
Hum in the presence of God, it will sustain you.
Again I am cold, as after weeping.
And I tremble – but there is no wind.

As a Fowl

As a fowl in the tall grass lies
Beneath the terror of the hawk,
The tressed white light crept
Whispering with hand on mouth mysterious
Hunting the leaping shadows in straight streets
By the white houses of old Flemish towns.

Far Back There

Far back there is a round pool,
Where trees reflected make sad memory,
Whose tense expectant surface waits
The ecstatic wave that ripples it
In sacrament of union,
The fugitive bliss that comes with the read tear
That falls from the middle-aged princess
(Sister to the princely Frog)
While she leans tranced in a dreamy curve,
As a drowsy wail in an Eastern song.

Musié

Over a void, a desert, a flat empty space,
Came in waves, like winds,
The sound of drums, in lines, sweeping the armies
… Dreams of soft notes
    Sail as a fleet at eve
    On a calm sea.

The Sunset

A coryphée, covetous of applause,
Loth to leave the stage,
With final diablerie, poises high her toe,
Displays scarlet lingerie of carmin'd clouds,
Amid the hostile murmurs of the stalls.

A Prayer to the Moon to Smile
(A Windy Night)

Through the driven clouds
The Moon
As a queen with unmoved face doth watch
Her dusky cavalry ride past
In mad manoeuvres,
Charging in mass, divide in swerving wings
On either side the throne,
Yet smiles she not at the show provided
By Wind,
Master of the Royal Masque.

What is the grief doth fix your face,
O Queen! in such immutability.
Is it that I, a poor versemaker,
In your royal presence walks unbidden
And through the chinks, without payment,
Steal a look!

Autumn (II)

Suddenly in the night, I came into
A valley deep, filled with forest dark.
Tall naked women seemed the trunks of trees,
Tall unnatural, limp with lassitude,
Bent with vague grief, like flags in failing wind,
The very ecstasy of Nature dead,
Nude flesh, yet agony of drapery,
Arms interlaced, like trellis 'gainst the sky
Covered with dark hair, impenetrable
Where tears were leaves that lay thick on the ground,
Dead memory of summer's passion past.
Tears dropped, fluttering slowly to the earth,
Blown idly by the wind, vain sigh of God,
Tears that vanished not, but lay red and brown
    Until the coming of forgetful Spring.

Sunset (II)

I love not the Sunset
That flaunts like a scarlet sore
O'er half a sick sky,
That calls aloud for all to gape
At its beauty
Like a wanton.

But Sunset when the sun comes home
Like a ship from the sea
With its round red sail
Shadowed against a clear sky,
Silent, in a cool harbour
At eve,
After labour.

Sunset

I love not the Sunset
That spréad like a scarlet sóre
O'er hálf a sick sky,
Or flaunts a tráiled red globe
Along the fretted edge of the city's roofs
Abóut the time of hómeward going crowds
Calling aloúd for all to gápe
At its beáuty
Like a wanton.

But sunsets
When the sún comes hóme
As a shíp from the séa
With its round red sáil
Shádowed sharp against the dárkening sky
Quíet – in a cóol harbour
At éve
After wórk

[Oh Lady – full of mystery]

Oh Lady – full of mystery
Is that blue sea, beyond your knee.

My dreaming languorous voyage take
To where that same blue sea doth break
In cambric surf all framed with lace
On white strands far from this dull place.

[Now though the skirt be fallen]

Now though the skirt be fallen,
Gone the vision of the sea.
Though braced (abominable feeling)
By the cold winds of common sense,
Still my seaman thoughts sail hence.
Still hears the murmur of the blue
Round the black cliffs of your shoe.

Trenches: St Eloi[2]
TEH Poem: Abbreviated from the Conversation of Mr T.E.H.

Over the flat slopes of St Eloi
A wide wall of sand bags.
Night,
In the silence desultory men
Pottering over small fires, cleaning their mess-tins:
To and fro, from the lines,
Men walk as on Piccadilly,
Making paths in the dark,
Through scattered dead horses,
Over a dead Belgian's belly.

The Germans have rockets. The English have no rockets.
Behind the line, cannon, hidden, lying back miles.
Before the line, chaos:

My mind is a corridor. The minds about me are corridors.
Nothing suggests itself. There is nothing to do but keep on.

Fragments[3]

Always I desire the great canvas for my lines and gestures.

*

Old houses were scaffolding once
                    and workmen whistling.

*

Three birds flew over the red wall
                    into the pit of the evening sun.
O daring, doométd birds that pass from my sight.

*

I lie alone in the little valley, in the noon heat,
In the kingdom of little sounds.
The hot air whispers lasciviously.
The lark sings like the sound of distant
                              Unattainable brooks.

*

The sky is the eye of labourer earth.
Last night late in the view he stayed.
Today, clouds pass, likes motes
Across his bleared vision.

*

As on a veiled stage, thin Anar
Trembles with listless arms hung limp
At the touch of the cold hand of Manar
Placed warning.

*

Raleigh in the dark tower prisoned
Dreamed of the blue sea and beyond
Where in strange tropic paradise
Grew musk…

*

Her skirt lifted as a dark mist
From the columns of amethyst.

*

This to all ladies gay I say.
Away, abhorréd lace, away.

*

The lark crawls on the cloud
Like a flea on a white body.

*

With a courtly bow the bent tree sighed,
May I present you to my friend the sun.

*

The mystic sadness of the sight
Of a far town seen in the night.

*

The after–black lies low along the hills
Like the trailed smoke of a steamer.

*

Sounds fluttered,
                    like bats in the dusk.

*

The flounced edge of a skirt,
      recoiling like waves off a cliff.

*

Down the long desolate street of stars.

*

The bloom of the grape has gone.

*

The magic momentary time.

*

Slowly died along the scented way.

*

When she speaks, almost her breasts touch me.
Backward leans her head.

*

Her head hung down
Looked fixedly at earth,
As the rabbit at the stoat,
Till she thinks the earth is the sky.

*

Somewhere the gods (the blanket-makers in the prairie
   of cold)
Sleep in their blankets.

['Religion is the expansive lie of temporary warmth']

*

I walked into the wood in June
And suddenly Beauty, like a thick scented veil,
Stifled me,
Tripped me up, tight round my limbs,
Arrested me.

Belated Romanticism

[*The New Age*, 4/17 (18 February 1909)]

To the Editor of The New Age

When Mr. Flint[1] compares the unclassed lyric assembly of the Poets' Club with that of Verlaine and his companions in obscure (sic.) cafés – he laughs. I can hear that laugh: sardonic, superior, and rather young.

When, oh, when, shall we finish sentimentalising about French poets in cafés! One hoped that with Mr. George Moore's entry into middle-age the end of it was nigh. But now comes Mr. Flint, a belated romantic born out of due time, to carry on the mythical tradition of the poètes maudits. Nurtured on Mürger, he is obsessed by the illusion that poets must be addicted to Circean excess and discoloured linen.

With all the sentimentality of an orthodox suburban, he dwells with pathetic fondness on perfectly ordinary habits, and with great awe reminds us how Verlaine hung his hat on a peg. We, like Verlaine, are natural. It was natural for a Frenchman to frequent cafés. It would be dangerous as well as affected for us to recite verse in a saloon bar.

Mr. Flint speaks with fine scorn of evening dress. It is time to protest against this exclusiveness of the Bohemian, that exotic creature of rare and delicate growth. Why should we be treated as outcasts by the new aristocracy of one suit?

Historically, Mr. Flint is inaccurate. The founders of the modern 'vers libres' movement were Kahn and Laforgue, the latter a court functionary 'épris de ton londonien' Kahn entertained at a banquet where Mallarmé (alas for the granitic Flint) in evening dress formally proposed his health.

I hereby invite Mr. Flint to come to the next dinner, on the 23rd, in any costume that suits him best, when that 'correct person' – Professor G.K. Chesterton – will lecture 'portentously'.

Café Tour d'Eiffel.   T.E. HULME, M.P.C.

Cinders[1]

[*Speculations*, 217-245]

For the Preface.

The history of philosophers we know, but who will write the history of the philosophic amateurs and readers? Who will tell us of the circulation of Descartes, who read the book and who understood it? Or do philosophers, like the mythical people on the island, take in each other's washing? Are they the only readers of each other's books? For I take it, a man who understands philosophy is inevitably irritated into writing it. The few who have learnt the jargon must repay themselves by employing it. A new philosophy is not like a new religion, a thing to be merely thankful for and accepted mutely by the faithful. It is more of the nature of food thrown to the lions; the pleasure lies in the fact that it can be devoured. It is food for the critics, and all readers of philosophy, I take it, are critics, and not faithful ones waiting for the new gospel. With this preface I offer my new kind of food to tickle the palate of the connoisseurs.[2]

A Sketch of a New Weltanschauung.

I. In spite of pretensions to absolute truth, the results of philosophy are always tested by the effects, and by the judgments of other philosophers. There is always an appeal to a circle of people. The same is true of values in art, in morals. A man cannot stand alone on absolute ground, but always appeals to his fellows.

II. Therefore it is suggested that there is no such thing as an absolute truth to be discovered. All general statements about truth, etc., are in the end only amplifications of man's appetites.

The ultimate reality is a circle of persons, *i.e.* animals who communicate.

There is a kind of gossamer web, woven between the real things, and by this means the animals communicate. For purposes of communication they invent a symbolic language. Afterwards this language, used to excess, becomes a disease, and we get the curious phenomena of men explaining themselves by means of the gossamer web that connects them. Language becomes a disease in the hands of the counter-word mongers. It must constantly be remembered that it is an invention for the convenience of men; and in the midst of Hegelians who triumphantly explain the world as a mixture of 'good' and 'beauty' and 'truth', this should be remembered. What would an intelligent animal (without the language disease), or a carter in the road, think of it all?

Symbols are picked out and believed to be realities. People imagine that all the complicated structure of the world can be woven out of 'good' and 'beauty'. These words are merely counters representing vague groups of things, to be moved about on a board for the convenience of the players.

III. Objection might be taken that this makes man the measure of the world, and that after all he is only an animal, who came late, and the world must be supposed to have existed before he evolved at all. The reply to this is as follows:

(i) Analogy of courage and capacity. Courage in the Wild West requires capacities different from those it requires in the city. But the phenomena are the same: A non-muscular man is inevitably physically a coward.

(ii) The mental qualities of men and animals are common, though they are realised by different means.

(iii) These qualities – *e.g.* the common return to egoism, the roundness of the world, the absence of all infinitude, the denial of all Utopias – are extended to the ultimate nature of the world.

(iv) These qualities extend to the amoeba and the inorganic world.

(v) It is these qualities with which the world is measured in I.

(vi) Hence in a sense 'Man is the measure of all things' and man (egoism) *has always existed and always will exist.*

IV. Just as no common purpose can be aimed at for the conflicting purposes of real people, *so* there is no common purpose in the world.

The world is a plurality.

A unity arrived at by stripping off essentials is not a unity. Compound is not an inner reality.

V. This plurality consists in the nature of an ash-heap. In this ash-pit of cinders, certain ordered routes have been made, thus constituting whatever unity there may be – a kind of manufactured chess-board laid on a cinder-heap. Not a real chess-board impressed on the cinders, but the gossamer world of symbolic communication already spoken of.

Cinders.

There is a difficulty in finding a comprehensive scheme of the cosmos, because there is none. The cosmos is only *organised* in parts; the rest is cinders.

Death is a breaking up into cinders. Hence partial truth of the old Greek conception of Hades (a place of less organisation and *no* happiness) .

Many necessary conditions must be fulfilled before the counters and the chess-board can be posed elegantly on the cinders. Illness and death easily disturb and give falls from this condition. Perhaps this is an illustration of Nietzsche's image of the tightrope walker. When all is arranged the counters are moved about. This is happiness, moving to enthusiastic conclusions, the musical note, perhaps Art. But it must be largely artificial. (Art prolongs it, and creates it by blur.)

The floating heroic world (built up of moments) and the cindery reality – can they be made to correspond to some fundamental constitution of the world? (An antithesis much more deep than the one which analyses all realities into forms of egoism. This latter only a particular case of the general law.)

The *absolute* is to be described not as perfect, but if existent as essentially imperfect, chaotic, and cinder-like. (Even this view is not ultimate, but merely designed to satisfy temporary human analogies and wants.)

World is indescribable, that is, not reducible to counters; and particularly it is impossible to include it all under one large counter such as 'God' or 'Truth' and the other verbalisms, or the disease of the symbolic language.

Cinders can never be counters except for certain practical purposes (good enough) – cf. rail lines and chess-board. The treatment of the soul as the central part of the nominalist position. Their habit of regarding it as a kind of round counter all red, which survives *whole* in all its redness and roundness (the redness as the character), a counter-like *distinct* separate entity, just as *word* itself is.

Why is it that London looks pretty by night? Because for the general cindery chaos there is substituted a simple ordered arrangement of a finite number of lights.

The two complementary phenomena: that each wash is a line, and that each line is a wash.

That the world is finite (atomism: there are no infinitudes except in art) and that it is yet an infinitude of cinders (there is no finite law encompassing all).

This new view may perhaps be caricatured by saying that the bad is fundamental, and that the good is artificially built up in it and out of it, like oases in the desert, or as cheerful houses in the storm.

(Two parts: 1 – All cinders; 2 – the part built up. So the question: How far built up and how far given us? The question of the pliability of the world.)

All is flux. The moralists, the capital letterists, attempt to find a framework outside the flux, a solid bank for the river, a pier rather than a raft. Truth is what helps a particular sect in the general flow.

School children at a fountain (moved mechanically by thirst) to someone looking down from above, appear as a pure instinctive mechanical act. Cf. ants – we are unable to ascertain the subtler reasons which move them. They all look alike. Hence humpty-dumpty's remark about human faces is seen to be the foundation of all science and all philosophy.

Only in the fact of consciousness is there a unity in the world. Cf. Oxford Street at 2 a.m. All the mud, endless, except where bound together by the spectator.

Unity is made in the world by drawing squares over it. We are able to get along these at any rate – cf. railway line in desert. (Always the elusive as seen in maps. *Ad infinitum.*)

The squares include cinders – always cinders.

No unity of laws, but merely of the sorting machine.

Formerly, one liked theories because they reduced the world to a single principle. Now the same reason disgusts us. The flats of Canada are incomprehensible on any single theory. The world only comprehensible on the cinder theory.

The same old fallacy persists – the desire to introduce a unity in the world: (1) The mythologists made it a woman or an elephant; (2) the scientists made fun of the mythologists, but themselves turned the world into the likeness of a mechanical toy. They were more concerned with models than with woman (woman troubled them and hence their particular form of anthropomorphism). One analogy is as good as another. The truth remains that the world is not any unity, but a house in the cinders (outside in the cold, primeval).

Contrast the Pythagorean ecstasies in the numbers 3 and 7. The cinder is the opposite prejudice. I am immediately up in arms if a book says a subject can be divided into three separate parts.

Most of our life is spent in buttoning and unbuttoning. Yes, quite so. This fact can be welcomed as fitting in with the general theory.

The unity of Nature is an extremely artificial and fragile bridge, a garden net.

The covers of a book are responsible for much error. They set a limit round certain convenient groups of ideas, when there are really no limits.

The aim of science and of all thought is to reduce the complex and inevitably disconnected world of grit and cinders to a few ideal counters, which we can move about and so form an ungritlike picture of reality – one flattering to our sense of power over the world.

In the end this is true too of mathematics, though at first it appears as a more complex symbolism. The conclusion of all mathematics is: that one counter stands in a certain relation to another. That counter maybe a simple number or an elliptic integral, but the final effect is the same. (All mathematics is deducible from numbers, which are nothing but counters.)

There is an *objective* world (?), a chaos, a cinder-heap. Gradually cases have been built up. Egos have grown as organised trees.

So not *idealist*, as that assumes that there is nothing but a fixed number of persons, and without them nothing. (So the Real New Realism is something beyond names. World can't be O because O is opposed to human psychology.)

A landscape, with occasional oases. So now and then we are moved – at the theatre, action, a love. But mainly deserts of dirt, ash-pits of the cosmos, grass on ash-pits. No universal ego, but a few definite persons gradually built up.

Nature as the accumulation of the memories of man.

Certain groups of ideas as huts for men to live in. The Act of Creation.

Truth is always seen to lie in a compromise. All clear cut ideas turn out to be wrong. Analogy to real things, which are artificially picked out of the general lava flow of cinders.

Cf. the wandering attention in the library. Sometimes one seems to have definite clear cut moments, but not afterwards.

I.   Nature. Scenery as built up by man. Oases in the desert of grit.
II. Extended to the whole of the world.
III. *But* the microscope. Things revealed, not created, but there before, and also seem to be in an order.
IV. Before man other powers created in the struggle.
V.   So man was gradually built up, and man's world was gradually built up at the same time.

Evolution of colour; dim perception of it in the amoeba; evolved –

the whole modern world of colour built up from this; gradually made more counter-like and distinct.

There is no inevitable order into which ideas must be shifted.

We live in a room, of course, but the great question for philosophy is: how far have we decorated the room, and how far was it made before we came? Did we merely decorate the room, or did we make it from chaos? The laws of nature that we certainly do find – what are they?

In an organised city it is not easy to see the cinder element of earth – all is banished. But it is easy to see it psychologically. What the Nominalists call the grit in the machine, I call the fundamental element of the machine.

Properly to estimate the true purpose of absolute philosophy, it should be realised as reducing everything to number, the only rational and logical solution from the point of view that dares to conceive relation as of more importance than the persons related.

The eyes, the beauty of the world, have been organised out of the faeces. Man returns to dust. So does the face of the world to primeval cinders.

A girl's ball-dress and shoes are symbolic of the world organised (in counters) from the mud. Separate from contact.

Only the isolated points seem to have any value, so how can the world be said to be designed? Rather we may say that gradually certain points are being designed.

Taken *mystically* – then all peculiarities of the human organism must have their counterpart in the construction of the world.
E.g. – Illness and a reversion to chaos.
Man is the chaos highly organised, but liable to revert to chaos at any moment. Happiness and ecstasy at present unstable. Walking in the street, seeing pretty girls (all chaos put into the drains: not seen)

and wondering what they would look like ill. Men laughing at a bar –
but wait till the fundamental chaos reveals itself.

The two moods in life. (i) Ill in bed, toothache, W.C. in the Atlantic
– the disorganised, withdrawn-into-oneself mood. (ii) Flying along in
the wind (wind in the hair, on a motor bus). *Or* evolving a new theory.
The impersonal feeling.

Ennui and disgust, the sick moments – not an occasional lapse or
disease, but the fundamental ennui and chaos out of which the world
has been built, and which is as necessary to it as the listeners are to
intellectuals. The old world order of queens and pawns.

The apparent scientific unity of the world may be due to the fact
that man is a kind of sorting machine.

'I must tell someone' as the final criterion of philosophy, the *raison
d'être* of the human circle symbol.

The sick disgusting moments are part of the fundamental cinders –
primeval chaos – the dream of impossible chaos.

The absolute is invented to reconcile conflicting purposes. But
these purposes are necessarily conflicting, even in the nature of Truth
itself. It is so absurd to construct an absolute which shall at each
moment just manage by artificial gymnastics to reconcile these
purposes.

Philosophical syntheses and ethical systems are only possible in
arm-chair moments. They are seen to be meaningless as soon as we get
into a bus with a dirty baby and a crowd.

Note the fact that all a writer's generalisations and truths can be
traced to the personal circumstances and prejudices of his class, expe-
rience, capacity and body. This, however, is not an instance of error or
hypocrisy. There is no average or real truth to be discerned among the
different fronts of prejudice. Each is a truth in so far as it satisfies the
writer.

We must judge the world from the status of animals, leaving out 'Truth', etc.

Animals are in the same state that men were before symbolic language was invented.

Philosophy is about people in clothes, not about the soul of man.

The fixed order of the world is woven in a gigantic way by the acts of men and animals.

The world lives in order to develop the lines on its face.

These little theories of the world, which satisfy and are then thrown away, one after the other, develop *not* as successive approximations to the truth, but like successive thirsts, to be satisfied at the moment, and not evolving to one great Universal Thirst.

Through all the ages, the conversation of ten men sitting together is what holds the world together.

Never think in a book: here are Truth and all the other capital letters; but think in a theatre and watch the audience. Here is the reality, here are human animals. Listen to the words of heroism and then at the crowded husbands who applaud. All philosophies are subordinate to this. It is not a question of the unity of the world and men afterwards put into it, *but* of human animals, and of philosophies as an elaboration of their appetites.

Words.
Heaven as the short summary paradise of words.

The ideal of knowledge: all cinders reduced to counters (words); these counters moved about on a chess-board, and so all phenomena made obvious.
Something is always lost in generalisation. A railway leaves out all the gaps of dirt between. Generalisations are only means of getting

about.

Cf. the words love, sex, nude, with the actual details.

I hate more than anything the vague long pretentious words of Wells – 'indefinable tendency in events', etc., etc.

Always seek the hard, definite, personal word.

The real levelheadedness: to be able to analyse a pretty girl at first sight, not to be intoxicated with clothes, to be able to imagine the effect of dipping in water – this is what one must be able to do for words, and for all embracing philosophies. We must not be taken in by the arm-chair moments.

The World is Round.

Disillusionment comes when it is recognised that all heroic actions can be reduced to the simple laws of egoism. But wonder can even then be found in the fact that there *are* such *different* and *clear-cut* laws and egoisms and that they have been created out of the chaos.

The pathetic search for the *different*. Where shall they find it? Never found in sex. All explored sex is the same.

World as finite, and so no longer any refuge in infinities of grandeur.

Atomism.

Resolution of apparent flexibility and continuity into atomic structure. Oratory and fluency mean a collection of phrases at fingers' ends. This seen in Hyde Park, the young men, Christian preachers.

Escapes to the infinite:
   (i) Art, blur, strangeness, music.
   (ii) Sentimentality.

The sentimental illusion of a man (invalid) who takes pleasure in resting his head in a woman's lap – it is a deliberate act, work on her part. While he may feel the sentimental escape to the infinite, she has to be uncomfortable and prosaic.

All experience tends to do away with all sentimental escapes to the infinite, but at the same time to provide many deliberated, observed, manufactured, artificial, spectacular, poised for seeing continuities and patterns.

The universal conspiracy: other people unconsciously provide the sentimental spectacle in which you luxuriate. The world is nothing more or less than a stage.

There may be an attitude which sees that most things are illusions, that experience is merely the gradual process of disillusionment, that the new as well as the old ideals turn out to be partial, non-continuous or infinite, but then in face of this decides that certain illusions or moods are pleasurable and exhilarating, and deliberately and knowingly encourages them. A judicious choice of illusions, leading to activities planned and carried out, is the only means of happiness, *e.g.* the exhilaration of regarding life as a procession or a war.

In opposition to socialism and utopian schemes comes the insistence on the fact of the unalterability of motives. Motives are the only unalterable and fixed things in the world. They extend to the animal kingdom. They are the only *rock*: physical bases change. They are more than human motives: they are the constitution of the world.

That great secret which all men find out for themselves, and none reveal – or if they do, like Cassandra, are not believed – that the world is round. The young man refuses to believe it.

Refuse World as a unit and take Person (in flight from the word fallacy).

But why person? Why is the line drawn exactly there in the discussion of counter words?

We are becoming so particular in the choice of words and the rejection of symbolism that we are in danger of *forgetting* that the world does really exist.

The truth is that there are no ultimate principles, upon which the whole of knowledge can be built once and for ever as upon a rock. But there are an infinity of analogues, which help us along, and give us a feeling of power over the chaos when we perceive them. The field is infinite and herein lies the chance for originality. Here there are some new things under the sun. (Perhaps it would be better to say that there are some new things under the moon, for here is the land pre-eminently of shadows, fancies and analogies.)

Danger.

One must recognise thought's essential independence of the imagery that steadies it. Subtle associations which similar images recall are insinuated into the thought.

Though perhaps we do not realise it, we are still governed by the analogy, by which spirit was first compared to the wind. The contrast the same as the one between the little box and space, between the court and cinders – that between the one that thinks of a man as an elaborately built-up pyramid, a constructed elaboration, easily upset and not flexible, only functioning in one direction, the one in which he was made, and the other that considers him as a flexible essence, a spirit, like a *fluid*.

We can all see that there is an eternal flexibility in the most obviously constituted man, but we realise the contrast best when looking at a tailor's model of a man in dress, whose limbs move and flex.

In the problem of ghosts which bend and flex lies the whole difference between the two world philosophies –

I. Flexible essence.
II. Built up stuff.

Philosophical Jargon.

There is this consoling thought, supporting us while wandering in the wilderness of which the priests alone pretend they have the secret. In all other uses of language, no matter for what purpose, the analogies used are quite simple, and even can be replaced, leaving the idea behind them just as real. The analogies a man uses to represent a state of soul, though personal, can be replaced, to produce almost the same effect. *No one* mistakes the analogies for the real thing they stand for.

The Dancer.

Dancing to express the organisation of cinders, finally emancipated (cf. bird).

I sat before a stage and saw a little girl with her head thrown back, and a smile. I knew her, for she was the daughter of John of Elton.

But she smiled, and her feet were not like feet, but ... [sic].

Though I knew her body.

All these sudden insights (*eg.* the great analogy of a woman compared to the world in Brussels) – all of these start a line, which seems about to unite the whole world logically. But the line stops. There is no unity. All logic and life are made up of tangled ends like that.

Always think of the fringe and of the cold walks, of the lines that lead nowhere.

Mind and Matter.

Realise that to take *one* or the *other* as absolute is to perpetrate the same old counter fallacy; both are mixed up in a cindery way and we extract them as counters.

Mathematics takes one group of counters, abstracts them and makes them absolute, down to Matter and Motion.

That *fringe of cinders* which bounds any ecstasy.

The tall lanky fellow with a rose, in a white moonlit field. But where does he sleep?

All heroes, great men, go to the outside, away from the Room, and wrestle with cinders.

And cinders become the Azores, the Magic Isles.

A house built is then a symbol, a Roman Viaduct; but the walk there and the dirt – this must jump right into the mind also.

Aphra's Finger.

There are moments when the tip of one's finger seems raw. In the contact of it and the world there seems a strange difference. The spirit lives on that tip and is thrown on the rough cinders of the world. All philosophy depends on that – the state of the tip of the finger.

When Aphra had touched, even lightly, the rough wood, this wood seemed to cling to his finger, to draw itself backward and forward along it. The spirit returned again and again, as though fascinated, to the luxurious torture of the finger.

The prediction of the stars is no more wonderful, and no more accurate, than the prediction of another person's conduct. There is no last refuge here for the logical structure of the world.

The phenomenon we study is not the immense world in our hand, but certain little observations we make about it. We put these on a table and look at them.

We study little chalk marks on a table (chalk because that shows the cindery nature of the division we make) and create rules near enough for them.

If we look at a collection of cinders from all directions, in the end, we are bound to find a shadow that looks regular.

The attempt to get a common element in personality, *i.e.* the old attempt to get a unity. Abstract an element and call that a fundamental.

The inner spirit of the world is miles and miles of ploughed fields.

Never speak of 'my unconquerable soul', or of any vulgarism of that sort. But thank God for the long note of the bugle, which moves all the world bodily out of the cinders and the mud.

There is only one *art* that moves me: architecture.

French.

The exact fault which is typical of French books: The taking of a few opinions, a few epigrams, a few literary *obiter dicta*, and arranging them symmetrically, finding a logical order, an underlying principle where there is one, and calling the whole a science.

I shall call my philosophy the 'Valet to the Absolute'. The Absolute not a hero to his own valet.

All these various little notes will never combine because in their nature they cannot. The facts of Nature are solid enough, but Man is a weathercock standing in the middle, looking first at one part and then at another. A little idea in one sentence appears to contain a whole new world philosophy. So it does. But then a world philosophy is only a certain direction, N. or S. It is quite easy to change this direction. Hence the astonishing power that philosophers appear to have at the summit of the sciences. Buy a book obviously literary, by an amateur, made of light combinations of words. It seems to change the world, but nothing is further from the truth. It just turns the weathercock to a new direction. The philosophic faculty is quite irresponsible, the easiest moving thing in nature, and quite divorced from nature.

So be sceptical of the first enthusiasm that a new idea gives.

The Eagle's eye.

The ruling analogy, which is quite false, must be removed. It is that of the eagle's eye. The metaphysician imagines that he surveys the world as with an eagle's eye. And the farther he flies, the 'purer' his knowledge becomes .

Hence we can see the world as pure geometry, and can make out its dividing lines.

But the eye is in the mud, the eye *is* mud.

Pure seeing of the whole process is impossible. Little fancies help us along, but we never get pure disinterested intellect.

Space.

I. Admitted the pragmatic criterion of any analogy that makes for clearness.

II. Now *space* is essential to clearness. A developed notion, perhaps, but now essential.

III. The idealists analyse space into a mode of arranging sensations. But this gives us an unimaginable world existing all at a point.

IV. Why not try the reverse process and put all ideas (purely mental states) into terms of *space* (cf. landscape thinking)?

The sense of reality is inevitably connected with that of *space* (the world existing before us).

Truths don't exist before we invent them. They respond to man's need of economy, just as beliefs to his need of faith.

The fountain turned on. It has a definite geometrical shape, but the shape did not exist before it was turned on. Compare the arguments about the pre-existence of the soul.
But the little pipes are there before, which give it that shape as soon as the water is turned on.
The water is the same though the geometrical figures of different fountains differ.
By analogy we may perhaps claim that there is no such thing as a personal soul. The personality of the soul depends on the bodily frame which receives it, *i.e.* on the shape of the pipes.
The soul is a spirit certainly, but undifferentiated and without personality. The personality is given by the bodily frame which receives and shapes it.

Ritual and Sentiment.
Sentiment cannot easily retire into itself in pure thought; it cannot live and feed on itself for very long. In wandering, thought is easily displaced by other matters. So that the man who deliberately sets himself the task of thinking continuously of a lover or dead friend has an impossible task. He is inevitably drawn to some form of ritual for the expression and outflow of the sentiment. Some act which requires less concentration, and which at an easy level fulfils his obligations to sentiment, which changes a morbid feeling into a grateful task and employment. Such as pilgrimages to graves, standing bareheaded and similar freaks of a lover's fancy. The same phenomena can be observed in religion. A man cannot deliberately make up his mind to think of the goodness of God for an hour, but he can perform some ritual act of admiration whether it be the offering of a sacrifice or merely saying amen to a set prayer. Ritual tends to be constant, even that seeming

exception the impromptu prayers of a Non-conformist minister are merely the stringing together in accidental order of set and well-known phrases and tags. The burning of candles to the Virgin if only one can escape from some danger. The giving of a dinner, or getting drunk in company as a celebration – a relief from concentrated thinking.

Body.

In Tube lift hearing the phrase 'fed up', and realising that all our analogies spiritual and intellectual are derived from purely physical acts. Nay more, all attributes of the absolute and the abstract are really nothing more (in so far as they mean anything) but elaborations of simple passions.

All poetry is an affair of the body—that is, to be real it must affect body.

Action.

Teachers, university lecturers on science, emancipated women, and other spectacled anaemics attending the plays at the Court Theatre remind me of disembodied spirits, having no body to rest in. They have all the intellect and imagination required for high passion, but no material to work on. They feel all the emotions of jealousy and desire, but these leading to no action remain as nothing but petty motives. *Passion is action* and without action but a child's anger.

They lack the bodies and the daggers. Tragedy never sits steadily on a chair, except in certain vague romantic pictures which are thus much affected (as real tragedy) by the moderns and the sedentary. Just as sentiment and religion require expression in ritual, so tragedy requires action.

Jealousy, desire to kill, desire for strong arms and knives, resolution to shake off social convention and to do it.

The knife order.

Why grumble because there is no end discoverable in the world? There is no end at all except in our own constructions.

Necessity of distinguishing between a vague philosophic statement
that 'reality always escapes a system', and the definite cinder, felt in a
religious way and being a criterion of nearly all judgment, philosophic
and aesthetic.

No Geist without ghost.
This is the only truth in the subject.
Is there here a possible violation of the cinder principle; an escape
back to the old fallacy? But without some definite assertion of this
kind... Some definite crossing beyond is necessary to escape poetic
overstatement, to relieve us.

Philosophy.
The strange quality, shade of feeling, one gets (a few people alone
in a position a little separated from the world); a ship's cabin, the last
bus.
If all the world were destroyed and only these left... That all the
gods, all the winged words (love...) exist *in them* on that fluid basis.

To take frankly that fluid basis and elaborate it into a solidity, that
the gods do not exist horizontally in space, but somehow vertically in
the isolated fragment of the tribe. There is another form of space
where gods, etc., do exist concretely.

Smoothness.
Hate it.
This is the obsession that starts all my theories.
Get other examples, other facets of the one idea.
Build them up by the catalogue method
(I)   in science;
(II)   in sex;
(III) in poetry.

Analogy.
I look at the reality, at London stream, and dirt, mud, power, and

then I think of the pale shadowy analogy that is used without thinking by the automatic philosophers, the 'stream of time'. The people who treat words without reverence, who use analogies without thinking of them: let us always remember that solid real stream and the flat thin voice of the metaphysician, '*the stream of time*'.

Extended clay. Looking at the Persian Gulf on a map and imagining the mud shore at night.

Pictures of low coasts of any country. We are all just above the sea.

Delight in perceiving the real cinder construction in a port. Upon mud as distinct from the clear-cut harbour on the map.

Travel is education in cinders; the merchants in Hakluyt, and the difference in song. (When we are all gathered together and when we are in a book.)

Must see these different manifestations of the cinders; otherwise we cannot work the extended clay.

A melancholy spirit, the mind like a great desert lifeless, and the sound of march music in the street, passes like a wave over that desert, unifies it, but then goes.

Notes on Language and Style[1]

[Michael Roberts, *T.E. Hulme*, 271–303]

Notes for a Preface

I believe that while the world cosmically cannot be reduced to unity as science proclaims (in the postulate of uniformity), yet on the contrary poetry can. At least its methods follow certain easily defined routes. (Anyone can be taught how to use poetry.)

Real work, history and scientific researches, the accidental, the excrescences, like digging, and necessary just as digging is. Poetry the permanent humanity, the expression of man freed from his digging, digging for poetry when it is over.

Clumsiness of prose – relation of language and the idea expressed

Analysis of the attitude of a man reading an argument

(i) Compare in algebra, the real things are replaced by symbols. These symbols are manipulated according to certain laws which are independent of their meaning. N.B. At a certain point in the proof we cease to think of x as having a meaning and look upon it as a mere counter to be manipulated.

(ii) An analogous phenomenon happens in reasoning in language. We replace meaning (i.e. *vision*) by words. These words fall into well-known patterns, i.e. into certain well-known phrases which we accept without thinking of their meaning, just as we do the x in algebra. *But* there is a constant movement above and below the line of meaning (representation).[2] And this is used in dialectical argument. At any stage we can ask the opponent to show his hand, that is to turn all his *words* into visions, in realities we can see.

Seeing 'solid' things

One facet of the idea may be expressed in this way. Refer back to note on the use of x in arithmetic and its analogy in expression. Habitually we may say that the reader takes words as x *without* the meaning attached. Aphra sees each word with an image sticking on to it, never a flat word passed over a board like a counter.

Perhaps the nearest analogy is the hairy caterpillar. Taking each segment of his body as a word, the hair on that segment is the vision the poet sees behind it.

It is difficult to do this, so that the poet is forced to use new analogies, and especially to construct a plaster model of a thing to express his emotion at the sight of the vision he sees, his wonder and ecstasy. If he employed the ordinary word, the reader would only see it as a segment, with no hair, used for getting along. And without this clay, spatial image, he does not feel that he has expressed at all what he sees.

The ordinary caterpillar for crawling along from one position to another. The hairy one for beauty, to build up a solid vision of realities.

All emotion depends on real solid vision or sound. It is physical.

But in *rhetoric* and expositional prose we get words divorced from any real vision. Rhetoric and emotion – here the connection is different.

So perhaps literary expression is from *Real* to *Real* with all the intermediate forms keeping their *real* value. In expositional reasoning, the intermediate terms have only counter value. Give an example of *counter* prose (boy's letter to paper).

Watching a class: the difference between their attitude to geography and that to mathematics. Probably having only spatial imagination, the geography is quite clear and comprehensible. If the mathematics could be got into the same flat form upon a map, with only relative distances to be observed, then their difficulties would vanish.

This suggests that the type of all reasoning is that of arranging counters on the flat, where they can be moved about, without the mind having to think in any involved way. (cf. this with note in the old book, about chess-board.)

The ideal of modern prose is to be all counters, i.e. to pass to conclusions without thinking.

Visual Poetry

Each *word* must be an image *seen*, not a counter.

That dreadful feeling of cheapness when we contemplate the profusion of words of modern prose. The true ideal – the little statue in Paris.

The contrast between (i) a firm simple prose, creating in a definite way a fairy story, a story of simple life in the country (in the old country). Here we have the microcosm of poetry. The pieces picked out from which it comes. Sun and sweat and all of them. Physical life and death fairies. And (ii) on the other hand, genteel poetry like Shelley's, which refers in elaborate analogies to the things mentioned in (i).

Gibbering ghosts and Morris's tales seem real, as (i). Transmigration of souls seems a drawing-room thrill, compounded of goodwill and long words.

Style

With perfect style, the solid leather for reading, each sentence should be a lump, a piece of clay, a vision seen; rather, a wall touched with soft fingers. Never should one feel light vaporous bridges between one solid sense and another. No bridges – all solid: then never exasperated.

A man cannot write without seeing at the same time a visual signification before his eyes. It is this image which precedes the writing and makes it firm.

The piece from Morris as an example of poetry always being a solid thing. Seen but not words.

Criticism

Rising disgust and impatience with the talking books, e.g. Lilly and the books about Life, Science, and Religion. All the books which seem to be the kind of talk one could do if one wished.

Rather choose those in old leather, which are *solid*. Here the man did not talk, but saw solid, definite things and described them. Solidity a pleasure.

It is seeing the real clay, that men in an agony worked with, that gives pleasure. To read a book which is *real clay* moulded by fingers that had to mould something, or they would clutch the throat of their maddened author. *No* flowing on of words, but tightly clutched tense fingers leaving marks in the clay. These are the only books that matter – and where are they to be found?

Style short, being forced by the coming together of many different thoughts, and generated by their contact. Fire struck between stones.

Mechanism of Creation

Get rid of the idea that out of vacuo can come writing. Generally following certain practical ends, we throw out writing – comes out as the one in the many. Not as a pure intellectual machine. A cindery thing done, not a pure thought made manifest in some counter-like way.

The idea is nothing: it is the holding on to the idea, through the absolutely transforming influence of putting it into definiteness. The holding on through waves.

That extraordinary difficulty in shaping any material, in moving from the idea to the matter. Seen even in simple matters like going to the tailor's. The difference between the idea and the choice. Material is never plastic. The extraordinary difficulty of the living material. Seen in everything, even in railway meetings, in people, in everything. Write essay on it.

The resistance of the ὕλη ἐυεργής.[3] The process of invention is that of gradually making solid the castles in the air.

Self-delusion

(i) Whence comes the excitement, the delusion of thinker's creation?

(ii) All inventions spring from the *idea*, e.g. Flaubert and the *purple* bases of Madame Bovary.

(iii) I have a *central* idea like that quite *unworked* out into detail.

(iv) I see a book *worked out* from the same central idea and I unconsciously imagine that I have worked it out myself, and that I could easily have been the author.

(v) But in the working out is required the multiplicity of detail that I lack. The central idea is nothing.

At last come to think that all expression is vulgar, that only the unexpressed and silent ...

Dead Analogies

All styles are means of subduing the reader.

(i) New phrases made in poetry, tested, and then employed in prose.

(ii) In poetry they are all glitter and new coruscation, in prose useful and not noticed.

(iii) Prose a museum where all the old weapons of poetry kept.

(iv) Poetry always the advance guard in language. The progress of language is the absorption of new analogies. (Scout, so nearest to flux and real basic condition of life.)

Expression (I)

If I say: putting in the 'finer touches', it expresses what I mean by the refinement of language.

But the damnable thing is that if I use that phrase to another person, it produces no equal effect on him. It is one of the rounded counters of language and so has the least possible meaning. What to me is an entirely physical thing, a real clay before me, moulded, an image, is when used nothing but an expression like 'in so far, etc.'.

The pity is that in this all the *meaning* goes.

A word to me is a board with an image or statue on it. When I pass the word, all that goes is the board, the statue remains in my imagination.

Transfer physical to language

Dome of Brompton in the mist. Transfer that to art. Dead things not men as the material of art. Everything for art is a thing in itself, cf. the café at Clapham as a thing in itself.

And the words moved until they became a dome, a solid, separate world, a dome in a mist, a thing of terror beyond us, and not of us. Definite heaven above worshippers, incense hides foundations. A definite *force majeure* (all the foundations of the scaffolding are in us, but we want an illusion, falsifying us, something independent of foundations). A long pillar.

Aphra took the words, and they grew into a round smooth pillar and the child wondered and the merchant caused. Putting a few bricks together to imitate the shape of a dome, but the mist effect, the transformation in words, has the art of pushing it through the door.

Example of Plastic Imagination

The two tarts walking along Piccadilly on tiptoe, going home, with hat on back of head. Worry until could find the exact model analogy that will reproduce the extraordinary effect they produce. Could be done at once by an artist in a blur. The air of absolute detachment, of being things in themselves. Objects of beauty with the qualification as the basis of it. Disinterestedness, as though saying: We may have evolved painfully from the clay, and be the last leaf on a tree. But now we have cut ourselves away from that. We are things-in-themselves. We exist out of time.

Language (I)

(i) Delightful sensation of power in looking at it, as a vehicle, a machine whose ages we can see. The relics of the extravagant fancies and analogies of dead and forgotten poets.

Regard each word as a picture, then a succession of pictures. Only the dead skeleton remains. We cut the leaves off. When the tree becomes a mast, the leaves become unnecessary. But now only the thick lines matter, and the accompanying pictures are forgotten.

(ii) An agricultural implement. Philosophy expressed in farmer's language. All the predominant metaphors are naturally agricultural, e.g. field of thought, flood, stream. Keep present in mind when we look at nature, the curious place of language which is founded on it and *subordinate* to it. When I see a stream now (such as Waterloo Bridge) I imagine it carrying down with it the impermeable language and the *begriffe* of philosophy.

If only the making and fixing of words had begun in the city stage in the evolution of society and not in the nomadic.

(But ideas expressed would have been the same. So thought and language not identical.)

Language (II)

The fallacy that language is logical, or that meaning is. Phrases have meaning for no reason, cf. with nature of truth.

(i) The metaphysical theory. Watching a woman in the street. Is the idea expressed anything like? so –

(ii) The idea is just as real as a landscape and there is the same difficulty in getting it on to paper. Each word is a different twist to it.

Something added. Each of the fifty possible sentences that will express it changes its character.

(iii) Another question: growing conviction of the Solidity of Ideas, as opposed to language.

Very often the idea, apart from the analogy or metaphor which clothes it, has no existence. That is, by a subtle combination of allusions we have artificially built up in us an idea, which apart from these, cannot be got at. As if a man took us on a rocky path and said look – and we saw the view. i.e. the analogy is the thing, not merely decoration. i.e. there is no such thing as.

Language (III)

Large clumsy instrument. Language does not naturally come with meaning. Ten different ways of forming the same sentence. Any style will do to get the meaning down (without childish effect). There is *no* inevitable simple style as there ought to be.

Language a cumbrous growth, a compound of old and new analogies. Does this apply to thought? Is there *no* simple thought, but only styles of thought?

Poetry is neither more nor less than a mosaic of words, so great exactness required for each one.

Language (IV)

(i) Thought is prior to language and consists in the simultaneous presentation to the mind of two different images.

(ii) Language is only a more or less feeble way of doing this.

(iii) All the connections in language, this term including not only prepositions, but all phrases (ready made), which only indicate the precise relation or attitude or politeness between the two simultaneously presented images.

(iv) Connect this with the old scorn, denoted by the black edge theory, cf. Rue de la limite. And hence see the solution of the difficulty, and the use of words for literary purposes, always inferior.

Thought

As merely the discovery of new analogies, when useful and sincere, and not mere paradoxes.

The things bring a kind of going straight, write them as analogy and call it literature, cf. marching in step, the great procession (analogy of creative and sexual pleasure).

Creation

Thought is the joining together of new analogies, and so inspiration is a matter of an accidentally seen analogy or unlooked-for resemblance. It is therefore necessary to get as large as possible change in sense impressions, cf. looking in shop windows, and war-game. The more change of shapes and sights there is the more chance of inspiration. Thoughts won by walking.

Fertility of invention means: remembrance of accidental occurrences *noted* and arranged. (cf. detective stories.)

Expression (II)

Think of sitting at that window in Chelsea and seeing the chimneys and the lights in the dusk. And then imagine that by contemplation this will transfer itself bodily on to paper.

This is the direct opposite of literature, which is never an absorption and meditation. But a deliberate choosing and working-up of analogies. The continued, close, compressed effort.

The demand for clear logical expression is impossible, as it would confine us to the use of flat counter-images only.

If you only admit that form of manipulating images as good, if you deny all the other grasps, hands, for the cards, all solid images, all patterns, then you can be clear, but not otherwise.

Expression (III)

(i) People who think, pen in hand. Like people who write at twenty, for *Eton College Chronicle*. Writers first, and then afterwards perhaps find thought.

(ii) Think in air. And then years afterwards acquire knack of writing.

Expression (IV)

The chessboard of language expression, where the two players put down counters one after the other. And the player who became interested in the pieces themselves and called them, and gazed at them in a kind of ecstasy.

Humour and Expression

A joke analysed and viewed as the decadent form into which all forms of literary expression can be shown to pass by degeneration of function (a suitable analogy for this).

(i) The surprise at the end. Resembles novel building.

(ii) Analogies in poetry, like the likenesses of babies, to be taken half seriously, with a smile.

Contempt for Language

Black Border

All literature as accident, a happy escape from platitude. Nothing new under the sun. Literature like pitching, how to throw phrases about, to satisfy a demand. An exercise for the time being, no eternal body to be added to. So learn phrases like 'ringed with gold', 'in a lens', etc.

To excite certain mild feelings of delight in the reader, to produce a pleasant warm feeling in brain as phrases run along.

Enlightenment when first see that literature is not a vision, but a voice, or a line of letters in a black border.

Vision the sight of the quaint shadows in things, of the lone trees on the hill, and the hills in life; not the deed, but the shadow cast by the deed.

The art of literature consists exactly in this *passage from the Eye to the Voice*. From the wealth of nature to that *thin* shadow of words, that gramophone. The Readers are the people who *see* things and want them expressed. The author is the Voice, or the conjuror who does tricks with that curious rope of letters, which is quite different from real passion and sight.

The prose writer drags meaning along with the rope. The poet makes it stand on end and hit you.

Prose

A sentence and a worm are the most stupid of animals and the most difficult to teach tricks. Tendency to crawl along requires genius, music, to make them stand up (snake charmer).

The dreadful limitations of all – so many lines. So many images enclosed in a black border.

Uncomfortable vision of all words as line. String lying on paper. Impossibility of getting mystery out of this. Words seen as physical things. Pull gently into rows. Want to make them *stand up*. Must invent new plan.

Words seen as physical thing like a piece of string, e.g. walking on dark boulevard. Girl hidden in trees passes on other side. How to get this.

Always a border round, to isolate the sentence as a thing in itself, a living worm to be taught tricks.

Facility in Manipulation

Phrases

Two people sitting talking at table. Delight in having counters ready to hand. (French.) Must not be taught how to *make* counters but a list of them.

(i) Collection of phrases. Words fit in and out of phrases. A *cadre* for grammar. Impossibility of grammar because can't think of end of sentence first. *Learn list* of sentences then fix grammar for them as do in English. Get grammar by ear.

(ii) No language but collection of phrases, but phrases on *different* subjects. One wanders as over a country. No fixed guide for everything. Start Good morning.

(iii) All one tense for past. *Je suis allé.*

Sentences

Sentences as units. Given a large *vocabulary of sentence units*, not of words, we are fluent and can express what we want.

Model sentences learnt perfectly. Perhaps three or four in each Berlitz lesson. Gradually get a definite *armoury* of sentences which will help you and be sufficient to you in conversation.

Physical need some people have to be able to make a comment, to exchange comments. Hence proverbs are the most popular authors. cf. with reading in W.C.

Never, never, never a simple statement. It has no effect. Always must have analogies, which make an other-world through-the-glass effect, which is what I want.

Danger that when all these notes are arranged, the order will kill them in commonplace. When isolated at least there is hope they suggest great unities, which I am at any rate at present quite unable to carry out.

All theories of how to teach a language, all in the air, all null and void, if *each day* you do not learn at your finger's-ends some new phrases. One new *word* and ten phrases as to how to employ it. Reading gives knowledge only of roots.

Each night. What new phrases. What new *cadres* for the word I already know?

Question of preposition etc. at end of sentence. *Il faut le faire payer.* Do we think of end first?

In learning foreign language and teaching your own, learn how little is your knowledge of your own. Hesitating for a phrase in your own language. Very few of us learn all the *possible phrases* in our own language, and we must have them all at the tips of our fingers to write well.

So adapt same method to *English*. Read and Read, and copy the phrases like the one about 'microscopic detail magnified'.

The Imaginary World and a Standard of Meaning

Literature always possible. Compared with peasant, it only deals with imaginary world. Even my attempt to get to reality (no long words) is in the end only another adjustment of the imaginary toy. Fields left unaltered.

Literary people work in imaginary land which all of us carry about in desert moments.

Not sufficient to find analogies. It is necessary to find those that add something to each, and give a sense of wonder, a sense of being united in another mystic world.

One must have something to overawe the *reader*. The fact outside him, e.g. in boasting. Take case of '*Oh, Richard, oh mon roi'*.

All literature and poetry is life seen in a mirror; it must be absolutely removed from reality, and can never be attained.

The exact relation between the expression and the inside image: (i)

Expression obviously partakes of the nature of cinders, cf. Red girl dancing. (ii) But on other hand, vague hell image common to everybody makes an infinite of limited *hard* expression.

> Over a large table, smooth, he leaned in ecstasies,
> In a dream.
> He had been to woods, and talked and walked with trees
> Had left the world
> And brought back round globes and stone images
> Of gems, colours, hard and definite.
> With these he played, in a dream,
> On the smooth table.

(cf. the red dancer in his head.)

Expression (Metaphysical)

A red dancer on the stage. A built-up complex of cinders so not due to any primeval essence. Cinders as foundations for (i) philosophy (ii) aesthetics.

The old controversy as to which is greater, the mind or the material in art.

Each dancer on the stage with her effects and her suggestions of intensity of meaning which are not possible, is not herself (that is a very cindery thing) but a synthesized state of mind in me. The red moving figure is a way of grouping some ideas together, just as powerful a means as the one called logic which is only an analogy to *counter-pushing*.

This can be considered more seriously. A picture like this, the cosmic dance, fading away into the margin (this the basis of all art), not [this][4] which gives the limitations, the furniture, etc.

Must be imaginary world. Trick it out with fancies. Analogies must be substituted for what suggests something, a cloud of fancies, e.g. Waterloo Bridge in the early morning.

The only intellectual pleasure in recognising old friends.

(i) At a race. Look first and see the horses in the paper described. Then excited about result.

(ii) Picture gallery. (a) recognition of *names*. (b) progress to recognition of characteristics. Galleries full of strange names no interest.

(iii) Climate and landscape. The only pleasure in comparison, e.g. Waterloo Bridge and Canada by the river in the morning.

Ideal

Typical phenomena – the yellow girl leaning from the window in the morning. The Baptist meeting seen through the drawing-room window in the evening.

For the first, if it reminds me of an expressible vague something, I must first have been educated into the idea that there was such a vague something.

Observe this something is quite different to the emotional crises of ordinary people when they speak of love and hate. There must be something on which we can hang our hat. Better something to which, when for a surging moment we have a feeling (really the cinders drunk for a minute) there must be something to which we can *refer* it.

Literature as the building-up of this *state of reference*. Must avoid the word, the Ideal, like a plague, for it suggests easy comprehension where there is no easy comprehension. It is used by Baptist young men to mean quite other things, it has *moral* contamination.

Ideas Staged

In a sense all ideals must be divorced, torn away from the reality where we found them and put on a stage. They must appear separate and far from all dirt and laughter at their low and common relations. They must be posed and moved dramatically, and above all, their gestures must express their emotions. This is the art of literature, the making of this *other* world.

They must wear high-heeled shoes which make them appear free movers, and not sprung from that low thing Earth. The separation of the high heel and the powdered face is essential to all emotions, in order to make a work of art.

Intensity of Meaning

'By thine agony and bloody sweat.' By common effort, all this many times repeated, gives an *intensity of meaning*. This 'intensity of meaning' is what is sought for.

Christian Mystics and Physical Expression

Read them as analogous with own temper. For the expression of states of soul by elaborate physical landscape analogies, cf. my own walking in the evening by the Thames. Also the Neo-Platonic philosophers. It is the physical analogies that hold me, true kindred spirits in that age, in own poetry, not the *vain* decorative and verbal images of the ordinary poets.

Feminine Form

The beauty of the feminine form, which came to be looked upon even by the halest of the four, as a typical vesture or symbol of Beauty herself, and perhaps also as the 'sovran shrine' of Melancholy.

Rossetti saw the spiritual element in face and form, and desired the spirit through his desire of the body, and at last did not know the one desire from the other, and pressed on, true mystic as he was, in ever-narrowing circles, to some third thing that seemed to lie behind both desires. 'Soul is form and doth the body make.'

Eye blur

Tennyson seems to have waited for his expression to come to him – to have brooded before a scene with its orchestra of sounds, in a kind of intense passiveness – until the thing beheld *became greatly different from what it was at any other moment or to any other man.*

Dwelling on a Point

Perhaps the difficulty that is found in expressing an idea, in making it long, in dwelling on it, by means of all kinds of analogy, has its roots in the nature of ideas and thought itself.

Dancing as the art of prolonging an idea, lingering on a point.

This clearly seen gives the relation between the author's and the reader's position. Both can see the points (as visions in their heads), e.g. Moore's hypostatization of the ideas as real. But I am quite unable to dwell on this point at the length of ten pages.

The author is the man who dwells on a point for the edification of the reader, and for his pleasure, thus prolonging the pleasure and luxury of thought in the mind of the reader.

Method: (i) quotation; (ii) analogies from all possible subjects.

Write down examples:

(i) Prose – of making a tremendous deal out of a point which can be noted down in one sentence. But perhaps the sentence only represents it to the writer. To get the same effect on the reader as it produces on him, he must work it up into a froth, like stirring eggs.

(ii) Dwelling on a point in poetry. The main function of analogy in poetry is to enable one to dwell and linger upon a point of excitement. To achieve the impossible and convert a point into a line. This can only be done by having ready-made lines in our heads, and so getting at the result by analogy.

The inner psychology of a poet at such a creative moment is like that of a drunkard who pushes his hand forward along a table, with an important gesture, and remains there pondering over it. In that relaxing gesture of pushing comes the inner psychology of all these moments.

Gradually one learns the art of dwelling on a point, of decorating it, of transforming it, until it produces in the reader the sense of novelty.

Reader and Writer

Personal

The popular idea of poet as in communion with the infinite, cf. account of Yeats walking in the woods, but remember Tennyson and his hair. (The deed and poem always greater than the man.)

The rubbish that authors write in their casual moments, when they talk. We haven't heard the kind of interview Shelley and Keats would have given.

Reason why Whitman did not go to the gold fields and become a frontiersman actually. His hatred of the particular, and desire to be the average American citizen, desire to find romance even in Brooklyn. Often at theatres, and a journalist and carpenter. When had made money would go for long holidays in the woods and by the sea. Always seen on bus-tops.

The bodily activity and position most favourable to thought requires coolness, comfort, and a table, a strenuous effort. Can't think without words or pencil.

Object and Readers of Poetry

Poetry after all for the amusement of bankers and other sedentary arm-chair people in after-dinner moods. No other. (Not for inspiration of progress.) So no infinite nobleness and function about that. (For one person in a thousand hence uselessness of school teaching.)

Entirely modern view of poet as something greater than a statesman, cf. Frederic the Great.

In old days merely to amuse warrior and after banquet.

(i) amuse banker.

(ii) for use of clerks in love to send to sweethearts.

(iii) temporary moods (in theatres) of cultivated artificial people.

(iv) songs of war.

Author and Reader

Just as Aristotle asserts that Matter the unlimited contains Forms embedded in it, and that they are not thrust upon it from some ideal world, so all the effects that can be produced by the literary man (here assuming his apprenticeship and marshalling of isolated moments to produce a mystic separation, aided by old metaphors), are to be found dormant, unused in the reader, and are thus awakened.

The Reader

The new art of the Reader. (i) The relation between banker and poetry. (ii) Sympathy with reader as brother, as *unexpressed* author.

Literature a method of sudden arrangement of commonplaces. The *suddenness* makes us forget the commonplace.

Complete theory, what was thought, in the old book, of relations between the poet and the reader seen suddenly at a glance in listening to boys going home from music-hall whistling a song. Chelsea Palace. Here a new way (a mental dance) found for them of synthesizing certain of their own emotions. (Even so with personal psychological poetry, mere putting down is for the reader a form of expression.)

Always seek the causes of these phenomena in their lowest elements – their lowest terms, i.e. literati in Chelsea.

The Writer

The effort of the literary man to find subtle analogies for the ordinary street feelings he experiences, leads to the differentiation and importance of those feelings. What would be unnoticed by others, and is nothing when not labelled, becomes an important emotion. A transitory artificial impression is deliberately cultivated into an emotion and written about. Reason here creates and modifies an emotion, e.g. standing at street corners. Hence the sudden joy these produce in the reader when he remembers a half-forgotten impression. 'How true!'

What is the difference between people who can write literature and people who can merely appreciate it. The faculty of disillusionment and cynicism, of giving the show away, possessed by readers. What is the necessary quality for creation?

Literary man always first completely disillusioned and then deliberately and purposely creative of illusions.

A writer always a feeble, balanced, artificial kind of person. The mood is cultivated feeling all the time. The vibrant and tense fingers, drawing up rhythm, which one knows could be broken at any moment by anyone coming into the room.

Do these doubts, as to authors, vitiate in any way the work they produce?

Poetry not for others, but for the poet. Nature infinite, but personality finite, rough, and incomplete. Gradually built up.

Poet's mood vague and passes away, indefinable. The poem he makes selects, builds up, and makes even his own mood more definite to him. Expression builds up personality.

The life of the literary man being always aiming at the production of these artificial deliberate poises in himself, and so at the creation of his own chess-board.

But what of the relation of this to ordinary life and people? They have their own hereditary (sentimental) chess-boards, which remain the same until changed by the survival of some of those of the literary man. The earnest striving after awkward and new points of view, such as that from a balloon, the useful seen from the non-useful attitude.

Literature as red counters moving on a chess-board, life as gradual shifting of cinders, and occasional consciousness.

Unfortunately can now see the trick, can see the author working his counters for the peroration. So very few more possible enthusiasms left. Grit and toothache still to be in any heaven or Utopia.

Literature as entirely the deliberate standing still, hovering and thinking oneself into an artificial view, for the moment, and not effecting any real actions at all. Sunsets no consolation in harvest-field. (Lovers' sentimental fancies in letters.)

A Poem

It was formerly my idea that a poem was made somewhat as follows: The poet, in common with many other people, occasionally experienced emotions which strangely moved him. In the case of the greengrocer this was satisfied by reading Tennyson and sending the lines he seemed to have experienced to his beloved. The poet on the contrary tried to find new images to express what he felt. These lines and vague collections of words he gradually built up into poems. But this I now see to be wrong; the very act of trying to find a form to fit the separate phrases into, itself leads to the creation of new images hitherto not felt by the poet. In a sense the poetry writes itself. This creation by happy chance is analogous to the accidental stroke of the brush which creates a new beauty not previously consciously thought of by the artist.

The form of a poem is shaped by the intention, vague phrases containing ideas which at past moments have strongly moved us: as the purpose of the poem is narrative or emotional the phrases become altered. The choice of a form is as important as the individual pieces and scraps of emotion of which the poem is made up. In the actual making accidental phrases are hit upon. Just as musician in striking notes on piano comes across what he wants, the painter on the canvas, so the poet not only gets the phrases he wants, but even from the words gets a *new* image.

Creative effort means *new* images. (Lobster and me.) The accidental discovery of effect, not conscious intellectual endeavour for it.

The theory that puts all phrases in a box and years later starts to arrange *all wrong*. Don't. Start creating *at once*, and in this very process new ideas spring up, accidentally. So *condemn* card system, red tape leads to nothing. The living method of arranging at once in temporary note-books.

Crowds

Drama
The effect produced by multitude (i) one by one as they left the hall; (ii) policemen's dance.

Actors can add to a comedy. All gestures unreal, but add to comedy and subtract and annoy in tragedy.

Music
Fortuitous assemblage of noises.

The mechanical model, music seen for an instant once during a hymn as smooth rolling.[5]

Conductor's baton and foundation in body rhythm.

Music in its power of seeming to hold an audience or crowd together into an organism. When plays low in park the atmosphere seems to fall to pieces and crowd becomes units again. cf. Band and Bard.

Sound a fluid beaten up by conductor.

Breaking of waves. Listening is like the motion in a ship.

Big Crowds
(i) Not found in streets which are routes, except in those which are meeting-places, as Oxford Street.

(ii) The old market-places, the gymnasia of the Greeks, Plato, and the pretty youths.

(iii) Churches and theatres to catch the prolific mood. Davidson and railway stations.

(iv) Secular churches in street, to sit, rest and look.

Beauty, Imitation, and Ecstasy

Tradition
Poetry always founded on tradition. So light-haired woman with upturned face in Regent Street. A bright moon in dark sky over Paddington. All books, history, etc., after all only a record of the opinions of a class, the artificial moments and poses of literary men. The other classes and little worlds inarticulate (cf. villages).

When artistic impressions of miners and artisans seen (Millet) they do not in any way have anything to do with the emotions of the miner, do not in any way dignify his life. Are only blurs in light and shade. There is no *depth* in the mirror.

Beauty

Art creates beauty (not art copies the beauty in nature: beauty does not exist by itself in nature, waiting to be copied, only organised pieces of cinders). Origin of this view, course of etchings has made cranes and chimneys at night seem beautiful.

Landscape makes the ordinary man think pieces of wood beautiful. 'Just like a picture.'

So one purpose of art to make people like the merely healthy. Necessary to correct false bias in favour of guilt. Plain steel. (Should make all art seem beautiful)

Beauty is usefulness seen from another point (cf. distant railway line, *not* the one you yourself are on). Point of view above, birds' eye, because *new*. The waiting engine in the trees, *one* line, red light, like animal waiting to kill.

Culture seeks romantic in far regions. Seeks passions and tragedies in peasants. Tolstoy. Then sees it in prostitutes. Why not abandon it all and take supernatural for art.

Whitman had a theory that every object under the sun comes within the range of poetry. But he was too early in the day. No use having a theory that motor-cars are beautiful, and backing up this theory by working up emotion not really felt. Object must cause the emotion before poem can be written. Whitman's theory, that everything in America must be glorious, was his snare, because it was only a theory.

Minor poets, with their romantic jewels, make same mistake from other side – a lost poetic content. Lexicon of beautiful is elastic, but walla-walla not yet poetically possible.

Continual effort necessary to think of things as they are, the constraint necessary to avoid great tendencies to use big words and common phrases without meaning. Cf. Nietzsche and his ambition to say everything in a paragraph.

Imitation

Tendency to begin a tale 'It began in the E. M. restaurant' and similarly in poems. The imitation makes one imagine that one is producing stuff of the same calibre and the same effect on other people.

Stupid little poems about flowers and spring, imitations. No *new* emotion in them. Or the infinitely fascinating man (fiction), cf G. Moore's novels, the infinitely beautiful woman.

Poetasters write in metre because poets have done so, poets because singing, not talking, is the obvious mode of expressing ecstasy. Whitman went wrong through deficiency of selective process. Even Turner had to shroud his railway train in vapour.

What is the exact difference which would be produced if chess or cinders were stated by Andrew Lang. How is the childishness made to disappear? Perhaps they don't state a thing baldly but hint at rounder and counter-like figures behind it.

People anxious to be literary men think there is no work, just as haymaking – but just as monotonous grinding it out. Concerned in the field with ecstasy, but the pains of birth and parturition are sheets and sheets of paper.

W.B. Yeats attempts to ennoble his craft by strenuously believing in supernatural world, race-memory, magic, and saying that symbols can recall these where prose couldn't. This an attempt to bring in an infinity again. Truth that occasionally have moments of poetic feelings in W.C. and other places, banging of doors, etc.

The beauty of London only seen in detached and careful moments, never continuously, always a conscious effort. On top of a bus, or the sweep of the avenue in Hyde Park. But to appreciate this must be in some manner detached, e.g. wearing workmen's clothes (when not shabby but different in kind) then opportunity for conscious reflection. It is the stranger that sees the romantic and the beautiful in the commonplace, cf. in New York, or in strange city, detached and therefore able to see beauty and romance.

Moments of enthusiasm due to a selection seen as a possible *continuously* happy future.

All attempts at beauty necessarily consciously made, open to reaction of the man who talks of 'nature', etc.

Life as a rule tedious, but certain things give us sudden lifts. Poetry comes with the jumps, cf. love, fighting, dancing. The moments of ecstasy.

Literature, like memory, selects only the vivid patches of life. The

art of abstraction. If literature (realistic) did really resemble life, it
would be interminable, dreary, commonplace, eating and dressing,
buttoning, with here and there a patch of vividness. Zola merely
selects an interesting group of sordid pieces.

Life composed of exquisite moments and the rest shadows of them.
The *gaps* – hence chess.

Drink

They followed the road with the knowledge that they were soaring
along in a supporting medium, possessed of original and profound
thoughts, themselves and surrounding nature forming an organism of
which all the parts harmoniously and joyously interpenetrate each
other.

Heroes occasionally, drink influence only for a time like effect of
church or music.

The literary man deliberately perpetrates a hypocrisy, in that he fits
together his own isolated moments of ecstasy (and generally deliberate
use of big words without personal meaning attached) and presents
them as a picture of higher life, thereby giving old maids a sense of
superiority to other people and giving mandarins the opportunity to
talk of 'ideals'. Then makes attempt to justify himself by inventing the
soul and saying that occasionally the lower world gets glimpses of this,
and that inferentially he is the medium. As a matter of fact being
certain moments of ecstasy perhaps brought on by drink. Surely
obvious that drink and drugs have nothing to do with a higher world
(cf. Q and his little safe yacht, a kind of mechanical ladder to the soul
world).

All theories as toys.

A Lecture on Modern Poetry[1]

[Michael Roberts, *T.E. Hulme*, 258-270]

I want to begin by a statement of the attitude I take towards verse. I do that in order to anticipate criticism. I shall speak of verse from a certain rather low but quite definite level, and I think that criticism ought to be confined to that level. The point of view is that verse is simply and solely the means of expression. I will give you an example of the position exactly opposite to the one I take up. A reviewer writing in the *Saturday Review* last week spoke of poetry as the means by which the soul soared into higher regions, and as a means of expression by which it became merged into a higher kind of reality. Well, that is the kind of statement that I utterly detest. I want to speak of verse in a plain way as I would of pigs: that is the only honest way. The President told us last week that poetry was akin to religion. It is nothing of the sort. It is a means of expression just as prose is and if you can't justify it from that point of view it's not worth preserving.

I always suspect the word soul when it is brought into discussion. It reminds me of the way that the medieval scientists spoke of God. When entirely ignorant of the cause of anything they said God did it. If I use the word soul, or speak of higher realities, in the course of my speech, you will know that at that precise point I didn't know of any real reason and was trying to bluff you. There is a tremendous amount of hocus-pocus about most discussions of poetry. Critics attempting to explain technique make mysterious passes and mumble of the infinite and the human heart, for all the world as though they were selling a patent medicine in the market-place.

There are two ways in which one can consider this. The first as a difficulty to be conquered, the second as a tool for use. In the first case we look upon poets as we look upon pianists, and speak of them as masters of verse. The other way is to consider it merely as a tool which we want to use ourselves for definite purposes. One daily paper compared us to the Mermaid Club but we are not. We are a number of modern people, and verse must be justified as a means of expression for us. I have not a catholic taste but a violently personal and prejudiced one. I have no reverence for tradition. I came to the subject of verse from the inside rather than from the outside. There were certain impressions which I wanted to fix. I read verse to find models but I could not find any that seemed exactly suitable to express that kind of impression, except perhaps a few jerky rhythms of Henley, until I came to read the French *vers-libre*, which seemed to exactly fit the case.

So that I don't want any literary criticism, that would be talking on another level. I don't want to be killed with a bludgeon and references to Dante, Milton and the rest of them.

The principle on which I rely in this paper is that there is an intimate connection between the verse form and the state of poetry at any period. All kinds of reasons are given by the academic critics for the efflorescence of verse at any period. But the true one is very seldom given. It is the invention or introduction of a new verse form. To the artist the introduction of a new art form is, as Moore says, like a new dress to a girl; he wants to see himself in it. It is a new toy. You will find the burst of poetic activity at the time of Elizabeth put down to the discovery of America. The discovery of America had about as much effect on the Courtier poets at that time as the discovery of a new asteroid would have had on the poetic activity of Swinburne. The real reason was, I take it, that the first opportunity was given for the exercise of verse composition by the introduction of all kinds of new matter and new forms from Italy and France.

It must be admitted that verse forms, like manners, and like individuals, develop and die. They evolve from their initial freedom to decay and finally to virtuosity. They disappear before the new man, burdened with the thought more complex and more difficult to express by the old name. After being too much used their primitive effect is lost. All possible tunes have been played on the instrument. What possibility is there in that for the new men, or what attraction? It would be different if poetry, like acting and dancing, were one of the arts of which no record can be kept, and which must be repeated for each generation. The actor has not to feel the competition of the dead as the poet has. Personally I am of course in favour of the complete destruction of all verse more than twenty years old. But that happy event will not, I am afraid, take place until Plato's desire has been realised and a minor poet has become dictator. Meanwhile it is necessary to realise that as poetry is immortal, it is differentiated from those arts which must be repeated. I want to call attention to this point – it is only those arts whose expression is repeated every generation that have an immutable technique. Those arts like poetry, whose matter is immortal, must find a new technique each generation. Each age must have its own special form of expression, and any period that deliberately goes out of it is an age of insincerity.

The latter stages in the decay of an art form are very interesting and worth study because they are peculiarly applicable to the state of poetry at the present day. They resemble the latter stages in the decay of religion when the spirit has gone and there is a meaningless reverence for formalities and ritual. The carcass is dead and all the flies are upon it. Imitative poetry springs up like weeds, and women whimper and whine of you and I alas, and roses, roses all the way. It becomes the expression of sentimentality rather than of virile thought.

The writers who would be able to use the old instrument with the old masters refuse to do so for they find it inadequate. They know the entirely empirical nature of the old rules and refuse to be cramped by them.

It is at these periods that a new art form is created; after the decay of Elizabethan poetic drama came the heroic couplet, after the decay of the couplet came the new lyrical poetry that has lasted till now. It is interesting to notice that these changes do not come by a kind of natural progress of which the artist himself is unconscious. The new forms are deliberately introduced by people who detest the old ones. Modern lyrical verse was introduced by Wordsworth with no pretence of it being a natural progress; he announced it in good set terms as a new method.

The particular example which has most connection with what I have to say is that of the Parnassian school about 1885:[2] itself beginning as a reaction from romanticism, it has come rapidly to decay; its main principle of an absolute perfection of rhyme and form was in harmony with the natural school of the time. It was a logical form of verse, as distinct from a symbolical one. There were prominent names in it, Monde, Prudhomme, etc., but they were not very fertile; they did not produce anything of great importance; they confined themselves to repeating the same sonnet time after time, their pupils were lost in a state of sterile feebleness.

I wish you to notice that this was not the kind of unfortunate accident which has happened by chance to a number of poets. This check to the Parnassian school marked the death of a particular form of French poetry which coincided with the birth and marvellous fertility of a new form. With the definite arrival of this new form of verse in 1880 came the appearance of a band of poets perhaps unequalled at any one time in the history of French poetry.

The new technique was first definitely stated by Kahn.[3] It consisted in a denial of a regular number of syllables as the basis of versification. The length of the line is long and short, oscillating with the images used by the poet; it follows the contours of his thoughts and is free rather than regular; to use a rough analogy, it is clothes made to order, rather than ready-made clothes. This is a very bald statement of it and I am not concerned here so much with French poetry as with English. The kind of verse I advocate is not the same as *vers-libre*, I merely use the French as an example of the extraordinary effect that an emancipation of verse can have on poetic activity.

The ancients were perfectly aware of the fluidity of the world and of its impermanence; there was the Greek theory that the whole world was a flux. But while they recognised it they feared it and endeavoured to evade it, to construct things of permanence which would stand fast in this universal flux which frightened them. They had the disease, the passion, for immortality. They wished to construct things which should be proud boasts that they, men, were immortal. We see it in a thousand different forms. Materially in the pyramids, spiritually in the dogmas of religion and in the hypostatised ideas of Plato. Living in a dynamic world they wished to create a static fixity where their souls might rest.

This I conceive to be the explanation of many of the old ideas on poetry. They wish to embody in a few lines a perfection of thought. Of the thousand and one ways in which a thought might roughly be conveyed to a hearer there was one way which was the perfect way, which was destined to embody that thought to all eternity, hence the fixity of the form of poem and the elaborate rules of regular metre. It was to be an immortal thing and the infinite pains taken to fit a thought into a fixed and artificial form are necessary and understandable. Even the Greek name ποίημα[4] seems to indicate the thing created once and for all, they believed in absolute duty as they believed in absolute truth. Hence they put many things into verse which we now do not desire to, such as history and philosophy. As the French philosopher Guyau put it, the great poems of ancient times resembled pyramids built for eternity where people loved to inscribe their history in symbolic characters. They believed they could realise an adjustment of idea and words that nothing could destroy.

Now the whole trend of the modern spirit is away from that; philosophers no longer believe in absolute truth. We no longer believe in perfection, either in verse or in thought, we frankly acknowledge the relative. We shall no longer strive to attain the absolutely perfect form in poetry. Instead of these minute perfections of phrase and words, the tendency will be rather towards the production of a general effect; this of course takes away the predominance of metre and a regular number of syllables as the element of perfection in words. We are no longer concerned that stanzas shall be shaped and polished like gems, but rather that some vague mood shall be communicated. In all the arts, we seek for the maximum of individual and personal expression, rather than for the attainment of any absolute beauty.

The criticism is sure to be made, what is this new spirit, which finds itself unable to express itself in the old metre? Are the things that a poet wishes to say now in any way different to the things that former poets say? I believe that they are. The old poetry dealt essentially with big things, the expression of epic subjects leads naturally to the anatomical matter and regular verse. Action can best be expressed in regular verse, e.g., the Ballad.

But the modern is the exact opposite of this, it no longer deals with heroic action, it has become definitely and finally introspective and deals with expression and communication of momentary phrases in the poet's mind. It was well put by Mr G.K. Chesterton in this way – that where the old dealt with the Siege of Troy, the new attempts to express the emotions of a boy fishing. The opinion you often hear expressed, that perhaps a new poet will arrive who will synthesise the whole modern movement into a great epic, shows an entire misconception of the tendency of modern verse. There is an analogous change in painting, where the old endeavoured to tell a story, the modern attempts to fix an impression. We still perceive the mystery of things, but we perceive it in entirely a different way – no longer directly in the form of action, but as an impression, for example Whistler's pictures.[5] We can't escape from the spirit of our times. What has found expression in painting as Impressionism will soon find expression in poetry in free verse. The vision of a London street at midnight with its long rows of light, has produced several attempts at reproduction in verse, and yet the war produced nothing worth mentioning, for Mr Watson is a political orator rather than a poet. Speaking of personal matters, the first time I ever felt the necessity or inevitableness of verse, was in the desire to reproduce the peculiar quality of feeling which is induced by the flat spaces and wide horizons of the virgin prairie of western Canada.

You see that this is essentially different to the lyrical impulse which has attained completion, and I think once and forever, in Tennyson, Shelley and Keats. To put this modern conception of the poetic spirit, this tentative and half-shy manner of looking at things, into regular metre is like putting a child into armour.

Say the poet is moved by a certain landscape, he selects from that certain images which put into juxtaposition in separate lines, serve to suggest and to evoke the state he feels. To this piling-up and juxtaposition of distinct images in different lines, one can find a fanciful analogy in music. A great revolution in music when for the melody that is one-dimensional music, was substituted harmony which moves in two. Two visual images form what one may call a visual chord. They unite to suggest an image which is different to both.

Starting then from this standpoint of extreme modernism, what are the principal features of verse at the present time? It is this: that it is read and not chanted. We may set aside all theories that we read verse internally as mere verbal quibbles. We have thus two distinct arts. The one intended to be chanted, and the other intended to be read in the study. I wish this to be remembered in the criticisms that are made on me. I am not speaking of the whole of poetry, but of this distinct new art which is gradually separating itself from the older one and becoming independent.

I quite admit that poetry intended to be recited must be written in regular metre, but I contend that this method of recording impressions by visual images in distinct lines does not require the old metric system.

The older art was originally a religious incantation; it was made to express oracles and maxims in an impressive manner, and rhyme and metre were used as aids to the memory. But why, for this new poetry, should we keep a mechanism which is only suited to the old?

The effect of rhythm, like that of music, is to produce a kind of hypnotic state, during which suggestions of grief or ecstasy are easily and powerfully effective, just as when we are drunk all jokes seem funny. This is for the art of chanting, but the procedure of the new visual art is just the contrary. It depends for its effect not on a kind of half sleep produced, but on arresting the attention, so much so that the succession of visual images should exhaust one.

Regular metre to this impressionist poetry is cramping, jangling, meaningless, and out of place. Into the delicate pattern of images and colour it introduces the heavy, crude pattern of rhetorical verse. It destroys the effect just as a barrel organ does, when it intrudes into the subtle interwoven harmonies of the modern symphony. It is a delicate and difficult art, that of evoking an image, of fitting the rhythm to the idea, and one is tempted to fall back to the comforting and easy arms of the old, regular metre, which takes away all the trouble for us.

The criticism is sure to be made that when you have abolished the regular syllabled line as the unit of poetry, you have turned it into prose. Of course this is perfectly true of a great quantity of modern verse. In fact one of the great blessings of the abolition of regular metre would be that it would at once expose all this sham poetry.

Poetry as an abstract thing is a very different matter, and has its own life, quite apart from metre as a convention.

To test the question of whether it is possible to have poetry written without a regular metre, I propose to pick out one great difference between the two. I don't profess to give an infallible test that would enable anyone to at once say:'This is, or is not, true poetry', but it will be sufficient for the purposes of this paper. It is this: that there are, roughly speaking, two methods of communication, a direct, and a conventional language. The direct language is poetry, it is direct because it deals in images. The indirect language is prose, because it uses images that have died and become figures of speech.

The difference between the two is, roughly, this: that while one arrests your mind all the time with a picture, the other allows the mind to run along with the least possible effort to a conclusion.

Prose is due to a faculty of the mind, something resembling reflex action in the body. If I had to go through a complicated mental process each time I laced my boots, it would waste mental energy; instead of that, the mechanism of the body is so arranged that one can do it almost without thinking. It is an economy of effort. The same process takes place with the images used in prose. For example, when I say that the hill was clad with trees, it merely conveys the fact to me that it was covered. But the first time that expression was used was by a poet, and to him it was an image recalling to him the distinct visual analogy of a man clad in clothes; but the image has died. One might say that images are born in poetry. They are used in prose, and finally die a long lingering death in journalists' English. Now this process is very rapid, so that the poet must continually be creating new images, and his sincerity may be measured by the number of his images.

Sometimes, in reading a poem, one is conscious of gaps where the inspiration failed him, and he only used metre of rhetoric. What happened was this: the image failed him, and he fell back on a dead image, that is prose, but kept an effect by using metre. That is my objection to metre, that it enables people to write verse with no poetic inspiration, and whose mind is not stored with new images.

As an example of this, I will take the poem which now has the largest circulation. Though consisting of only four verses it is six feet long. It is posted outside the Pavilion Music-hall. We instinctively shudder at these clichés or tags of speech. The inner explanation is this: it is not that they are old, but that being old they have become dead, and so evoked no image. The man who wrote them not being a poet, did not see anything definitely himself, but imitated other poets' images.

This new verse resembles sculpture rather than music; it appeals to the eye rather than to the ear. It has to mould images, a kind of spiritual clay, into definite shapes. This material, the ὕλη[6] of Aristotle, is image and not sound. It builds up a plastic image which it hands over to the reader, whereas the old art endeavoured to influence him physically by the hypnotic effect of rhythm.

One might sum it all up in this way: a shell is a very suitable covering for the egg at a certain period of its career, but very unsuitable at a later age. This seems to me to represent fairly well the state of verse at the present time. While the shell remains the same, the inside character is entirely changed. It is not addled as a pessimist might say, but has become alive, it has changed from the ancient art of chanting to the modern impressionist, but the mechanism of verse has remained the same. It can't go on doing so. I will conclude, ladies and gentlemen, by saying, the shell must be broken.

Romanticism and Classicism[1]

[*Speculations*, 113–40]

I want to maintain that after a hundred years of romanticism, we are in for a classical revival, and that the particular weapon of this new classical spirit, when it works in verse, will be fancy. And in this I imply the superiority of fancy – not superior generally or absolutely, for that would be obvious nonsense, but superior in the sense that we use the word good in empirical ethics – good for something, superior for something. I shall have to prove then two things, first that a classical revival is coming, and, secondly, for its particular purposes, fancy will be superior to imagination.

So banal have the terms Imagination and Fancy become that we imagine they must have always been in the language.[2] Their history as two differing terms in the vocabulary of criticism is comparatively short. Originally, of course, they both mean the same thing; they first began to be differentiated by the German writers on aesthetics in the eighteenth century.

I know that in using the words 'classic' and 'romantic' I am doing a dangerous thing. They represent five or six different kinds of antitheses, and while I may be using them in one sense you may be interpreting them in another. In this present connection I am using them in a perfectly precise and limited sense. I ought really to have coined a couple of new words, but I prefer to use the ones I have used, as I then conform to the practice of the group of polemical writers who make most use of them at the present day, and have almost succeeded in making them political catchwords. I mean Maurras, Lasserre and all the group connected with L'Action Française.[3]

At the present time this is the particular group with which the distinction is most vital. Because it has become a party symbol. If you asked a man of a certain set whether he preferred the classics or the romantics, you could deduce from that what his politics were.

The best way of gliding into a proper definition of my terms would be to start with a set of people who are prepared to fight about it – for in them you will have no vagueness. (Other people take the infamous attitude of the person with catholic tastes who says he likes both.)

About a year ago, a man whose name I think was Fauchois gave a lecture at the Odéon on Racine, in the course of which he made some disparaging remarks about his dullness, lack of invention and the rest of it. This caused an immediate riot: fights took place all over the house; several people were arrested and imprisoned, and the rest of the series of lectures took place with hundreds of gendarmes and detectives scattered all over the place. These people interrupted because the classical ideal is a living thing to them and Racine is the great classic. That is what I call a real vital interest in literature. They regard romanticism as an awful disease from which France had just recovered.

The thing is complicated in their case by the fact that it was romanticism that made the revolution. They hate the revolution, so they hate romanticism.

I make no apology for dragging in politics here; romanticism both in England and France is associated with certain political views, and it is in taking a concrete example of the working out of a principle in action that you can get its best definition.

What was the positive principle behind all the other principles of '89? I am talking here of the revolution in as far as it was an idea; I leave out material causes – they only produce the forces. The barriers which could easily have resisted or guided these forces had been previously rotted away by ideas. This always seems to be the case in successful changes; the privileged class is beaten only when it has lost faith in itself, when it has itself been penetrated with the ideas which are working against it.

It was not the rights of man – that was a good solid practical warcry. The thing which created enthusiasm, which made the revolution practically a new religion, was something more positive than that. People of all classes, people who stood to lose by it, were in a positive ferment about the idea of liberty. There must have been some idea which enabled them to think that something positive could come out of so essentially negative a thing. There was, and here I get my definition of romanticism. They had been taught by Rousseau that man was by nature good, that it was only bad laws and customs that had suppressed him. Remove all these and the infinite possibilities of man would have a chance. This is what made them think that something positive could come out of disorder, this is what created the religious enthusiasm. Here is the root of all romanticism: that man, the individual, is an infinite reservoir of possibilities; and if you can so rearrange society by the destruction of oppressive order then these possibilities will have a chance and you will get Progress.

One can define the classical quite clearly as the exact opposite to this. Man is an extraordinarily fixed and limited animal whose nature is absolutely constant. It is only by tradition and organisation that anything decent can be got out of him.

This view was a little shaken at the time of Darwin. You remember his particular hypothesis, that new species came into existence by the cumulative effect of small variations – this seems to admit the possibility of future progress. But at the present day the contrary hypothesis makes headway in the shape of De Vries's mutation theory, that each new species comes into existence, not gradually by the accumulation of small steps, but suddenly in a jump, a kind of sport, and that once in existence it remains absolutely fixed. This enables me to keep the classical view with an appearance of scientific backing.

Put shortly, these are the two views, then. One, that man is intrinsically good, spoilt by circumstance; and the other that he is intrinsically limited, but disciplined by order and tradition to something fairly decent. To the one party man's nature is like a well, to the other like a bucket. The view which regards man as a well, a reservoir full of possibilities, I call the romantic; the one which regards him as a very finite and fixed creature, I call the classical.

One may note here that the Church has always taken the classical view since the defeat of the Pelagian heresy and the adoption of the sane classical dogma of original sin.

It would be a mistake to identify the classical view with that of materialism. On the contrary it is absolutely identical with the normal religious attitude. I should put it in this way: That part of the fixed nature of man is the belief in the Deity. This should be as fixed and true for every man as belief in the existence of matter and in the objective world. It is parallel to appetite, the instinct of sex, and all the other fixed qualities. Now at certain times, by the use of either force or rhetoric, these instincts have been suppressed – in Florence under Savonarola, in Geneva under Calvin, and here under the Roundheads. The inevitable result of such a process is that the repressed instinct bursts out in some abnormal direction. So with religion. By the perverted rhetoric of Rationalism, your natural instincts are suppressed and you are converted into an agnostic. Just as in the case of the other instincts, Nature has her revenge. The instincts that find their right and proper outlet in religion must come out in some other way. You don't believe in a God, so you begin to believe that man is a god. You don't believe in Heaven, so you begin to believe in a heaven on earth. In other words, you get romanticism. The concepts that are right and proper in their own sphere are spread over, and so mess up, falsify and blur the clear outlines of human experience. It is like pouring a pot of treacle over the dinner table. Romanticism then, and this is the best definition I can give of it, is spilt religion.

I must now shirk the difficulty of saying exactly what I mean by romantic and classical in verse. I can only say that it means the result of these two attitudes towards the cosmos, towards man, in so far as it gets reflected in verse. The romantic, because he thinks man infinite, must always be talking about the infinite; and as there is always the bitter contrast between what you think you ought to be able to do and what man actually can, it always tends, in its later stages at any rate, to be gloomy. I really can't go any further than to say it is the reflection of these two temperaments, and point out examples of the different spirits. On the one hand I would take such diverse people as Horace, most of the Elizabethans and the writers of the Augustan age, and on the other side Lamartine, Hugo, parts of Keats, Coleridge, Byron, Shelley and Swinburne.

I know quite well that when people think of classical and romantic in verse, the contrast at once comes into their mind between, say, Racine and Shakespeare. I don't mean this; the dividing line that I intend is here misplaced a little from the true middle. That Racine is on the extreme classical side I agree, but if you call Shakespeare romantic, you are using a different definition to the one I give. You are thinking of the difference between classic and romantic as being merely one between restraint and exuberance. I should say with Nietzsche that there are two kinds of classicism, the static and the dynamic. Shakespeare is the classic of motion.

What I mean by classical in verse, then, is this. That even in the most imaginative flights there is always a holding back, a reservation. The classical poet never forgets this finiteness, this limit of man. He remembers always that he is mixed up with earth. He may jump, but he always returns back; he never flies away into the circumambient gas.

You might say if you wished that the whole of the romantic attitude seems to crystallise in verse round metaphors of flight. Hugo is always flying, flying over abysses, flying up into the eternal gases. The word infinite in every other line.

In the classical attitude you never seem to swing right along to the infinite nothing. If you say an extravagant thing which does exceed the limits inside which you know man to be fastened, yet there is always conveyed in some way at the end an impression of yourself standing outside it, and not quite believing it, or consciously putting it forward as a flourish. You never go blindly into an atmosphere more than the truth, an atmosphere too rarefied for man to breathe for long. You are always faithful to the conception of a limit. It is a question of pitch; in romantic verse you move at a certain pitch of rhetoric which you know, man being what he is, to be a little high-falutin. The kind of thing you get in Hugo or Swinburne. In the coming classical reaction that will feel just wrong. For an example of the opposite thing, a verse written in the proper classical spirit, I can take the song from *Cymbeline* beginning with 'Fear no more the heat of the sun'. I am just using this as a parable. I don't quite mean what I say here. Take the last two lines:

> 'Golden lads and girls all must,
> Like chimney sweepers come to dust.'[4]

Now, no romantic would have ever written that. Indeed, so ingrained is romanticism, so objectionable is this to it, that people have asserted that these were not part of the original song.

Apart from the pun, the thing that I think quite classical is the word lad. Your modern romantic could never write that. He would have to write golden youth, and take up the thing at least a couple of notes in pitch.

I want now to give the reasons which make me think that we are nearing the end of the romantic movement.

The first lies in the nature of any convention or tradition in art. A particular convention or attitude in art has a strict analogy to the phenomena of organic life. It grows old and decays. It has a definite period of life and must die. All the possible tunes get played on it and then it is exhausted; moreover its best period is its youngest. Take the case of the extraordinary efflorescence of verse in the Elizabethan period. All kinds of reasons have been given for this – the discovery of the new world and all the rest of it. There is a much simpler one. A new medium had been given them to play with – namely, blank verse. It was new and so it was easy to play new tunes on it.

The same law holds in other arts. All the masters of painting are born into the world at a time when the particular tradition from which they start is imperfect. The Florentine tradition was just short of full ripeness when Raphael came to Florence, the Bellinesque was still young when Titian was born in Venice. Landscape was still a toy or an appanage of figure-painting when Turner and Constable arose to reveal its independent power. When Turner and Constable had done with landscape they left little or nothing for their successors to do on the same lines. Each field of artistic activity is exhausted by the first great artist who gathers a full harvest from it.

This period of exhaustion seems to me to have been reached in romanticism. We shall not get any new efflorescence of verse until we get a new technique, a new convention, to turn ourselves loose in.

Objection might be taken to this. It might be said that a century as an organic unity doesn't exist, that I am being deluded by a wrong metaphor, that I am treating a collection of literary people as if they were an organism or state department. Whatever we may be in other things, an objector might urge, in literature in as far as we are anything at all – in as far as we are worth considering – we are individuals, we are persons, and as distinct persons we cannot be subordinated to any general treatment. At any period at any time, an individual poet may be a classic or a romantic just as he feels like it. You at any particular moment may think that you can stand outside a movement. You may think that as an individual you observe both the classic and the romantic spirit and decide from a purely detached point of view that one is superior to the other.

The answer to this is that no one, in a matter of judgment of beauty, can take a detached standpoint in this way. Just as physically you are not born that abstract entity, man, but the child of particular parents, so you are in matters of literary judgment. Your opinion is almost entirely of the literary history that came just before you, and you are governed by that whatever you may think. Take Spinoza's example of a stone falling to the ground. If it had a conscious mind it would, he said, think it was going to the ground because it wanted to. So you with your pretended free judgment about what is and what is not beautiful. The amount of freedom in man is much exaggerated. That we are free on certain rare occasions, both my religion and the views I get from metaphysics convince me. But many acts which we habitually label free are in reality automatic. It is quite possible for a man to write a book almost automatically. I have read several such products. Some observations were recorded more than twenty years ago by Robertson on reflex speech, and he found that in certain cases of dementia, where the people were quite unconscious so far as the exercise of reasoning went, that very intelligent answers were given to a succession of questions on politics and such matters. The meaning of these questions could not possibly have been understood. Language here acted after the manner of a reflex. So that certain extremely complex mechanisms, subtle enough to imitate beauty, can work by themselves – I certainly think that this is the case with judgments about beauty.

I can put the same thing in slightly different form. Here is a question of a conflict of two attitudes, as it might be of two techniques. The critic, while he has to admit that changes from one to the other occur, persists in regarding them as mere variations to a certain fixed normal, just as a pendulum might swing. I admit the analogy of the pendulum as far as movement, but I deny the further consequence of the analogy, the existence of the point of rest, the normal point.

When I say that I dislike the romantics, I dissociate two things: the part of them in which they resemble all the great poets, and the part in which they differ and which gives them their character as romantics. It is this minor element which constitutes the particular note of a century, and which, while it excites contemporaries, annoys the next generation. It was precisely that quality in Pope which pleased his friends, which we detest. Now, anyone just before the romantics who felt that, could have predicted that a change was coming. It seems to me that we stand just in the same position now. I think that there is an increasing proportion of people who simply can't stand Swinburne.

When I say that there will be another classical revival I don't necessarily anticipate a return to Pope. I say merely that now is the time for such a revival. Given people of the necessary capacity, it may be a vital thing; without them we may get a formalism something like Pope. When it does come we may not even recognise it as classical. Although it will be classical it will be different because it has passed through a romantic period. To take a parallel example: I remember being very surprised, after seeing the Post Impressionists, to find in Maurice Denis's account of the matter that they consider themselves classical in the sense that they were trying to impose the same order on the mere flux of new material provided by the impressionist movement, that existed in the more limited materials of the painting before.

There is something now to be cleared away before I get on with my argument, which is that while romanticism is dead in reality, yet the critical attitude appropriate to it still continues to exist. To make this a little clearer: For every kind of verse, there is a corresponding receptive attitude. In a romantic period we demand from verse certain qualities. In a classical period we demand others. At the present time I should say that this receptive attitude has outlasted the thing from which it was formed. But while the romantic tradition has run dry, yet the critical attitude of mind, which demands romantic qualities from verse, still survives. So that if good classical verse were to be written tomorrow very few people would be able to stand it.

I object even to the best of the romantics. I object still more to the receptive attitude. I object to the sloppiness which doesn't consider that a poem is a poem unless it is moaning or whining about something or other. I always think in this connection of the last line of a poem of John Webster's which ends with a request I cordially endorse:

'End your moan and come away.'[5]

The thing has got so bad now that a poem which is all dry and hard, a properly classical poem, would not be considered poetry at all. How many people now can lay their hands on their hearts and say they like either Horace or Pope? They feel a kind of chill when they read them.

The dry hardness which you get in the classics is absolutely repugnant to them. Poetry that isn't damp isn't poetry at all. They cannot see that accurate description is a legitimate object of verse. Verse to them always means a bringing in of some of the emotions that are grouped round the word infinite.

The essence of poetry to most people is that it must lead them to a beyond of some kind. Verse strictly confined to the earthly and the definite (Keats is full of it) might seem to them to be excellent writing, excellent craftsmanship, but not poetry. So much has romanticism debauched us, that, without some form of vagueness, we deny the highest.

In the classic it is always the light of ordinary day, never the light that never was on land or sea. It is always perfectly human and never exaggerated: man is always man and never a god.

But the awful result of romanticism is that, accustomed to this strange light, you can never live without it. Its effect on you is that of a drug.

There is a general tendency to think that verse means little else than the expression of unsatisfied emotion. People say: 'But how can you have verse without sentiment?' You see what it is: the prospect alarms them. A classical revival to them would mean the prospect of an arid desert and the death of poetry as they understand it, and could only come to fill the gap caused by that death. Exactly why this dry classical spirit should have a positive and legitimate necessity to express itself in poetry is utterly inconceivable to them. What this positive need is, I shall show later. It follows from the fact that there is another quality, not the emotion produced, which is at the root of excellence in verse. Before I get to this I am concerned with a negative thing, a theoretical point, a prejudice that stands in the way and is really at the bottom of this reluctance to understand classical verse.

It is an objection which ultimately I believe comes from a bad metaphysic of art. You are unable to admit the existence of beauty without the infinite being in some way or another dragged in.

I may quote for purposes of argument, as a typical example of this kind of attitude made vocal, the famous chapters in Ruskin's *Modern Painters*, Vol. II, on the imagination. I must say here, parenthetically, that I use this word without prejudice to the other discussion with which I shall end the paper. I only use the word here because it is Ruskin's word. All that I am concerned with just now is the attitude behind it, which I take to be the romantic.

Imagination cannot but be serious; she sees too far, too darkly, too solemnly, too earnestly, ever to smile. There is something in the heart of everything, if we can reach it, that we shall not be inclined to laugh at... Those who have so pierced and seen the melancholy deeps of things, are filled with intense passion and gentleness of sympathy. (Part III, Chap. III, § 9)

There is in every word set down by the imaginative mind an awful undercurrent of meaning, and evidence and shadow upon it of the deep places out of which it has come. It is often obscure, often half-told; for he who wrote it, in his clear seeing of the things beneath, may have been impatient of detailed interpretation; for if we choose to dwell upon it and trace it, it will lead us always securely back to that metropolis of the soul's dominion from which we may follow out all the ways and tracks to its farthest coasts. (Part III, Chap. III, § 5)[6]

Really in all these matters the act of judgment is an instinct, an absolutely unstateable thing akin to the art of the tea taster. But you must talk, and the only language you can use in this matter is that of analogy. I have no material clay to mould to the given shape; the only thing which one has for the purpose, and which acts as a substitute for it, a kind of mental clay, are certain metaphors modified into theories of aesthetic and rhetoric. A combination of these, while it cannot state the essentially unstateable intuition, can yet give you a sufficient analogy to enable you to see what it was and to recognise it on condition that you yourself have been in a similar state. Now these phrases of Ruskin's convey quite clearly to me his taste in the matter.

I see quite clearly that he thinks the best verse must be serious. That is a natural attitude for a man in the romantic period. But he is not content with saying that he prefers this kind of verse. He wants to deduce his opinion like his master, Coleridge, from some fixed principle which can be found by metaphysic.

Here is the last refuge of this romantic attitude. It proves itself to be not an attitude but a deduction from a fixed principle of the cosmos.

One of the main reasons for the existence of philosophy is not that it enables you to find truth (it can never do that) but that it does provide you a refuge for definitions. The usual idea of the thing is that it provides you with a fixed basis from which you can deduce the things you want in esthetics. The process is the exact contrary. You start in the confusion of the fighting line, you retire from that just a little to the rear to recover, to get your weapons right. Quite plainly, without metaphor this – it provides you with an elaborate and precise language in which you really can explain definitely what you mean, but what you want to say is decided by other things. The ultimate reality is the hurly-burly, the struggle; the metaphysic is an adjunct to clear-headedness in it.

To get back to Ruskin and his objection to all that is not serious. It seems to me that involved in this is a bad metaphysical aesthetic. You have the metaphysic which in defining beauty or the nature of art always drags in the infinite. Particularly in Germany, the land where theories of aesthetics were first created, the romantic aesthetes collated all beauty to an impression of the infinite involved in the identification of our being in absolute spirit. In the least element of beauty we have a total intuition of the whole world. Every artist is a kind of pantheist.

Now it is quite obvious to anyone who holds this kind of theory that any poetry which confines itself to the finite can never be of the highest kind. It seems a contradiction in terms to them. And as in metaphysics you get the last refuge of a prejudice, so it is now necessary for me to refute this.

Here follows a tedious piece of dialectic, but it is necessary for my purpose. I must avoid two pitfalls in discussing the idea of beauty. On the one hand there is the old classical view which is supposed to define it as lying in conformity to certain standard fixed forms; and on the other hand there is the romantic view which drags in the infinite. I have got to find a metaphysic between these two which will enable me to hold consistently that a neo-classic verse of the type I have indicated involves no contradiction in terms. It is essential to prove that beauty may be in small, dry things.

The great aim is accurate, precise and definite description. The first thing is to recognise how extraordinarily difficult this is. It is no mere matter of carefulness; you have to use language, and language is by its very nature a communal thing; that is, it expresses never the exact thing but a compromise – that which is common to you, me and everybody. But each man sees a little differently, and to get out clearly and exactly what he does see, he must have a terrific struggle with language, whether it be with words or the technique of other arts. Language has its own special nature, its own conventions and communal ideas. It is only by a concentrated effort of the mind that you can hold it fixed to your own purpose. I always think that the fundamental process at the back of all the arts might be represented by the following metaphor. You know what I call architect's curves – flat pieces of wood with all different kinds of curvature. By a suitable selection from these you can draw approximately any curve you like. The artist I take to be the man who simply can't bear the idea of that 'approximately'. He will get the exact curve of what he sees whether it be an object or an idea in the mind. I shall here have to change my metaphor a little to get the process in his mind. Suppose that instead of your curved pieces of wood you have a springy piece of steel of the same types of curvature as the wood. Now the state of tension or concentration of mind, if he is doing anything really good in this struggle against the ingrained habit of the technique, may be represented by a man employing all his fingers to bend the steel out of its own curve and into the exact curve which you want. Something different to what it would assume naturally.

There are then two things to distinguish, first the particular faculty of mind to see things as they really are, and apart from the conventional ways in which you have been trained to see them. This is itself rare enough in all consciousness. Second, the concentrated state of mind, the grip over oneself which is necessary in the actual expression of what one sees. To prevent one falling into the conventional curves of ingrained technique, to hold on through infinite detail and trouble to the exact curve you want. Wherever you get this sincerity, you get the fundamental quality of good art without dragging in infinite or serious.

I can now get at that positive fundamental quality of verse which constitutes excellence, which has nothing to do with infinity, with mystery or with emotions.

This is the point I aim at, then, in my argument. I prophesy that a period of dry, hard, classical verse is coming. I have met the preliminary objection founded on the bad romantic aesthetic that in such verse, from which the infinite is excluded, you cannot have the essence of poetry at all.

After attempting to sketch out what this positive quality is, I can get on to the end of my paper in this way: That where you get this quality exhibited in the realm of the emotions you get imagination, and that where you get this quality exhibited in the contemplation of finite things you get fancy.

In prose as in algebra concrete things are embodied in signs or counters which are moved about according to rules, without being visualised at all in the process. There are in prose certain type situations and arrangements of words, which move as automatically into certain other arrangements as do functions in algebra. One only changes the X's and the Y's back into physical things at the end of the process. Poetry, in one aspect at any rate, may be considered as an effort to avoid this characteristic of prose. It is not a counter language, but a visual concrete one. It is a compromise for a language of intuition which would hand over sensations bodily. It always endeavours to arrest you, and to make you continuously see a physical thing, to prevent you gliding through an abstract process. It chooses fresh epithets and fresh metaphors, not so much because they are new, and we are tired of the old, but because the old cease to convey a physical thing and become abstract counters. A poet says a ship 'coursed the seas' to get a physical image, instead of the counter word 'sailed'. Visual meanings can only be transferred by the new bowl of metaphor; prose is an old pot that lets them leak out. Images in verse are not mere decoration, but the very essence of an intuitive language. Verse is a pedestrian taking you over the ground, prose – a train which delivers you at a destination.

I can now get on to a discussion of two words often used in this connection, 'fresh' and 'unexpected'. You praise a thing for being 'fresh'. I understand what you mean, but the word besides conveying the truth conveys a secondary something which is certainly false. When you say a poem or drawing is fresh, and so good, the impression is somehow conveyed that the essential element of goodness is freshness, that it is good because it is fresh. Now this is certainly wrong, there is nothing particularly desirable about freshness *per se*. Works of art aren't eggs. Rather the contrary. It is simply an unfortunate necessity due to the nature of the language and technique that the only way the element which does constitute goodness, the only way in which its presence can be detected externally, is by freshness. Freshness convinces you, you feel at once that the artist was in an actual physical state. You feel that for a minute. Real communication is so very rare, for plain speech is unconvincing. It is in this rare fact of communication that you get the root of aesthetic pleasure.

I shall maintain that wherever you get an extraordinary interest in a thing, a great zest in its contemplation which carries on the contemplator to accurate description in the sense of the word accurate I have just analysed, there you have sufficient justification for poetry. It must be an intense zest which heightens a thing out of the level of prose. I am using contemplation here just in the same way that Plato used it, only applied to a different subject; it is a detached interest. 'The object of aesthetic contemplation is something framed apart by itself and regarded without memory or expectation, simply as being itself, as end not means, as individual not universal.'

To take a concrete example. I am taking an extreme case. If you are walking behind a woman in the street, you notice the curious way in which the skirt rebounds from her heels. If that peculiar kind of motion becomes of such interest to you that you will search about until you can get the exact epithet which hits it off, there you have a properly aesthetic emotion. But it is the zest with which you look at the thing which decides you to make the effort. In this sense the feeling that was in Herrick's mind when he wrote 'the tempestuous petticoat'[7] was exactly the same as that which in bigger and vaguer matters makes the best romantic verse. It doesn't matter an atom that the emotion produced is not of dignified vagueness, but on the contrary amusing; the point is that exactly the same activity is at work as in the highest verse. That is the avoidance of conventional language in order to get the exact curve of the thing.

I have still to show that in the verse which is to come, fancy will be the necessary weapon of the classical school. The positive quality I have talked about can be manifested in ballad verse by extreme directness and simplicity, such as you get in 'On Fair Kirkconnel Lea'. But the particular verse we are going to get will be cheerful, dry and sophisticated, and here the necessary weapon of the positive quality must be fancy.

Subject doesn't matter; the quality in it is the same as you get in the more romantic people.

It isn't the scale or kind of emotion produced that decides, but this one fact: Is there any real zest in it? Did the poet have an actually realised visual object before him in which he delighted? It doesn't matter if it were a lady's shoe or the starry heavens.

Fancy is not mere decoration added on to plain speech. Plain speech is essentially inaccurate. It is only by new metaphors, that is, by fancy, that it can be made precise.

When the analogy has not enough connection with the thing described to be quite parallel with it, where it overlays the thing it described and there is a certain excess, there you have the play of fancy – that I grant is inferior to imagination.

But where the analogy is every bit of it necessary for accurate description in the sense of the word accurate I have previously described, and your only objection to this kind of fancy is that it is not serious in the effect it produces, then I think the objection to be entirely invalid. If it is sincere in the accurate sense, when the whole of the analogy is necessary to get out the exact curve of the feeling or thing you want to express – there you seem to me to have the highest verse, even though the subject be trivial and the emotions of the infinite far away.

It is very difficult to use any terminology at all for this kind of thing. For whatever word you use is at once sentimentalised. Take Coleridge's word 'vital'. It is used loosely by all kinds of people who talk about art, to mean something vaguely and mysteriously significant. In fact, vital and mechanical is to them exactly the same antithesis as between good and bad.

Nothing of the kind; Coleridge uses it in a perfectly definite and what I call dry sense. It is just this: A mechanical complexity is the sum of its parts. Put them side by side and you get the whole. Now vital or organic is merely a convenient metaphor for a complexity of a different kind, that in which the parts cannot be said to be elements as each one is modified by the other's presence, and each one to a certain extent is the whole. The leg of a chair by itself is still a leg. My leg by itself wouldn't be.

Now the characteristic of the intellect is that it can only represent complexities of the mechanical kind. It can only make diagrams, and diagrams are essentially things whose parts are separate one from another. The intellect always analyses – when there is a synthesis it is baffled. That is why the artist's work seems mysterious. The intellect can't represent it. This is a necessary consequence of the particular nature of the intellect and the purposes for which it is formed. It doesn't mean that your synthesis is ineffable, simply that it can't be definitely stated.

Now this is all worked out in Bergson, the central feature of his whole philosophy. It is all based on the clear conception of these vital complexities which he calls 'intensive' as opposed to the other kind which he calls 'extensive', and the recognition of the fact that the intellect can only deal with the extensive multiplicity. To deal with the intensive you must use intuition.

Now, as I said before, Ruskin was perfectly aware of all this, but he had no such metaphysical background which would enable him to state definitely what he meant. The result is that he has to flounder about in a series of metaphors. A powerfully imaginative mind seizes and combines at the same instant all the important ideas of its poem or picture, and while it works with one of them, it is at the same instant working with and modifying all in their relation to it and never losing sight of their bearings on each other – as the motion of a snake's body goes through all parts at once and its volition acts at the same instant in coils which go contrary ways.

A romantic movement must have an end of the very nature of the thing. It may be deplored, but it can't be helped – wonder must cease to be wonder.

I guard myself here from all the consequences of the analogy, but it expresses at any rate the inevitableness of the process. A literature of wonder must have an end as inevitably as a strange land loses its strangeness when one lives in it. Think of the lost ecstasy of the Elizabethans. 'Oh my America, my new found land,'[8] think of what it meant to them and of what it means to us. Wonder can only be the attitude of a man passing from one stage to another, it can never be a permanently fixed thing.

Review of Tancrède de Visan's *L'attitude du Lyrisme Contemporain*[1]

[*The New Age*, 9/17 (24 August 1911)]

This is an extremely good and an extremely interesting book. I recommend those who either know nothing of modern French poetry or who, knowing something, want their knowledge systematised, to buy it at once. (True inwardness of movement.)

I confess that its goodness was a surprise to me. When I first picked it up I saw that it was a collection of essays on all the poets that one has known about for some time. The names on the cover – Verhaeren, De Régnier, Mockel, Paul Fort, Maeterlinck, and Vielé-Griffin – seem just the same as those in Beaunier's book, *La Poésie Nouvelle*, that I read some five or six years ago. There were no new names. I found this to be an illustration of one of my favourite theories – that French verse, after a short period of great interest, the most vital that had occurred for centuries, had now arrived at comparative stagnation, and had been succeeded by a period during which French philosophy, also for the first time for centuries, was to dominate Europe.

However, when I commenced to read the book I found it vastly different to what I had expected. It is not a mere collection of disconnected, though intelligent, essays on the fashionable moderns that we all of us know, the kind of thing which any literary man who is in the know can turn out at his leisure, but is really a definitely-thought-out attempt to exhibit all these poets as particular manifestations of the same general current of ideas.

It starts out from this thesis. That there is in each generation what Taine called a 'temperature morale', which is to be found at the same epoch in all the different orders of mental activity, and which constitutes 'l'état général de l'esprit de moeurs environnantes'. To any tendency of poetry at a given time there is a corresponding tendency of philosophy. The psychology of one of Corneille's heroes corresponds to the pure Cartesian doctrine. To the Positivism of Comte and Littré corresponds in literature the spread of naturalism and the 'Parnasse'. The criticism of Taine, the poetry of Leconte de Lisle, the novels of Flaubert, the painting of Courbet, all live in one common atmosphere.

The question then arises, what similar parallelism holds good of modern French literature and philosophy – Monsieur De Visan's book is a reasoned attempt to prove that the spirit which finds expression in the Symboliste movement in poetry is the same as that represented by Bergson in philosophy.

They are both reactions against the definite and the clear, not for any preference for the vague as such, not for any mere preference for sentiment, but because both feel, one by a kind of instinctive, unconscious process and the other as the result of reasoning, that the clear conceptions of the intellect are a definite distortion of reality. Bergson represents a reaction against the atomic and rational psychology of Taine and Spencer, against the idea that states of mind can be arrived at by the summation of more elementary states. He asserts the mental states from a continuous and unanalysable state of flux which cannot from its nature be ever represented clearly by the intellect, but must be seized by a process of intuition. The Symbolist reaction against the Parnasse is exactly the same reaction in a different region of thought. For what was the Parnassian attitude? It was an endeavour always to keep to accurate description. It was an endeavour to create poetry of 'clear' ideas. They employed always clear and precise descriptions of external things and strove by combinations of such 'atoms of the beautiful' to manufacture a living beauty. To the Symbolists this seems an impossible feat. For life is a continuous and unanalysable curve which cannot be seized clearly, but can only be felt as a kind of intuition. It can only be got at by a kind of central vision as opposed to analytic description, this central vision expressing itself by means of symbols. M. Visan would then define Symbolism as an attempt by means of successive and accumulated images to express and exteriorise such a central lyric intuition. This is the central idea of the book, and the working of it out in the detailed study of the poets of the movement is extremely well done. It is very interesting to see how a complex thought like that of Bergson should be unconsciously anticipated and find a tentative expression in a purely literary movement.

One amusing expression should be noted. He gives an interesting description of the eager little sets of students who used to attend Bergson's lectures at the Collège de France, and contrasts it with the present-day, when it is impossible to find a seat and the hall is overpowered by the feathers and 'blasphemous scents' of women.

German Chronicle

[*Poetry and Drama*, 2 (June 1914), 221–8.]

Prefatory Note. – How do I take my duties as a chronicler? Rather lightly perhaps. My tale will be rather haphazard. I do not intend to make a careful *inventory* of current literature, either by honestly tasting everything, or by collecting current opinions. I shall make no special effort. I shall not read anything on your behalf that I should not naturally have read for my own amusement. I intend merely to give an account of the things which reach me naturally, as I sit nightly gossiping at the Café des Westens (the Café Royal of Berlin, immortalised by Rupert Brooke's poem)[1]. I am actually on the spot. I walk down Tauenzienstrasse in the afternoon. I know many of the people I have to write about. I daily contemplate the Kaiser Wilhelm Gedächtniskirche (so frequently mentioned in modern verse), and derive certain advantages from this physical fact. This is the extent of my superiority. I make no claim to judicial estimate of tendencies, but humbly communicate the 'latest thing' – quite a useful function when you remember that by ordinary channels of print it takes twenty years for an idea to get from one country to another, while even a hat takes six months.

After all, it is time that German had this kind of treatment. It has been written about by people who felt that the literature of the country was a phenomenon of the same kind as its rainfall or its commerce, and deserved periodical notice and report. Careful chronicles of this kind put the whole situation in an entirely wrong perspective. You have to mention writers whom the native never considers.

Nobody seems to have written about German for fun. The natural motive for such writing, the fact that you have discovered something exciting and want to communicate your excitement, seems to have been entirely lacking here. It seems rather as if men who at some trouble to themselves had learnt German, had looked round for suitable means of revenging themselves on others who had not had that trouble. French, on the contrary, has been written about by people who possessed the curious characteristic of insisting on reading only what amused them.

One can account for the fact that this type of enthusiastic amateur does not write about German, by a rather curious reason. It lies in a certain difference between the two literatures, which makes the one more easily accessible to the amateur of this kind that the other. Every speech is at once a language serving the purposes of the will, expressing intimate desires and commands, and at the same time a language expressing thoughts by a sequence of concepts. The second aspect of a language can be readily grasped by a foreigner who has learned the language in the usual literary way. The first, depending as it does on the emotional values attaching to simple words, can only be appreciated when one has oneself used the language as a weapon of daily abuse. The qualities inherent in the direct use of speech cannot be deliberately learnt. Here comes the point I am trying to make clear. Both French and German are in an equal degree used for these two purposes. But as far as literature itself is concerned, I should be inclined to assert that while the qualities of French literature are to be found in the use of language as a sequence of concepts, the essential qualities of German literature depend on its more homely use as a language of will and emotion.

While the essential qualities of French literature are thus easily seizable by a foreigner who has learnt the language in the usual way – i.e., as a descriptive conceptual language – those of German are not. It may seem rather paradoxical, in view of the qualities of German as a philosophical language, to assert it is less a conceptual language than French. I am not, however, speaking of the languages inherently, but only of the qualities they exhibit in literature. If one is not studying 'comparative literature', but just reading foreign literature in the spirit in which one reads one's own, one is apt, for this reason, at first to be repelled by German. It does not lie open at once as French does. It is only when one comes across the old peasant poems and songs in dialect, which exhibit prominently of course the qualities of a speech as a 'language of will', that one begins to appreciate it. Then one begins also to recognise these qualities in classical German literature and find it more bearable. One sees it most familiarly in the extraordinary homeliness and solidity of certain parts of Goethe.

These, I repeat again, are qualities which cannot be appreciated by the literary amateur who has learnt German as he has learnt French.

* * *

To turn now to contemporary German verse. A consideration of its immediate past is of some importance. Its roots do not go very deep. One should always bear in mind that German literature had no important Victorian period. Between the classical period of 1780-1830 and the moderns lies a gap. I am quite aware that this is an exaggeration, and that anyone who has ever read a manual of German literature could supply a continuous list of names stretching from one period to the other. But that would not affect the truth of what I assert. If you read Nietzsche's denunciation of German literature about 1870 you will see what is meant. It is only when one realises the state of German literature at the time that his denunciations become comprehensible. I point this out because it does seem to me to be important. The literary cabaret I speak of later commenced by a reading of these passages from Nietzsche's 'What the Germans lack.' This is not a mere dead fact from history, but throws light on the present.

The roots of the present lie only thirty years back. They resemble strawberry runners, springing from a mother root – in this case situated in Paris, Norway and elsewhere. The history of this period divides naturally into three decades. In 1880 also comes the beginning of the modern period with the influence of Zola, Ibsen and Tolstoi. A few years later come the German names Conrad, Hauptmann and Hart. About 1892 you get a new tendency showing itself, 'Los von Naturalismus'.[2] The principal names of this generation are Liliencron and Dehmel; Stephan Georg, Max Dauthendey, and Hofmannsthal, the group associated with *Blätter für die Kunst* ; Mombert, Peter Hille, Bierbaum, Falke, and Arno Holz, who perhaps belongs to the previous generation. From 1900 till 1910 you get another change. Naturalism is quite dead – but no formula can be given to describe this period. Carl Spitteler does not, properly speaking, belong to this generation, but I put him here because it was only at this time that his poems began to be read. The best poet of the period seems to me to be undoubtedly Rainer Maria Rilke. Other names are Schaukal, Eulenberg, and, among those who are not, properly speaking, poets, Wedekind, Heinrich, and Thomas Mann; Paul Ernst, Loublinski, and 'the Neo-Classical Movement', of which I hope to say something more later.

The generation that I am to write about is the one since this.

Before doing this, however, I should like to interpolate a list of papers and reviews where new work may be found: *Pan*, 6d. weekly, published by Cassirer, very lively indeed; *Die weissen Blätter*, a 2/- monthly, which, at present at any rate, includes some of the best of the younger men; *Der neue Rundschau*, a 2/- monthly something like the *English Review*; *Der Sturm*, a 4d. fortnightly, in reality a Futurist and Cubist art-paper, but always containing verse of Futurist type, well worth taking in; *Aktion*, a 2d. weekly, publishing good modern verses; *Der lose Vogel*; and finally two 3d. weeklies something like *The Academy*, *Die literarische Echo* and *Die Gegenwart*.

* * *

I can only give certain haphazard impressions of this last generation. Someone is sure to say that I have mistaken a small clique for contemporary poetry but I take the risk. I attempt to give only my impressions. I attended a meeting of the 'Cabaret Gnu.' This takes place every month in a Café. The Cabaret has a president who calls on various poets to get up and read their poems. All do so without any diffidence whatever, and with a certain ferocity. It is all much pleasanter than a reading here, for having paid to go in, you are free to talk and laugh if the poem displeases you. Moreover, the confidence and the ferocity of the poets is such that you do not feel bound to encourage them. To anyone accustomed to ordinary German, the language is very surprising. Very short sentences are used, sometimes so terse and elliptical as to produce a blunt and jerky effect. It does not send you to sleep like the diffuse German of the past, but is, on the other hand, so abrupt that the prose itself at times almost resembles Futurist verse. The result is not always happy but it is clear that a definite attempt is being made to use the language in a new way, an attempt to cure it of certain vices. That this reaction is a conscious one is shown, I suppose, by the opening reading of the passage from Nietzsche I have mentioned above. One feels that the language is passing through a period of experiment. Whether this is a local and unimportant fashion, or whether something will come of it, one cannot of course say. But there it is, an undoubted fact. The same reaction against softness and diffusiveness seems to me to be observable in the verse as in the prose.

As conveniently representing this present generation of poets, I take the anthology *Der Kondor* (edited by Kurt Hiller, published by Weissbach in Heidelberg, 1912). I might compare it with the Georgian Anthology. Though it has shown no signs yet of passing from edition to edition, like its remarkable English prototype, it yet attracted a certain amount of notice and criticism. Whatever its merits may be, it does represent the literary group with the greatest amount of life in it at the present moment. The editor, Kurt Hiller, was the conductor of the Cabaret Gnu I mentioned above.

The editor writes a short preface. Protesting in the first place against certain influences from which he imagines the present generation must make itself free – Stephan Georg and his school – the aristocratic view of art, 'we ourselves understand the value of strict technique, but we reject Hochnäsigkeit[3] as the constitutive principle of poetry.'

Secondly, he protests against those who mistake a metaphysical and pantheistic sentimentality for poetry.

Der Kondor then is to be a manifesto, a Dichter Sezession, 'a rigorous collection of radical strophes. It is to include only those verse writers who can be called artists. It is to give a picture of all the artists of a generation.' The eldest were born at the end of the 70's, the youngest in 1890. In the opinion of the editor it includes the best verse that has been written in German since Rilke.

To turn now to the verse itself, I obviously cannot give any detailed criticism of the fourteen poets included. I propose, therefore to quote one or two and then give my general impression.

Take first Ernst Blass, whose book *Die Strassen komme ich entlang geweht* has appeared with the same publisher as *Der Kondor* itself. I quote his 'Sonnenuntergang':

> Noch traüm ich von den Ländern, wo die roten
> Palastfassaden wie Gesichter stieren
> Der Mond hängt strotzend
> Weiss er von den Toten?
> Ich gehe an den weichen Strand spazieren.
> Schräg durch Bekannte. (Schrieen nicht einst Löwen?)
> Vom Kaffeegarten kommt Musike her,
> Die grosse Sonne fährt mit seidnen Möwen.
> Über das Meer.[4]

Else Lasker-Schüler, the best known of those included in the volume, in reality belongs to a slightly earlier generation. Some of her poems, for example, are translated in *Contemporary German Poetry* (Walter Scott, 1/-). She is a very familiar figure in the Café des Westens; her short hair, extraordinary clothes and manly stride are easily recognisable in the neighbourhood of the Kurfürstendamm. Her prose, however, is extremely feminine, and anyone who is interested in gossip about the poets of this generation will find *Mein Herz* amusing. (It is put in the form of letters addressed to her former husband, Herwath Walden, the editor of the Futurist paper, *Der Sturm*.)

> *Ein Alter Tibetteppich*
> Deine Seele, die die meine liebet,
> Ist verwirkt mit ihr im Teppichtibet,
>
> Strahl in Strahl, verliebte Farben,
> Sterne, die sich himmellang umwarben.
>
> Unsere Füsse ruhen auf der Kostbarkeit
> Maschentausendabertausendweit.
>
> Süsser Lamasohn auf Moschuspflanzenthron
> Wie lange küsst dein Mund den meinen wohl
> Und Wang die Wange buntgeknüpfte Zeiten schon?[5]

Then Georg Heym, who can be compared to Richard Middleton, in that he died young, leaving behind him a volume of verse and some short stories:

> Beteerte Fässer rollten von den Schwellen
> Der dunklen Speicher auf die hohen Kähne.
> Die Schlepper zogen an. Des Rauches Mähne
> Hing russig nieder auf die öligen Wellen.
>
> Zwei Dampfer kamen mit Musikkapellen.
> Den Schornstein kappten sie am Brückenbogen.
> Rauch, Russ, Gestank lag auf den schmutzigen Wogen
> Der Gerbereien mit den braunen Fellen.
>
> In allen Brücken, drunter uns die Zille
> Hindurchgebracht, ertönten die Signale

Gleichwie in Trommeln wachsend in der Stille.

Wir liessen los und trieben im Kanale
An Gärten langsam hin. In dem Idylle
Sahn wir der Riesenschlote Nachtfanale.[6]

Arthur Drey's 'Kloster':

Und Mauern stehen ohne sich zu rühren
Wir graue Fäuste, die im Wind erfrieren,[7]

like several other poems in the volume, illustrates the use, which has now become epidemic, of the word *Und* at the beginning of every other line (derived probably from Hugo von Hofmannsthal's well-known 'Ballade des Äusseren Lebens').

From René Schickele's *Auf der Friedrichstrasse bei Sonnenuntergang*:

An der Ecke steht ein Mann
Mit verklärtem Gesicht
Du stösst ihn an,
Er merkt es nicht.

Starrt empor mit blassem Blick
Schlaff die Arme herunter
Tiefer gestaltet sich sein Geschick
Und der Himmel bunter.[8]

I have no space to quote any more, but I give the names of the other poets and their books: Franz Werfel, *Der Weltfreund* and *Wir Sind*; Alfred Lichtenstein, *Dämmerung*; Max Brod, *Tagebuch in Versen*; Schickele, *Weiss und Rot*, published by Paul Cassirer; Crossberger, *Exhibitionen*, published by Meister, Heidelberg.

The group has to a certain extent divided. Kurt Hiller is writing for *Die Weissen Blätter*, a review which commenced last autumn, while Kronfeld told me when I saw him that he and Ernst Blass were starting a new review this spring, of which I hope to say something in my next chronicle.

As to my general impression of the whole group. First of all must be placed to their credit the fact that none of the poems can be described as pretty. They are not sentimentally derivative, they are the product of some constructive intelligence, but I doubt whether this intelligence is one making for poetry. I doubt it, because the poems are so recognisably those which intelligent people would write.

To explain in more detail, I assume that the sensibility of the poet is possessed by many who themselves are not poets. The differentiating factor is something other than their sensibility. To simplify matters then, suppose a poet and an intelligent man both moved in exactly the same way by some scene; both desire to express what they feel; in what way does the expression differ? The difficulty of expression can be put in an almost geometrical way. The scene before you is a picture in two dimensions. It has to be reduced to verse, which being a line of words has only one dimension. However, this one-dimensional form has other elements of rhythm, sound, etc., which form as it were an emotional equivalent for the lost dimension. The process of transition from the one to the other in the case of the poet is possibly something of this kind. First, as in the case of all of us, the emotional impression. Then probably comes *one* line of words, with a definite associated rhythm – the rest of the poem follows from this.

Now here comes the point. This first step from the thing clearly 'seen' to this almost blind process of development in verse, is the characteristic of the poet, and the step which the merely intelligent man cannot take. He sees 'clearly' and he must construct 'clearly'. This obscure mixture of description and rhythm is one, however, which cannot be *constructed* by a rational process, *i.e.*, a process which keeps all its elements clear before its eyes all the time.

The handicap of the intelligent man who is not a poet is that he cannot trust himself to this obscure world from which rhythm springs. All that he does must remain 'clear' to him as he does it. How does he then set about the work of composition? All that he can do is to mention one by one the elements of the scene and the emotions it calls up. I am moved in a certain way by a dark street at night, say. When I attempt to express this mood, I make an inventory of all the elements which make up that mood. I have written verse of that kind myself, I understand the process. The result is immediately recognisable. Qualities of sincere first-hand observation may be constantly shown, but the result is not a poem.

The Germans I have been writing about seem to me to be in this position. The qualities they display are destined rather to alter German prose than to add to its poetry.

Modern Art and its Philosophy[1]

[*Speculations*, 75–109]

I

My title is perhaps misleading, in that it lays emphasis on modern art itself, rather than on its philosophy. Only the last half of what I am going to say deals with the art itself; the first part is devoted to entirely general considerations, which seem to me to be necessary to its proper understanding. I know that this may appear an unnecessary and rather fantastic superstructure. An artist might feel that I was merely bringing in all kinds of vague literary considerations, which have very little to do with the art itself. New movements in art are generally accompanied by muddle-headed but enthusiastic attempts to connect them with quite unconnected movements in philosophy, which appear to the journalist's mind to be coloured by the same quality of excitement. There are people, for example, who try to connect cubism with Plato. The artist, recognising these interpretations as the mere confused sentimentality that they are, may yet accept them good-humouredly, in as far as they lend some kind of support to a new movement.

But it seems to me that there is another way of dealing with an art from a general point of view which follows the contours of the thing itself a little more closely. It may be justified in that it attempts to deal, not so much with the art itself, as with the language in which the artist or critic attempts to explain that art. The critic in explaining a new direction often falsifies it by his use of a vocabulary derived from the old position. The thought or vocabulary of one's period is an extraordinarily difficult thing to break away from. While an artist may have emancipated himself from his own period as far as his art is concerned, while a spectator may have emancipated himself by looking at the art of other periods in museums, yet the mental, or more accurately speaking, the linguistic emancipations of the two, may not have gone forward parallel with the artistic one.

Quite definitely what I mean is this: I think that the new art differs not in degree, but in kind, from the art we are accustomed to, and that there is a danger that the understanding of the new may be hindered by a way of looking on art which is only appropriate to the art that has preceded it. The general considerations I put forward are of this kind. This new art is geometrical in character, while the art we are accustomed to is vital* and organic. It so happens that there have been many other geometric arts in the past. I think that a consideration of these arts may help one to understand what is coming, and to avoid the falsification I have spoken of. I may also by this method be enabled to remove certain prejudices which stand in the way of appreciation of this art.

My remarks are likely to appear confused, as my argument, such as it is, is composed of three or four parts, only one of which I have space enough to develop in detail. I can perhaps give them more shape, by laying down to begin with certain theses which I assert to be true, but do not attempt to prove here:

(1) There are two kinds of art, geometrical and vital, absolutely distinct in kind from one another. These two arts are not modifications of one and the same art but pursue different aims and are created for the satisfaction of different necessities of the mind.

(2) Each of these arts springs from and corresponds to a certain general attitude towards the world. You get long periods of time in which only one of these arts with its corresponding mental attitudes prevails. The vital art of Greece and the Renaissance corresponded to a certain attitude of mind and the geometrical has always gone with a different general attitude, of greater intensity than this.

And (3) – this is really the point I am making for – that the re-emergence of geometrical art may be the precursor of the re-emergence of the corresponding attitude towards the world, and so, of the break up of the Renaissance humanistic attitude. The fact that this change comes first in art, before it comes in thought, is easily understandable for this reason. So thoroughly are we soaked in the spirit of the period

---

* I might add here on my use of the word vital. This word instead of having the specific meaning it should have, has come to have the meaning of living in the sense of strong and creative as opposed to weak and imitative. In fact the difference between vital and non-vital has simply come to be the difference between good and bad. It need perhaps hardly be pointed out that my use of the word vital in this lecture has nothing whatever to do with this sense of the word. Vital and mechanical or geometrical arts may both be vital or non-vital in the current use of the word. A man might conceivably say that the geometrical Byzantine art displayed a certain lack of vitality in this sense. I might dispute that; but even if I did not I think that my use of the word vital, defined as I have defined it, is permissible.

we live in, so strong is its influence over us, that we can only escape from it in an unexpected way, as it were, a side direction like art.

I am emphasising then, the absolute character of the difference between these two arts, not only because it is important for the understanding of the new art itself, but because it enables me to maintain much wider theses.

That is the logical order in which I present my convictions. I did not naturally arrive at them in that order. I came to believe first of all, for reasons quite unconnected with art, that the Renaissance attitude was coming to an end, and was then confirmed in that by the emergence of this art. I commenced by a change in philosophy and illustrated this by a change in art rather than vice versa. A thesis like my last one is so sweeping that it sounds a little empty. It would be quite ludicrous for me to attempt to state such a position in the space of the half page I intend to devote to it, but perhaps I can make it sound more plausible by saying how I came personally to believe it. You will have to excuse my putting it in autobiographical shape, for, after all, the break-up of a general attitude if it ever occurs will be a collection of autobiographies. First of all comes the conviction that in spite of its apparent extraordinary variety, European philosophy since the Renaissance does form a unity. You can separate philosophy into two parts, the technical and scientific part, that which more properly would be called metaphysics, and another part in which the machinery elaborated in the first is used to express the philosopher's attitude towards the world, what may be called his conclusions. These emerge in the last chapter of the book. In the first chapters the philosopher may be compared to a man in armour; he intimidates you, as a kind of impersonal machine. In the last chapter you perceive him naked, as perfectly human. Every philosopher says the world is other than it seems to be; in the last chapter he tells you what he thinks it is. As he has taken the trouble to prove it, you may assume that he regards the final picture of the world he gives as satisfactory.

Now here is my point. In a certain sense, all philosophy since the Renaissance is satisfied with a certain conception of the relation of man to the world. Now what is this conception? You get the first hint of it in the beginnings of the Renaissance itself, in a person like Pico Della Mirandola, for example. You get the hint of an idea there of something, which finally culminates in a doctrine which is the opposite of the doctrine of original sin: the belief that man as a part of nature was after all something satisfactory. The change which Copernicus is supposed to have brought about is the exact contrary of the fact. Before Copernicus, man was not the centre of the world; after Copernicus he was. You get a change from a certain profundity and intensity to that flat and insipid optimism which, passing through its first stage of decay in Rousseau, has finally culminated in the state of slush in which we have the misfortune to live. If you want a proof of the radical difference between these two attitudes, you have only to look at the books which are written now on Indian religion and philosophy. There is a sheer anaemic inability to understand the stark uncompromising bleakness of this religious attitude.

It may seem paradoxical in view of the extraordinary emphasis laid on life by philosophy at the present day, to assert that this Renaissance attitude is coming to an end. But I think that this efflorescence is its last effort.

About the time that I arrived at this kind of conviction I saw Byzantine mosaics for the first time. This led me a step further towards the conviction I have expressed in this thesis. I had got myself away from the contemporary view, and (as I shall illustrate later in the case of art, the first attempt to formulate a different attitude being always a return to archaism) I was inclined to hold a view not very different from that of that period. At that time, then, I was impressed by these mosaics, not as by something exotic, but as expressing quite directly an attitude I agreed with. Owing to this accident, I was able to see a geometrical art, as it were from the inside. I then saw how essential and necessary a geometrical character is in endeavouring to express a certain intensity.

Finally I recognised this geometrical character re-emerging in modern art. I am thinking particularly of certain pieces of sculpture I saw some years ago, of Mr Epstein's.[2]

I had here then, very crudely, all the elements of the position that I put before in my three theses. At that time, in an essay by Paul Ernst[3] on Byzantine art, I came across a reference to the work of Riegl[4] and Worringer.[5] In the latter particularly I found an extraordinarily clear statement, founded on an extensive knowledge of the history of art, of a view very like the one I had tried to formulate. This last year I heard

him lecture and had some conversation with him at the Berlin
Congress of Aesthetics. What follows is practically an abstract of
Worringer's views.

II

You have these two different kinds of art. You have first the art which
is natural to you, Greek art and modern art since the Renaissance. In
these arts the lines are soft and vital. You have other arts like Egyptian,
Indian and Byzantine, where everything tends to be angular, where
curves tend to be hard and geometrical, where the representation of
the human body, for example, is often entirely non-vital, and distorted
to fit into stiff lines and cubical shapes of various kinds.

What is the cause of the extraordinary difference between these
geometrical arts and the arts we are accustomed to admire? Why do
they show none of the qualities which we are accustomed to find in art?

We may at once put on one side the idea that the difference between
archaic and later art is due to a difference of capacity, the idea that
geometrical shapes are used because the artist had not the technical
ability necessary for carving the more natural representation of the
body. The characteristics of archaic art are not due to incapacity. In
Egypt, at the time when the monumental sculpture showed a stylifica-
tion as great as any we find in archaic art, the domestic art of the period
exhibited a most astonishing realism. In pure technical ability in
mastery of raw material, the Egyptians have never been surpassed. It is
quite obvious that what they did was intentional.

We are forced back on the idea, then, that geometrical art differs
from our own because the creators of that art had in view an object
entirely different from that of the creators of more naturalistic art. The
idea that an art is a satisfaction of some specific mental need, and so,
that in looking at a work of art of this type it is necessary not only to
think of the object itself, but of the desire it is intended to satisfy, is
one which it is very difficult for us to realise for the following reason.
The subjective side of an art is never forced on our notice, because it
so happens that the arts with which we are familiar, the classical and
our own, have the same subjective element. It never occurs to us there-
fore that classical art is the satisfaction of one among other possible

desires, since we always think that this art is the satisfaction of *the* desire which must inevitably be behind all art. We thus erect the classical and our own conception of art into an absolute and look on all art before the classical as imperfect strivings towards it, and all after as decadence from it.

It is necessary to realise that all art is created to satisfy a particular desire – that when this desire is satisfied, you call the work beautiful; but that if the work is intended to satisfy a desire and mental need different from your own, it will necessarily appear to you to be grotesque and meaningless. We naturally do not call these geometrical arts beautiful because beauty for us is the satisfaction of a certain need, and that need is one which archaic art never set out to satisfy. What from our standpoint appears as the greatest distortion must have been, for the people who produced it, the highest beauty and the fulfilment of some desire. Consider the differences between these two kinds, then, from this point of view.

Take first the art which is most natural to us. What tendency is behind this, what need is it designed to satisfy?

This art as contrasted with geometrical art can be broadly described as naturalism or realism – using these words in their widest sense and entirely excluding the mere imitation of nature. The source of the pleasure felt by the spectator before the products of art of this kind is a feeling of increased vitality, a process which German writers on aesthetics call empathy (*Einfühlung*). This process is perhaps a little too complicated for me to describe it shortly here, but putting the matter in general terms, we can say that any work of art we find beautiful is an objectification of our own pleasure in activity, and our own vitality. The worth of a line or form consists in the value of the life which it contains for us. Putting the matter more simply we may say that in this art there is always a feeling of liking for, and pleasure in, the forms and movements to be found in nature. It is obvious therefore that this art can only occur in a people whose relation to outside nature is such that it admits of this feeling of pleasure in its contemplation.

Turn now to geometrical art. It most obviously exhibits no delight in nature and no striving after vitality. Its forms are always what can be described as stiff and lifeless. The dead form of a pyramid and the suppression of life in a Byzantine mosaic show that behind these arts there must have been an impulse, the direct opposite of that which finds satisfaction in the naturalism of Greek and Renaissance art.

This is what Worringer calls the *tendency to abstraction*.

What is the nature of this tendency? What is the condition of mind of the people whose art is governed by it?

It can be described most generally as a feeling of separation in the face of outside nature.

While a naturalistic art is the result of a happy pantheistic relation between man and the outside world, the tendency to abstraction, on the contrary, occurs in races whose attitude to the outside world is the exact contrary of this. This feeling of separation naturally takes different forms at different levels of culture.

Take first, the case of more primitive people. They live in a world whose lack of order and seeming arbitrariness must inspire them with a certain fear. One may perhaps get a better description of what must be their state of mind by comparing it to the fear which makes certain people unable to cross open spaces. The fear I mean here is mental, however, not physical. They are dominated by what Worringer calls a kind of spiritual 'space-shyness' in face of the varied confusion and arbitrariness of existence. In art this state of mind results in a desire to create a certain abstract geometrical shape, which, being durable and permanent shall be a refuge from the flux and impermanence of outside nature. The need which art satisfies here, is not the delight in the forms of nature, which is a characteristic of all vital arts, but the exact contrary. In the reproduction of natural objects there is an attempt to purify them of their characteristically living qualities in order to make them necessary and immovable. The changing is trans-lated into something fixed and necessary. This leads to rigid lines and dead crystalline forms, for pure geometrical regularity gives a certain pleasure to men troubled by the obscurity of outside appearance. The geometrical line is something absolutely distinct from the messiness, the confusion, and the accidental details of existing things.

It must be pointed out that this condition of fear is in no sense a necessary presupposition of the tendency to abstraction. The neces-sary presupposition is the idea of disharmony or separation between man and nature. In peoples like the Indian or the Byzantine this feeling of separation takes quite another form.

To sum up this view of art then: it cannot be understood by itself, but must be taken as one element in a general process of adjustment between man and the outside world. The character of that relation determines the character of the art. If there is a difference of 'potential' between man and the outside world, if they are at different levels, so that the relation between them is, as it were, a steep inclined plane, then the adjustment between them in art takes the form of a tendency to abstraction. If on the contrary there is no disharmony between man and the outside world, if they are both on the same level, on which man feels himself one with nature and not separate from it, then you get a naturalistic art.

The art of a people, then, will run parallel to its philosophy and general world outlook. It is a register of the nature of the opposition between man and the world. Each race is in consequence of its situation and character inclined to one of these two tendencies, and its art would give you a key to its psychology.

It is easy to trace these parallel changes. I have spoken of that feeling of space-shyness which produced the tendency to abstraction in primitive art. This tendency would have been impossible in the case of a people like the Greeks at the time when they had finally got free from the oriental elements of their origins and had not fallen afresh to oriental tendencies. In such a people you get a feeling of confidence in face of the world which expresses itself in religion in a certain anthropomorphism. The feeling of disharmony with the world had been destroyed by certain favourable conditions and by increased knowledge (Rationalism). You can speak here, then, of a classical religious period as you speak of a classical art period. Both are only different manifestations of the same classical conception which Goethe defined as that in which man 'feels himself one with nature and consequently looks upon the outside world not as something strange, but as something which he recognises as answering to his own feelings'.

In the case of the orientals the feeling of separation from the world could not be dispelled by knowledge. Their sense of the unfathomable existence was greater than that of the Greeks. A satisfaction with appearances is limited to Europe. It is only there that the superhuman abstract idea of the divine has been expressed by banal representation. No knowledge could damp down the Indian inborn fear of the world, since it stands, not as in the case of primitive man before knowledge, but above it. Their art consequently remained geometrical.

It is in the light of this tendency to abstraction that I wish to deal with modern art. Before doing that, however, I want to make the tendency clearer by giving some concrete examples of its working in sculpture.

In the endeavour to get away from the flux of existence, there is an endeavour to create in contrast, an absolutely enclosed material individuality. Abstraction is more difficult in the round than in the flat. With three dimensions we get the relativism and obscurity of appearance. A piece of sculpture in the round seems quite as lost in its context as does the natural object itself. There is consequently stronger stylification used in the round than is necessary in the relief. In archaic Greek sculpture, for example, the arms are bound close to the body, any diversion of the surface is as far as possible avoided and unavoidable divisions and articulations are given in no detail. The first gods were always pure abstractions without any resemblance to life. Any weakening of these abstract forms and approximation to reality would have let in change and life and so would have done what it was desired to avoid – it would have taken the thing out of eternity and put it into time. In monumental art, the abstract and inorganic is always used to make the organic seem durable and eternal. The first rule of monumental art must be a strong inclosure of cubical forms. It is ridiculous to suppose that the masons who carved the face of an archaic figure did not possess the capacity to separate the arms or legs from the body. The fact that they did so later in classical Greek art was not due to a progress in technical ability. The Greeks left behind the intensity of these cubical forms and replaced the abstract by the organic simply because, as their attitude to the world changed, they had different intentions. Having attained a kind of optimistic rationalism they no longer felt any desire for abstraction. They did not create gods like these earlier ones because they no longer possessed any religious intensity.

When we turn to Egyptian art, we find that in the endeavour to escape from anything that might suggest the relative and impermanent there is always the same tendency to make all the surfaces as flat as possible. In the sitting figures the legs and the body form a cubical mass out of which only the shoulders and head appear as necessary individualisation. The treatment of drapery and hair is only another example of this desire to make what is most obviously flexible and impermanent look fixed.

III

I come now to the application of the distinction thus elaborately constructed between geometrical and vital art to what is going on at the present moment.

If the argument I have followed is correct, I stand committed to two statements:

(1) ... that a new geometrical art is emerging which may be considered as different in kind from the art which preceded it, it being much more akin to the geometrical arts of the past, and

(2) ... that this change from a vital to a geometrical art is the product of and will be accompanied by a certain change of sensibility, a certain change of general attitude, and that this new attitude will differ in kind from the humanism which has prevailed from the Renaissance to now, and will have certain analogies to the attitude of which geometrical art was the expression in the past.

Naturally both of these sweeping statements run a good deal ahead of the facts and of my ability to prove them. I must here, therefore, make the same qualification and warning about both of the statements. Though both the new *Weltanschauung* and the new geometrical art will have certain analogies with corresponding periods in the past, yet it is not for a moment to be supposed that there is anything more than an analogy here. The new geometrical art will probably in the end not in the least resemble archaic art, nor will the new attitude to the world be very much like the Byzantine, for example. As to what actually they both will culminate in, it would obviously be ludicrous for me to attempt to say. It would be more ludicrous to attempt to do this in the case of the general attitude, than it would in the case of the art itself. For one of my points at the beginning of this paper was that one's mind is so soaked in the thought and language of the period, that one can only perceive the break-up of that period in a region like art which is – when one's mind is focused on thought itself – a kind of side activity.

One can only make certain guesses at the new attitude by the use of analogy. Take two other attitudes of the past which went with geometrical art: say primitive and Byzantine. There is a certain likeness and a certain unlikeness in relation to man and the outside world. The primitive springs from what we have called a kind of mental space-shyness, which is really an attitude of fear before the world; the Byzantine from what may be called, inaccurately, a kind of contempt for the world. Though these two attitudes differ very much, yet there is a common element in the idea of separation as opposed to the more intimate feeling towards the world in classical and renaissance thought. In comparison with the flat and insipid optimism of the belief in progress, the new attitude may be in a certain sense inhuman, pessimistic. Yet its pessimism will not be world-rejecting in the sense in which the Byzantine was.

But one is on much surer ground in dealing with the art itself. On what grounds does one base this belief that a new geometrical art is appearing? There is first the more negative proof provided by a change of taste.

You get an extraordinary interest in similar arts in the past, in Indian sculpture, in Byzantine art, in archaic art generally, and this interest is not as before a merely archaeological one. The things are liked directly, almost as they were liked by the people who made them, as being direct expressions of an attitude which you want to find expressed. I do not think for a moment that this is conscious. I think that under the influence of a false conception of the nature of art, that most people, even when they feel it, falsify their real appreciation by the vocabulary they use – naïve, fresh, charm of the exotic, and so on.

A second and more positive proof is to be found in the actual creation of a new modern geometrical art.

You get at the present moment in Europe a most extraordinary confusion in art, a complete breaking away from tradition. So confusing is it that most people lump it altogether as one movement and are unaware that it is in fact composed of a great many distinct and even contradictory elements, being a complex movement of parts that are merely reactionary, parts that are dead, and with one part only containing the possibility of development. When I speak of a new complex geometrical art then, I am not thinking of the whole movement. I am speaking of one element which seems to be gradually hardening out, and separating itself from the others. I don't want anyone to suppose, for example, that I am speaking of futurism which is, in its logical form, the exact opposite of the art I am describing, being the deification of the flux, the last efflorescence of impressionism. I also exclude a great many things which – as I shall attempt to show later –

were perhaps necessary preliminaries to this art, but which have now been passed by – most of the work in fact which is included under the term post-impressionism – Gauguin, Maillol, Brancusi.

If space allowed I could explain why I also exclude certain elements of cubism, what I might call analytical cubism – the theories about interpenetration which you get in Metzinger[6] for example.

IV

Before dealing actually with this work I ought to qualify what I have said a little. I have put the matter in a rather too ponderous way by talking about the new general attitude. That is perhaps dealing with the matter on the wrong plane. It would have been quite possible for this change to come about without the artists themselves being conscious of this change of general attitude towards the world at all. When I say 'conscious' I mean conscious in this formulated and literary fashion. The change of attitude would have taken place, but it might only have manifested itself in a certain change of sensibility in the artist, and in so far as he expresses himself in words, in a certain change of vocabulary. The change of attitude betrays itself by changes in the epithets that a man uses, perhaps disjointedly, to express his admiration for the work he admires. Most of us cannot state our position, and we use adjectives which in themselves do not explain what we mean, but which, for a group for a certain time, by a kind of tacit convention become the 'porters' or 'bearers' of the complex new attitude which we all recognise that we have in company, but which we cannot describe or analyse. At the present time you get this change shown in the value given to certain adjectives. Instead of epithets like graceful, beautiful, etc., you get epithets like austere, mechanical, clear cut, and bare, used to express admiration.

Putting on one side all this talk of a 'new attitude' of which the artist in some cases may not be conscious at all, what is the nature of the new sensibility which betrays itself in this change of epithets? Putting it at its lowest terms, namely that a man was unconscious of any change of aim, but only felt that he preferred certain shapes, certain forms, etc., and that his work was moulded by that change of sensibility, what is the nature of that change of sensibility at the present moment?

Expressed generally, there seems to be a desire for austerity and bare-
ness, a striving towards structure and away from the messiness and
confusion of nature and natural things. Take a concrete matter like the
use of line and surface. In all art since the Renaissance, the lines used
are what may be called vital lines. In any curve there is a certain empir-
ical variation which makes the curve not mechanical. The lines are
obviously drawn by a hand and not by a machine. You get Ruskin
saying that no artist could draw a straight line. As far as sensibility goes
you get a kind of shrinking from anything that has the appearance of
being mechanical. An artist, suppose, has to draw a part of a piece of
machinery, where a certain curve is produced by the intersection of a
plane and a cylinder. It lies in the purpose of the engine and it is obvi-
ously the intention of the engineer that the line shall be a perfect and
mechanical curve. The artists in drawing the two surfaces and their
intersection would shrink from reproducing this mechanical accuracy,
would instinctively pick out all the accidental scratches which make
the curve empirical and destroy its geometrical and mechanical char-
acter. In the new art on the contrary there is no shrinking of that kind
whatever. There is rather a desire to avoid those lines and surfaces
which look pleasing and organic, and to use lines which are clean,
clear-cut and mechanical. You will find artists expressing admiration
for engineers' drawings, where the lines are clean, the curves all
geometrical, and the colour, laid on to show the shape of a cylinder for
example, gradated absolutely mechanically. You will find a sculptor
disliking the pleasing kind of patina that comes in time on an old
bronze and expressing admiration for the hard clean surface of a piston
rod. If we take this to be in fact the new sensibility, and regard it as the
culmination of the process of breaking-up and transformation in art,
that has been proceeding since the impressionists, it seems to me that
the history of the last twenty years becomes more intelligible. It
suddenly enables one to look at the matter in a new light.

Put the matter in an a priori way. Admitting the premiss that a new
direction is gradually defining itself, what would you expect to
happen? As a help to this reconstruction, recall what was said about the
relation between the various geometrical arts of the past at the begin-
ning of the last part of my paper, to the effect that there are always
certain common elements, but also that each period has its own
specific qualities. This new art, towards which things were working,

was bound, then, to have certain elements in common with past geometric archaic arts, but at the same time as an art springing up today, it would necessarily exhibit certain original and peculiar qualities due to the fact. Consider then the beginning of the movement. No man at the beginning of a movement of this kind can have any clear conception of its final culmination – that would be to anticipate the result of a process of creation. Of which of the two elements of the new geometric art – that which it has in common with similar arts in the past, or that which is specific and peculiar to it – is an artist most likely to be conscious at the beginning of a movement? Most obviously of those elements which are also to be found in the past. Here then you get the explanation of the fact which may have puzzled some people, that a new and modern art, something which was to culminate in a use of structural organisation akin to machinery, should have begun by what seemed like a romantic return to barbarous and primitive art, apparently inspired by a kind of nostalgia for the past.

Another cause reinforcing the tendency to the archaic is the difficulty of at once finding an appropriate method of expression. Though the artist feels that he must have done with the contemporary means of expression, yet a new and more fitting method is not easily created. The way from intention to expression does not come naturally, as it were from in outwards. A man has first to obtain a foothold in this, so to speak, alien and external world of material expression, at a point near the one he is making for. He has to utilise some already existing methods of expression and work from them to the one that expresses his own personal conception more accurately and naturally. What happened then was this – a certain change of direction took place, beginning negatively with a feeling of dissatisfaction with, and reaction against, existing art. You get a breaking away from contemporary methods of expression, a new direction, an intenser perception of things striving towards expression, and as this intensity was fundamentally the same kind of intensity as that expressed in certain archaic arts, it quite naturally and legitimately found a foothold in these archaic yet permanent formulae. A certain archaicism then, just as it is at the beginning helpful to an artist though he may afterwards repudiate it, is an almost necessary stage in the preparation of a new movement. This seems to me to be the best way of describing and understanding the movement that has had the label of post-impressionism affixed to it in

England. Though perhaps the individual artists of that time would never have gone further than they did, yet looking at them from this general point of view, it is best to regard them as the preliminary and temporary stage of experimentation in the preparation of a suitable method of expression for a new and intenser sensibility. It is not necessary to do more than mention an obvious example such as Gauguin.

The case of Cézanne is more important for it is out of him that the second stage of the movement that I have called analytical cubism has developed. It is also interesting since it is only lately that it has been recognised how fundamentally Cézanne differed from his contemporaries, the impressionists. It was against their fluidity that he reacted. He wanted, so he said, to make of impressionism something solid and durable like old art.

Before commenting on this, I must recall again the distinction I have used between naturalism and abstraction. I want to point out that even in a period of natural and vital art a certain shadow of the tendency to abstraction still remains in the shape of formal composition. Some kinds of composition are attempts to make the organic look rigid and durable.

In most landscapes, of course, the composition is rhythmical and not formal in this extreme sense, and so it is not an expression of a tendency to abstraction. With this in mind, look at one of Cézanne's latest pictures, 'Women Bathing', where all the lines are ranged in a pyramidal shape, and the women are distorted to fit this shape. You will, if you are accustomed to look for pleasing rhythmical composition in a picture, be repelled rather than attracted by this pyramidal composition. The form is so strongly accentuated, so geometric in character, that it almost lifts the painting out of the sphere of 'vital' art into that of abstract art. It is much more akin to the composition you find in the Byzantine mosaic (of the empress Theodora) in Ravenna, than it is to any thing which can be found in the art of the Renaissance.

If you deny the existence of a 'tendency to abstraction' at all in art, you will naturally deny the apparent appearance of it in Cézanne. You will say that the simplification of planes (out of which of course cubism grew), is not due to any 'tendency to abstraction', but is the result of an effort to give a more solid kind of reality in the object. You will assert that when Cézanne said that the forms of nature could be reduced to the cone, the cylinder, and the sphere, that he meant something quite different from the obvious meaning of his words. This misconception of Cézanne results from the fact that you have refused to see the obvious truth, that there is in him a hint of that 'tendency to abstraction' that is found in certain arts of the past. The difference between the use of planes in Cézanne and in the cubists themselves, is not that between a simplification based on observation of nature and a mere playing about with formulae. Both simplifications are based on the research into nature, but their value to the artist does not lie in their origin, but in the use that is made of them.

That is, I think, how one ought to look on these painters, quite apart from the qualities they show as painters belonging to the past vital period of painting. They are interesting to us as showing the first gradual emergence in a state of experimentation, of this new geometrical art which will be created by a tendency to abstraction. I should, properly speaking, now attempt to define the characteristics of the new art as they emerge from this experimental stage, but that is difficult for me to do as the thing itself is still to a large extent experimental. I cannot say what artists will make of this method; the construction of this is their business, not mine. That is the fun of the thing. I await myself the development of that art with the greatest impatience. My feeling about the matter is this. I look at most cubist pictures with a certain feeling of depression. They are from a certain point of view, confused. If I may be allowed to go against my own principles for a minute, and to describe abstract things in a metaphor borrowed from organic life, I should say they look rather like embryos. I think they will soon open out and grow distinct. I picture what is about to happen in this way. A man whose form is, as it were, dimly discerned in hay, stands up, shakes the hay off him, and proceeds to walk, i.e. he proceeds to do something. Dropping the metaphor then, cubism ceases to be analytical, and is transformed into a constructive geometrical art. The elements and the method patiently worked out by analysis begin to be used. If you want a concrete example of the difference I mean, compare the work illustrated in Metzinger's book on cubism, with that of Mr Epstein and Mr Lewis.[7] This difference seems to me to be important for this reason. There are many who, when the matter has been explained to them, can understand what the early cubists are trying to do. They follow the sort of analysis they have made, but they cannot for the life of them see how it can go on, or how it can develop into a new art. And I believe that this is in reality the source of the baffled feeling of most people when confronted by such art.

V

In conclusion, I might hazard some conjectures as to the probable nature of the specific and peculiar quality which will differentiate this new geometrical art from its predecessors. As far as one can see, the new 'tendency towards abstraction' will culminate, not so much in the simple geometrical forms found in archaic art, but in the more complicated ones associated in our minds with the idea of machinery. In this association with machinery will probably be found the specific differentiating quality of the new art. It is difficult to define properly at the present moment what this relation to machinery will be. It has nothing whatever to do with the superficial notion that one must beautify machinery. It is not a question of dealing with machinery in the spirit, and with the methods of existing art, but of the creation of a new art having an organisation, and governed by principles, which are at present exemplified unintentionally, as it were, in machinery. It is hardly necessary to repeat at this stage of the argument, that it will not aim at the satisfaction of that particular mental need, which in a vital art results in the production of what is called beauty. It is aiming at the satisfaction of a different mental need altogether. When Mr Roger Fry, therefore, talks as he did lately, of 'machinery being as beautiful as a rose' he demonstrates what is already obvious from his work, that he has no conception whatever of this new art, and is in fact a mere verbose sentimentalist.

This association of art and machinery suggests all kinds of problems. What will be the relation to the artist and the engineer? At present the artist is merely receptive in regard to machinery. He passively admires, for example, the superb steel structures which form the skeletons of modern buildings, and whose gradual envelopment in a parasitic covering of stone is one of the daily tragedies to be witnessed in London streets. Will the artist always remain passive, or will be take a more active part? The working out of the relation between art and machinery can be observed at present in many curious ways. Besides the interest in machinery itself, you get the attempt to create in art, structures whose organisation, such as it is, is very like that of machinery. Most of Picasso's paintings, for instance, whatever they may be labelled, are at bottom studies of a special kind of machinery.

But here an apparently quite legitimate objection might be raised. The desire to create something mechanical in this sense might be admitted as understandable, but the question would still be asked, 'Why make use of the human body in this art, why make that look like a machine?' Those who are accustomed to a vital art, the basis of whose appreciation of art is what I have called empathy, and who consequently derive pleasure from the reproduction of the actual details of life, are repulsed by an art in which something which is intended to be a body, leaves out all these details and qualities they expect.

Take for example one of Mr Wyndham Lewis's pictures. It is obvious that the artist's only interest in the human body was in a few abstract mechanical relations perceived in it, the arm as a lever and so on. The interest in living flesh as such, in all that detail that makes it vital, which is pleasing, and which we like to see reproduced, is entirely absent.

But if the division that I have insisted on in this paper – the division between the two different tendencies producing two different kinds of art – is valid, then this objection falls to the ground. What you get in Mr Lewis's pictures is what you always get inside any geometrical art. All art of this character turns the organic into something not organic, it tries to translate the changing and limited, into something unlimited and necessary. The matter is quite simple. However strong the desire for abstraction, it cannot be satisfied with the reproduction of merely inorganic forms. A perfect cube looks stable in comparison with the flux of appearance, but one might be pardoned if one felt no particular interest in the eternity of a cube; but if you can put man into some geometrical shape which lifts him out of the transience of the organic, then the matter is different. In pursuing such an aim you inevitably, of course, sacrifice the pleasure that comes from reproduction of the natural.

Another good example to take, would be Mr Epstein's latest work, the drawings for sculpture in the first room of his exhibition. The subjects of all of them are connected with birth. They are objected to because they are treated in what the critics are pleased to term a cubistic manner. But this seems to me a most interesting example of what I have just been talking about. The tendency to abstraction, the desire to turn the organic into something hard and durable, is here at work, not on something simple, such as you get in the more archaic work, but on something much more complicated. It is, however, the same tendency at work in both. Abstraction is much greater in the second case, because generation, which is the very essence of all the qualities which we have here called organic, has been turned into something as hard and durable as a geometrical figure itself.

The word machinery here suggests to me a point which requires a short discussion. You admit here this change of sensibility. You find the artists seeking out and using forms and surfaces which artists of our immediate past have always shrunk from. What is the cause of this change of sensibility? Any one who has agreed with the historical part of this paper will probably agree that this change of sensibility follows from a certain change in intention in art, the tendency towards abstraction instead of towards empathy. But another explanation may be given which, while it has an appearance of making the thing reasonable, seems to me to be fallacious. It may be said that an artist is using mechanical lines because he lives in an environment of machinery. In a landscape you would use softer and more organic lines. This seems to me to be using the materialist explanation of the origin of an art which has been generally rejected. Take the analogous case of the influence of raw material on art. The nature of material is never without a certain influence. If they had not been able to use granite, the Egyptians would probably not have carved in the way they did. But then the material did not produce the style. If Egypt had been inhabited by people of Greek race, the fact that the material was granite, would not have made them produce anything like Egyptian sculpture. The technical qualities of a material can thus never create a style. A feeling for form of a certain kind must always be the source of an art. All that can be said of the forms suggested by the technical qualities of the material is that they must not contradict this intended form. They can only be used when the inclination and taste to which they are appropriate already exist. So, though steel is not the material of the new art, but only its environment, we can, it seems to me, legitimately speak of it exercising the kind of influence that the use of granite did on Egyptian art, no more and no less.

The point I want to emphasise is that the use of mechanical lines in the new art is in no sense merely a reflection of mechanical environment. It is a result of a change of sensibility which is, I think, the result of a change of attitude which will become increasingly obvious.

Finally I think that this association with the idea of machinery takes away any kind of dilettante character from the movement and makes it seem more solid and more inevitable.

It seems to me beyond doubt that this, whether you like it or not, is the character of the art that is coming. I speak of it myself with enthusiasm, not only because I appreciate it for itself, but because I believe it to be the precursor of a much wider change in philosophy and general outlook on the world.

Mr Epstein and the Critics[1]

[*The New Age*, 14/8 (25 December 1913]

I begin with an apology. All through this article I write about Mr Epstein's work in a way which I recognise to be wrong, in that it is what an artist would call literary. The appreciation of a work of art must be plastic or nothing. But I defend myself in this way, that I am not so much writing directly about Mr Epstein's work, as engaged in the more negative and quite justifiable business of attempting to protect the spectator from certain prejudices which are in themselves literary. This is an article then not so much on Epstein as on his critics. When I see the critics attempting to corrupt the mind of the spectator and trying to hinder their appreciation of a great artist, I feel an indignation which must be my excuse for these clumsy, hurriedly-written and unrevised notes.

An attack on critics could not have a better subject matter than the Press notices on Mr Epstein's show. They exhibit a range and variety of fatuousness seldom equalled. It is not necessary to spend any time over notices which, like that of 'C.B' in the *Athenaeum*, are merely spiteful, or that in the *Illustrated London News*, which compared him unfavourably with the Exhibition of Humorous Artists. I propose rather to deal with those which, in appearance at any rate, profess to deal seriously with his work.

Take first the merely nervous. Their method is continually to refer to Mr Epstein as a great artist and at the same time to deplore everything he does. It reminds one of the old philosophical disputes about substance.

Would anything remain of a 'thing' if all its qualities were taken away? What is the metaphysical nature of an artist's excellence that seems to manifest itself in no particular thing he does? The truth is, of course, that they dare not say what they really think. The particular kind of gift which enables a man to be an art critic is not the possession of an instinct which tells them what pictures are good or bad, but of a different kind of instinct which leads them to recognise the people who do know. This is, of course, in itself a comparatively rare instinct. Once they have obtained a 'direction' in this way, their own literary capacity enables them to expand it to any desired length. You can, however, always tell this from a certain emptiness in their rhetoric (cf. Arthur Symons' article on Rodin). There is no one to give them a 'direction' about Mr Epstein's drawings, and they are at a loss. They seek refuge in praise of the 'Romilly John', which has been universally admitted to be one of the finest bronzes since the Renaissance. It shows how incapable the critics are of judging even Mr Epstein's earlier work, that one critic has been found to couple this superb head with Mr John's thin and unconvincing painting of a child, at present exhibited in the New English Art Club.[2]

I come now to the most frequent and the most reasonable criticism: that directed against the 'Carvings in Flenite'. It is generally stated in a rather confused way, but I think that it can be analysed out into two separate prejudices. The first is that an artist has no business to use formulae taken from another civilisation. The second is that, even if the formula the artist uses is the natural means of expressing certain of his emotions, yet these emotions must be unnatural in him, a modern Western. I shall attempt to show that the first objection really has its root in the second, and that this second prejudice is one which runs through almost every activity at the present time. These 'Carvings in Flenite', we are told, are 'deliberate imitations of Easter Island carvings'. This seems to me to depend on a misconception of the nature of formulae. Man remaining constant, there are certain broad ways in which certain emotions must, and will always naturally be expressed, and these we must call formulae. They constitute a constant and permanent alphabet. The thing to notice is that the use of these broad formulae has nothing to do with the possession of or lack of individuality in the artist. That comes out in the way the formulae are used. If I or the King of the Zulus want to walk, we both put one leg before the other; that is the universal formula, but there the resemblance ends. To take another illustration, which I don't want to put forward as literally true, but which I only use for purposes of illustration. A certain kind of *nostalgie* and attenuated melancholy is expressed in Watteau by a formula of tall trees and minute people, and a certain use of colour (I am also aware that he got this feeling, in the Gilles, for example, by a quite other formula, but I repeat I am only giving a sort of hypothetical illustration). It would be quite possible at the present day for a painter, wishing to express the same kind of emotion, to use the same broad formula quite naturally and without any imitation of Watteau. The point is, that given the same emotion, the same broad formula comes naturally to the hands of any people in any century. I may say that I have not, as a matter of fact, any great admiration for the particular painters who use this particular formula, but I am trying to give an illustration of a formula which the critics who attack Mr Epstein would not have attacked. To be legitimate, of course, the formula used must be a natural expression of the feeling you are getting at and not a mere imitation of an exotic or a romantic past. The form follows the need in each case. It may quite easily be the same need divided by many civilisations.

I think that in this way we can force these people back on to the real root of their objection, the second prejudice I mentioned, the feeling that it is unnatural for a modern to have the kind of emotion which these formulae naturally express. In getting at this, one is getting at something that is really fundamental in modern life. I do think that there is a certain general state of mind which has lasted from the Renaissance till now, with what is, in reality, very little variation. It is impossible to characterise it here, but it is perhaps enough to say that, taking at first the form of the 'humanities', it has in its degeneracy taken the form of a belief in 'Progress' and the rest of it. It was in its way a fairly consistent system, but is probably at the present moment breaking up. In this state of break-up, I think that it is quite natural for individuals here and there to hold a philosophy and to be moved by emotions which would have been unnatural in the period itself. To illustrate big things by small ones I feel, myself, a repugnance towards the *Weltanschauung* (as distinct from the technical part) of all philosophy since the Renaissance. In comparison with what I can vaguely call the religious attitude, it seems to me to be trivial. I am moved by Byzantine mosaic, not because it is quaint or exotic, but because it expresses an attitude I agree with. But the fate of the people who hold these views is to be found incomprehensible by the 'progressives' and to be labelled reactionary; that is, while we arrive at such a *Weltanschauung* quite naturally, we are thought to be imitating the past.

I have wandered into this by-path merely to find therein an illustration which will help us to understand the repugnance of the critic to the 'Carvings in Flenite'. It is, says the critic, 'rude savagery, flouting respectable tradition vague memories of dark ages as distant from modern feeling as the loves of the Martians'. Modern feeling be damned! As if it was not the business of every honest man at the present moment to clean the world of these sloppy dregs of the Renaissance. This carving, by an extreme abstraction, by the selection of certain lines, gives an effect of tragic greatness. The important point about this is that the tragedy is of an order more intense than any conception of tragedy which could fit easily into the modern progressive conception of life. This, I think, is the real root of the objection to these statues, that they express emotions which are, as a matter of fact, entirely alien and unnatural to the critic. But that is a very different thing from their being unnatural to the artist. My justification of these statues would be then (1) that an alien formula is justifiable when it is the necessary expression of a certain attitude; and (2) that in the peculiar conditions in which we find ourselves, which are really the breaking up of an era, it has again become quite possible for people here and there to have the attitude expressed by these formulae.

I have dealt with these in rather a literary way, because I think that in this case it is necessary to get semi-literary prejudices out of the way, before the carvings can be seen as they should be seen, i.e., plastically.

To turn now to the drawings which have been even more misunderstood by the critics than the carvings. I only want to make a few necessary notes about these, as I am dealing with them at greater length in an essay elsewhere. I need say very little about the magnificent drawing reproduced in this paper, for it stands slightly apart from the others and seems to have been found intelligible even by the critics. I might, perhaps, say something about the representative element in it – a man is working a Rock Drill mounted on a tripod, the lines of which, in the drawing continue the lines of his legs. The two lines converging on the centre of the design are indications of a rocky landscape. It is the other drawings which seem to have caused the most bewildered criticism; they have been called prosaic representations of anatomical details, 'medical drawings', and so on. It is perfectly obvious that they are not that. What prevents them being understood as expressions of ideas is quite a simple matter. People will admire the 'Rock Drill', because they have no preconceived notion as to how the thing expressed by it should be expressed. But with the other drawings concerned with birth the case is different. Take for example the drawing called 'Creation', a baby seen inside many folds. I might very roughly say that this was a non-sentimental restatement of an idea which, presented sentimentally and in the traditional manner, they would admire – an idea something akin to the 'Christmas crib' idea. If a traditional symbol had been used they would have been quite prepared to admire it. They cannot understand that the genius and sincerity of an artist lies in extracting afresh, from outside reality, a new means of expression. It seems curious that the people who in poetry abominate clichés and know that Nature, as it were, presses in on the poet to be used as metaphor, cannot understand the same thing when it occurs plastically. They seem unable to understand that an artist who has something to say will continually 'extract' from reality new methods of expression, and that these being personally felt will inevitably lack prettiness and will differ from traditional clichés. It must also be pointed out that the critics have probably themselves not been accustomed to think about generation, and so naturally find the drawings not understandable. I come now to the stupidest criticism of all, that of Mr Ludovici. It would probably occur to anyone who read Mr Ludovici's article that he was a charlatan, but I think it worth while confirming this impression by further evidence. His activities are not confined to art. I remember coming across his name some years ago as the author of a very comical little book on Nietzsche, which was sent me for review.

I shall devote some space to him here then, not because I consider him of the slightest importance, but because I consider it a duty, a very pleasant duty and one very much neglected in this country, to expose charlatans when one sees them. Apart from this general ground, the book on Nietzsche is worth considering, for it displays the same type of mind at work as in the article on art.

What, very briefly then, is the particular type of charlatan revealed in this book on Nietzsche. It gave one the impression of a little Cockney intellect which would have been more suitably employed indexing or in a lawyer's office, drawn by a curious kind of vanity into a region the realities of which must for ever remain incomprehensible to him. Mr Ludovici, writing on Nietzsche, might be compared to a child of four in a theatre watching a tragedy based on adultery. The child would observe certain external phenomena, but as to the real structure of the tragedy, its real moving forces, it would naturally be rather hazy. You picture then a spruce little mind that has crept into the complicated rafters of philosophy – you imagine him perplexed, confused – you would be quite wrong, the apperceptive system acts like a stencil, it blots out all the complexity which forms the reality of the subject, so that he is simply unaware of its existence. He sees only what is akin to his mind's manner of working, as dogs out for a walk only scent other dogs, and as a Red Indian in a great town for the first time sees only the horses. While thus in reality remaining entirely outside the subject, he can manage to produce a shoddy imitation which may pass here in England, where there is no organised criticism by experts, but which in other countries, less happily democratic in these matters, would at once have been characterised as a piece of fudge. I have only drawn attention to this in order to indicate the particular type of charlatan we have to deal with, so that you may know what to expect when you come to consider him as an art critic. I want to insist on the fact that you must expect to find a man dealing with a subject which is in reality alien to him, ignorant of the aims of the actors in that subject and yet maintaining an appearance of adequate treatment with the help of a few tags.

That a man should write stupid and childish things about Nietzsche does not perhaps matter very much; after all, we can read him for ourselves. But when a little bantam of this kind has the impertinence to refer to Mr Epstein as a 'minor personality of no interest to him', then the matter becomes so disgusting that it has to be dealt with. The most appropriate means of dealing with him would be a little personal violence. By that method one removes a nuisance without drawing more attention to it than its insignificance deserves. But the unworthy sentiment of pity for the weak, which, in spite of Nietzsche, still moves us, prevents us dealing drastically, with this rather light-weight superman. To deal definitely then with his criticism. He dismissed Mr Epstein with the general principle 'Great art can only appear when the artist is animated by the spirit of some great order or scheme of life.' I agree with this. Experience confirms it. We find that the more serious kind of art that one likes sprang out of organic societies like the Indian, Egyptian, and Byzantine. The modern obviously imposes too great a strain on an artist, the double burden of not only expressing something, but of finding something in himself to be expressed. The more organic society effects an economy in this. Moreover, you might go so far as to say that the imposition of definite forms does not confine the artist but rather has the effect of intensifying the individuality of his work (of Egyptian portraits). I agree then with his general principle: we all agree. It is one of those obvious platitudes which all educated people take for granted, in conversation and in print. It seems almost too comic for belief, but I begin to suspect from Mr Ludovici's continued use of the word 'I' in connection with this principle, that he is under the extraordinary hallucination that the principle is a personal discovery of his own. Really, Mr Ludo, you mustn't teach your grandmother to suck eggs in this way. That you should have read of these truths in a book and have seen that they were true is so much to the good. It is a fact of great interest to your father and mother, it shows that you are growing up; but I can assure you it is a matter of no public interest.

Admitting then, as I do, that the principle is true, I fail to see how it enables Mr Ludovici to dismiss Mr Epstein in the way he does, on a priori grounds. The same general principle would enable us to dismiss every artist since the Renaissance. Take two very definite examples. Michelangelo and Blake, neither of whom expressed any general 'scheme of life' imposed on them by society, but 'exalted the individual angle of vision of minor personalities'.

The whole thing is entirely beside the point. The business of an art critic is not to repeat tags, but to apply them to individual works of art. But of course that is precisely what a charlatan of the kind I have just described cannot do. It is quite possible for him in each gallery he goes to, to find some opportunity of repeating his tags, but when (as he was in his book on Nietzsche) he is entirely outside the subject, when he is really unaware of the nature of the thing which artists are trying to do, when he gets no real fun out of the pictures themselves, then, when he is pinned down before one actual picture and not allowed to wriggle away, he must either be dumb or make an ass of himself. It is quite easy to learn to repeat tags about 'balance', but put the man before one picture and make him follow with his finger, the lines which constitute that 'balance' and he can only shuffle and bring out more tags.

Now apply this test to Mr Ludovici. We have seen him dismiss Mr Epstein with a tag. When he makes individual judgments about individual pictures in The New English Art Club, what kind of judgments

are they? We start off with Mr John. Here he thinks he may be fairly
safe; here is a reputation ten years old which has at last reached him.
But, alas! we are not dealing with Mr John as a painter, but with one
painting by Mr John. Mr Ludovici falls. He picks out for extravagant
praise Mr John's cartoon 'The Flute of Pan', a thing universally
admitted to be the worst thing John has ever exhibited, a macédoine of
Botticelli-Mantegna drapery, Rossetti faces, rocky backgrounds from
Leonardo, and a ridiculous girl on the right pretending to be dancing
in order that she may show a Botticelli leg and foot, on the left a sort of
crapulous Michelangelo and the little Peter Pan boy so much admired
by Mr Ludovici, the whole messy, smudged and in parts badly drawn,
the design itself so clumsy that the right third of the picture is left so
empty that one feels a girder should be run up from the corner to prop
up the rest, which seems in imminent danger of toppling over. The
whole thing expresses, with the impotence of old age, the kind of
dream appropriate to puberty. It lacks precisely that quality of virility
which Mr Ludovici find in it, and is admired by precisely those 'spin-
sterly', sloppy and romantic people whom, he imagines, dislike it. It is
the result of no personal creative idea, but is entirely a derivative
conglomeration of already existing pretty ideas. I emphasise this point
because your critic insists so much on a picture being the expression of
a definite 'scheme of life'. I am not dealing with this picture as Mr
Ludovici did with Mr Epstein, contemptuously, but pointing out that
it marks a degeneration, temporary perhaps, of a great talent.

Of the other pictures that he praises, it is only necessary to mention
Van Glehn's No.2, which is merely a bad fake, and Mr D.G. Well's
hackneyed Victorian cliché, and Mr Steer's 'Sunset', which expresses
nothing but a romantic nostalgia. Are these the feeble derivative things
the 'creators of new values' admire?

That a critic of this calibre should attempt to patronise Mr Epstein
is disgusting. I make this very hurried protest in the hope that I may
induce those people who have perhaps been prejudiced by ignorant
and biased criticism to go and judge for themselves.

Modern Art

I: The Grafton Group[1]

[*The New Age*, 14/11 (15 January 1914)]

I am attempting in this series of articles to define the characteristics of a new constructive geometric art which seems to me to be emerging at the present moment. In a later series, to be called the 'Break up of the Renaissance', I shall attempt to show the relation between this art and a certain general changed outlook.

I am afraid that my use of the word 'new' here will arouse a certain prejudice in the minds of the kind of people that I am anxious to convince. I may say then that I use the word with no enthusiasm. I want to convince those people who regard the feeble romanticism which is always wriggling and vibrating to the stimulus of the word 'new', with a certain amount of disgust, that the art which they incline to condemn as decadent is in reality the new order for which they are looking. It seems to me to be the genuine expression of abhorrence of slop and romanticism which has quite mistakenly sought refuge in the conception of a classical revival. By temperament I should adopt the classical attitude myself. My assertion then that a 'new' art is being formed is not due to any desire on my part to perceive something 'new' but is forced on me almost against my inclination by an honest observation of the facts themselves.

In attempting thus to define the characteristics of a new movement a certain clearance of the ground is necessary. A certain work of dissociation and analysis is required, in connection with what is vaguely thought of as 'modern' in art. A writer on art may perform a useful function in pointing out that what is generally thought of as one living movement consists really of many parts, some of which are as a matter of fact quite dead. The words, 'modern', 'Post-Impressionist' and 'Cubist' are used as synonyms, not only in the more simple form of instinctive reaction to an unpleasing phenomena, but also in a more positive way, the psychology of which seems to me to be rather interesting. The Post-Impressionist or Cubist appearances, at first perceived chaotically as 'queer' and rejected as such, became after a

mysterious act of conversion, a signal for exhilarated acceptance, irre-
spective of the quality of the painting itself. They give every picture,
good or bad, which possesses them, a sort of cachet. But although this
complex of qualities passes from the stage in which it is repulsive to
that in which it is attractive, yet for most people it remains unanalysed.
It must be pointed out that what has been grouped together as one,
really contains within itself several diverse and even contradictory
tendencies. One might separate the modern movement into three
parts, to be roughly indicated as Post-Impressionism, analytical
Cubism and a new constructive geometrical art. The first of these, and
to a certain extent the second, seem to me to be necessary but entirely
transitional stages leading up to the third, which is the only one
containing possibilities of development.

This show at the Alpine Club provides a convenient illustration of
these points. Mr Fry organised the first Post-Impressionist exhibition
in London and was thought to have established a corner in the move-
ment. He probably regards himself, and is certainly regarded by many
others, as the representative of the new direction in art. The earlier
shows of the Grafton group were sufficiently comprehensive and
varied to make this opinion seem plausible. . . . There was a mixture of
a sort of aesthetic archaism and a more vigorous cubism which corre-
sponded very well to the loose use of the words 'modern art' which I
have just mentioned, and helped to maintain the illusion that the
whole formed in reality one movement. But the departure of Mr
Wyndham Lewis, Mr Etchells,[2] Mr Nevinson[3] and several others has
left concentrated in a purer form all the worked-out and dead elements
in the movement. It has become increasingly obvious that Mr Fry and
his group are nothing but a kind of backwater, and it seems to me to be
here worth while pointing out the character of this backwater. As you
enter the room you almost know what to expect, from the effect of the
general colour. It consists almost uniformly of pallid chalky blues,
yellows and strawberry colours, with a strong family resemblance
between all the pictures; in every case a kind of anaemic effect showing
no personal or constructive use of colour. The subjects also are signif-
icant. One may recognise the whole familiar bag of tricks the usual
Cézanne landscapes, the still lifes, the Eves in their gardens, and the
botched Byzantine. As the Frenchmen exhibited here have really no
connection with the Grafton group, I will omit them and confine

myself to the English painters. In Mr Fry's landscape you can see his inability to follow a method to its proper conclusion. The colour is always rather sentimental and pretty. He thus accomplishes the extraordinary feat of adapting the austere Cézanne into something quite fitted for chocolate boxes. It is too tedious to go on mentioning mediocre stuff, so I should like to point out the two things which are worth seeing, No. 29, a very interesting pattern by Mr Roberts,[4] and M. Gaudier-Brzeska's[5] sculpture.

However, I find it more interesting to escape from this show for a minute, by discussing a general subject which is to a certain extent suggested by it – the exact place of archaism in the new movement. I want to maintain (i) that a certain archaism was a natural stage in the preparation of a new method of expression, and (ii) that the persistence of a feeble imitation of archaism, such as one gets in this show, is an absolutely unnecessary survival when this stage has been passed through.

In the first place then, how does it come about that a movement towards a new method of expression should contain so many archaic elements? How can a movement whose essence is the exact opposite of romanticism and *nostalgie*, which is striving towards a hard and definite structure in art, take the form of archaism? How can a sensibility so opposed to that which generally finds satisfaction in the archaic, make such use of it? What happens, I take it, is something of this kind: a certain change of direction takes place which begins negatively with a feeling of dissatisfaction with and reaction against existing art. But the new tendency, admitting that it exists, cannot at once find its own appropriate expression. But although the artist feels that he must have done with contemporary means of expression, yet a new and more fitting method is not easily created. Expression is by no means a natural thing. It is an unnatural, artificial, and, as it were, external thing which a man has to install himself in before he can manipulate it. The way from intention to expression does not come naturally as it were from in outwards. It in no way resembles the birth of Minerva. A gap between the intention and its actual expression in material exists, which cannot be bridged directly. A man has first to obtain a foothold in this, so to speak, alien and external world of material expression, at a point near to the one he is making for. He has to utilise some already existing method of expression, and work from that to the one that expresses his own personal conception more accurately and naturally. At the present moment this leads to archaism because the particular change of direction in the new movement is a striving towards a certain intensity which is already expressed in archaic form. This perhaps supplements what I said about the archaism of Mr Epstein's 'Carvings in Flenite'. It perhaps enables me to state more clearly the relation between those works and the more recent work represented by the drawings. You get a breaking away from contemporary methods of expression, a new direction, an intenser perception of things striving towards expression. And as this intensity is fundamentally the same kind of intensity as that expressed in certain archaic arts, it quite naturally and legitimately finds a foothold in these archaic yet permanent formulae. But as this intensity is at the same time no romantic revival, but part of a real change of sensibility occurring now in the modern mind, and is coloured by a particular and original quality due to this fact, it quite as naturally develops from the original formula one which is for it, a purer and more accurate medium of expression. (That the great change in outlook is coming about naturally at the present moment, I shall attempt to demonstrate later by a consideration which has nothing whatever to do with art. I shall then be able to explain what I meant by the 'dregs of the Renaissance'.)

To return then to the discussion from which I started. A certain archaism it seems is at the beginning a help to an artist. Although it may afterwards be repudiated, it is an assistance in the construction of a new method of expression. Most of the artists who prepared the new movement passed through this stage. Picasso, for example, used many forms taken from archaic art, and other examples will occur to everyone. It might be objected that a direct line of development could be traced through Cézanne showing no archaic influence. But I think it would be true to say of Cézanne, even in much of his later work, that he seeks expression through forms that are to a certain extent archaic. So much then for the function of archaism. Apply this to what you find in the Grafton group. If it were only a matter of serious experimentation in archaic forms, after the necessity for that experimentation had passed by, the thing would be regrettable but not a matter for any violent condemnation. But you do not find anything of that kind, but merely a cultured and anaemic imitation of it. What in the original was a sincere effort towards a certain kind of intensity, becomes in its

English dress a mere utilisation of the archaic in the spirit of the aesthetic. It is used as a plaything to a certain quaintness. In Mr Duncan Grant's 'Adam and Eve', for example, elements taken out of the extremely intense and serious Byzantine art are used in an entirely meaningless and pointless way. There is no solidity about any of the things; all of them are quite flimsy. One delightful review of the show described Mr Fry's landscapes as having 'the fascination of reality seen through a cultured mind'. The word 'cultured' here explains a good deal. I feel about the whole show a typically Cambridge sort of atmosphere. I have a very vivid impression of what I mean here by Cambridge, as I have recently had the opportunity of observing the phenomenon at close quarters. I know the kind of dons who buy these pictures, the character of the dilettante appreciation they feel for them. It is so interesting and clever of the artist to use the archaic in this paradoxical way, so amusing to make Adam stand on his head, and the donkey's ear continue into the hills – gentle little Cambridge jokes.

It is all amusing enough in its way, a sort of aesthetic playing about. It can best be described in fact as a new disguise of aestheticism. It is not a new art, there is nothing new and creative about it. At first appearance the pictures seem to have no resemblance to Pre-Raphaelitism. But when the spectator has overcome his first mild shock and is familiarised with them, he will perceive the fundamental likeness. Their 'queerness', such as it is, is not the same serious queerness of the Pre-Raphaelites, it is perhaps only quaint and playful; but essentially the same English aesthetic is behind both, and essentially the same cultured reminiscent pleasure is given to the spectator. This being the basic constituent of both arts, just as the one ultimately declined into Liberty's, so there is no reason why the other should not find its grave in some emporium which will provide the wives of young and advanced dons with suitable house decoration.

What is living and important in new art must be looked for elsewhere.

II: A Preface Note and Neo-Realism[1]

[*The New Age*, 14/15 (12 February 1914)]

As in these articles I intend to skip about from one part of my argument to another, as occasion demands, I might perhaps give them a greater appearance of shape by laying down as a preliminary three theses that I want to maintain.

1. There are two kinds of art, geometrical or abstract, and vital and realistic art, which differ absolutely in kind from the other. They are not modifications of one and the same art, but pursue different aims and are created to satisfy a different desire of the mind.

2. Each of these arts springs from, and corresponds to, a certain general attitude towards the world. You get long periods of time in which only one of these arts and its corresponding mental attitude prevails. The naturalistic art of Greece and the Renaissance corresponded to a certain rational humanistic attitude towards the universe, and the geometrical has always gone with a different attitude of greater intensity than this.

3. The re-emergence of geometrical art at the present day may be the precursor of the re-emergence of the corresponding general attitude towards the world, and so of the final break-up of the Renaissance.

This is the logical order in which I state the position. Needless to say, I did not arrive at it in that way. I shall try to make a sweeping generalisation like the last a little less empty by putting the matter in an autobiographical form. I start with the conviction that the Renaissance attitude is breaking up and then illustrate it by the change in art, and not vice versa. First came the reaction against the Renaissance philosophy, and the adoption of the attitude which I said went with the geometrical art.

Just at this time I saw Byzantine mosaic for the first time. I was then impressed by these mosaics, not as something exotic or 'charming', but as expressing quite directly an attitude which I to certain extent agreed with. The important thing about this for me was that I was then, owing to this accidental agreement, able to see a geometrical art, as it were, from the inside. This altered my whole view of such arts. I realised for the first time that their geometrical character is essential to the expression of the intensity they are aiming at. It seemed clear that they differed absolutely from the vital arts because they were pursuing a different intention, and that what we, expecting other qualities from art, look on as dead and lifeless, were the necessary means of expression for this other intention.

Finally I recognised this geometrical re-emerging in modern art. I had here then very crudely all the elements of the position that I stated in my three theses. At that time, in an essay by Paul Ernst on religious art, I came across a reference to the work of Riegl and Worringer. In the latter particularly I found an extraordinarily clear statement founded on an extensive knowledge of the history of art, of a view very like the one I had tried to formulate. I heard him lecture last year and had an opportunity of talking with him at the Berlin Aesthetic Congress. I varied to a certain extent from my original position under the influence of his vocabulary, and that influence will be seen in some, at any rate, of the articles.

* * *

To turn now to Mr Ginner's defence of Neo-Realism. His article having somewhat the character of a painter's apologia, inevitably raises points over the whole range of the subject. I confine myself therefore to the main argument, which, put shortly, is that (1) All good art is realistic. Academism is the result of the adoption by weak painters of the creative artist's personal method of interpreting nature, and the consequent creation of formulae, without contact with nature. (2) The new movement in art is merely an academic movement of the kind, springing from the conversion of Cézanne's mannerisms into formulae. (3) The only remedy is a return to realism. Only a realistic method can keep art creative and vital.

These statements are based on such an extraordinarily confused and complicated mass of assumptions that I cannot give any proper refutation. I shall just try to show exactly what assumptions are made, and to indicate in a series of notes and assertions an opposite view of art to Mr Ginner's. I can only give body to these assertions and prove them much later in the series.

Taking first his condemnation of the new movement as academic, being based on the use of formulae. My reply to this is that the new movement does not use *formulae*, but *abstractions*, quite a different thing. Both are 'unlike nature', but while the one is unlike, owing to a lack of vitality in the art, resulting in dead conventions, the other is unlike, of deliberate intent, and is very far from being dead. Mr Ginner's misconception of the whole movement is due to his failure to make this distinction, a failure ultimately arising from the assumption that art must be realistic. He fails to recognise the existence of the abstract geometric art referred to in my prefatory note.

If you will excuse the pedantry of it, I think I can make the matter clearer by using a diagram:

$$R \ldots \ldots p_{(r)} \ldots \ldots a_{(r)} \ldots \ldots A$$

I take (R) to represent reality. As one goes from left to right one gets further and further from reality. The first step away being $p_{(r)}$ that is the artist's interpretation of nature. The next step $a_{(r)}$ being an art using abstractions (a), with a certain representative element $_{(r)}$. The element (a) owes its significance to, and is dependent on the other end (A) of this kind of spectrum – a certain 'tendency to abstraction'. I assert that these are two arts, the one focused round (R), which is moved by a delight in natural forms, and the other springing from the other end, making use of abstractions as a method of expression. I am conscious that this is the weak point of my argument, for I cannot give body to this conception of the 'expressive use of abstraction' till later on in the series.

Looking at the matter from this point of view, what is the source of Mr Ginner's fallacy? He admits that $p_{(r)}$ is the personal interpretation of reality, but as he would deny the possibility of an abstract art altogether, any further step away from reality must appear to him as decay, and the only way he can explain the (a) in a $_{(r)}$ is to look on it as a degeneration of (p) in $p_{(r)}$. An abstraction to him then can only mean the decay of mannerism in formulae which comes about when the artist has lost contact with nature, and there is no personal first-hand observation. When, therefore, Mr Ginner says the adoption of formulae leads to the decay of an art, it is obvious that this must be true if by art you mean realistic art. Inside such art, whose raison d'être is its connection with nature, the use of formulae, i.e., a lack of personal, creative and sincere observation, must inevitably lead to decay. But here comes the root of the whole fallacy. Realistic art is not the only kind of art. If everything hangs on the (R) side of my diagram then the (a) in a (r) must seem a decayed form of (p) in p(r). But in this other abstract art the (a) in a (r) gets its whole meaning and significance from its dependence on the other end of the scale A, i.e., from its use by a creative artist as a method of expression. Looked at from this point of view, the position of *abstraction* is quite a different one. The *abstractions* used in this other art will not bring about a decadence, they are an essential part of its method. Their almost geometrical and non-vital character is not the result of weakness and lack of vitality in the art. They are not dead conventions, but the product of a creative process just as active as that in any realist art. To give a concrete example of the difference between formula and abstraction. Late Greek art decays into formulae. But the art before the classical made deliberate use of certain abstractions differing in kind from the formulae used in the decadence. They were used with intention, to get a certain kind of intensity. The truth of this view is conveniently illustrated by the history of Greek ornament, where abstract and geometrical forms precede natural forms instead of following them.

To these abstractions, the hard things Mr Ginner says about formulae have no application.

We shall never get any clear argument on this subject, then, until you agree to distinguish these two different uses of the word formula. (1) Conventional dead mannerism. (2) Abstraction, equally unlike nature, but used in a creative art as a method of expression.

The first effort of the realists then to give an account of abstraction comes to grief. Abstractions are not formulae. In their effort to make the matter seem as reasonable as possible the realists have a second way of conceiving the nature of abstractions which is equally misleading. They admit the existence of *decorative* abstractions. When they have managed to give partial praise to the new movement in this way, they then pass on to condemn it. They assert that the repetition of empty decorative forms must soon come to an end, that pure pattern does not contain within itself the possibility of development of a complete art. But their modified approval and their condemnation are alike erroneous. This second misconception of abstractions as being decorative formulae, is as mistaken as the first conception of them as being conventionalised mannerisms. Like the first, it springs from a refusal to recognise the existence of an art based on the creative use of abstraction, an art focused on the right hand side (A) of my diagram. As long as that is denied, then abstractions must inevitably be either conventionalised mannerisms or decorative. They are neither.

Now to apply the first distinction between *formulae* and *abstraction* to Mr Ginner's argument about the new movement in art. This art undoubtedly uses abstraction. Are these abstractions *formulae* in his sense of the word or not? If they are, then his argument is valid and we are in presence of a new academic movement.

I deny, however, that the abstractions to be found in the new art are dead *formulae*. For the moment, I do not intend to offer any proof of this assertion, as far as Cubist art itself is concerned. I intend to deal rather with the precursor of the movement, that is Cézanne himself. The point at issue here then is narrowed down to this. The Cubists claim that the beginnings of an abstract art can be found in Cézanne. Mr Ginner, on the contrary, asserts that Cézanne was a pure realist. It is to be noticed that even if he proved his case, he would not have attacked the new art itself, but only its claimed descent from Cézanne.

One must be careful not to treat Cézanne as if he actually were a Cubist; he obviously is not. One must not read the whole of the later movement into him. But there are in his paintings elements which quite naturally develop into Cubism later. You get, as contrasted with the Impressionists, a certain simplification of places, an emphasis on three-dimensional form, giving to some of his landscapes what might be called a Cubist appearance. It is true that this simplification and abstraction, this seeing of things in simple forms, as a rule only extends to details. It might be said that simplifications are, as it were, 'accepted' passively, and are not deliberately built up into a definite organisation and structure.

The first thing to be noticed is that even supposing that Cézanne's intentions were entirely realistic, he initiated a break-up of realism and provided the material for an abstract art. Picasso came along and took over these elements isolated by Cézanne, and organised them. If the simplifications in Cézanne had passed beyond details and become more comprehensive, they would probably of themselves have forced him to build up definite structures.

But not only are the elements of an abstract art present in Cézanne, I should say also that there was an embryo of the creative activity which was later to organise these elements.

I put again the opposed view to this. I have already said that the simplification of planes is based on that actually suggested by nature. The realist intention, it might be said, is directed towards weight and three-dimensional form, rather than towards light, yet it still remains realist. This is quite a conceivable view. It is quite possible that a realist of this kind might prepare the material of an abstract art automatically. The abstractions might be produced accidentally, with no attempt to use them creatively as means of expression.

It seems to me, however, that there are many reasons against the supposition that this was the case with Cézanne. In looking for any traces of this abstract organising tendency, one must remember that Cézanne was extraordinarily hampered by the realism of his period; in some ways he might be said to have carried out the complete impressionist programme. Yet showing through this you do get traces of an opposed tendency. I should base this assertion on two grounds:

(1) Though the simplification of planes may appear passive and prosaic, entirely dictated by a desire to reproduce a certain solidity, and from one point of view almost fumbling, yet at the same time one may say that in this treatment of detail, there is an energy at work which, though perhaps unconscious, is none the less an energy which is working towards abstraction and towards a feeling for structure. If one thinks of the details, rather than of the picture as a whole, one need not even say this energy is unconscious. In this respect Cézanne does seem to have been fairly conscious, and to have recognised what he was after better than the contemporary opinion which looked upon him as an impressionist. I should say that expressions like 'everything is spherical or cylindrical', and all the forms of nature 'peuvent se ramener au cône, au cylindre et la sphère', yet show the working of a creative invention, which had to that extent turned away from realism and showed a tendency towards abstraction. (It is obvious that these words were not used in the sense in which a Cubist might use them; they apply to details rather than to wholes. Yet a denial of the wider application does not, as many people seem to suppose, justify the idea that they were meant in the sense in which a Cubist might understand them.) These sentences seem to me to destroy the whole of Mr Ginner's argument, unless, of course, you go a step further than those who explain Cézanne's painting as the result of astigmatism and incompetence, and assert that the poor man could not even use his

mother tongue. The simplification of planes itself, then, does seem to show a tendency to abstraction which is working itself free. (2) But the fact that this simplification is not entirely realistic and does come from a certain feeling after structure, seems to me to be demonstrated in a more positive way by pictures like the well-known 'Bathing Women'. Here you get a use of distortion and an emphasis on form which is constructive. The pyramidal shape, moreover, cannot be compared to decoration, or to the composition found in the old masters. The shape is so hard, so geometrical in character, that it almost lifts the picture out of the realistic art which has lasted from the Renaissance to now, and into the sphere of geometric art. It is in reality much nearer to the kind of geometrical organisations employed in the new art.

That is a theoretical statement of the errors Mr Ginner makes. I think it might be worth while to go behind these errors themselves, to explain the prejudices which are responsible for their survival.

As a key to his psychology, take the sentence which he most frequently repeats. 'It is only this intimate relation between the artist and the object which can produce original and great works. Away from nature, we fall into unoriginal and monotonous formulae'. In repeating this he probably has at the back of his mind two quite different ideas, (1) the idea that it is the business of the artist to represent and interpret nature, and (2) the assumption that even if it is not his duty to represent nature that he must do so *practically*, for away from nature the artist's invention at once decays. He apparently thinks of an artist using abstractions as of a child playing with a box of tricks. The number of interesting combinations must soon be exhausted.

The first error springs from a kind of Rousseauism which is probably much too deeply imbedded in Mr Ginner's mind for me to be able to eradicate. I merely meet it by the contrary assertion that I do not think it is the artist's only business to reproduce and interpret Nature, 'source of all good', but that it is possible that the artist may be creative. This distinction is obscured in Mr Ginner's mind by the highly coloured and almost ethical language in which he puts it. We are exhorted to stick to Mother Nature. Artists who attempt to do something other than this are accused of 'shrinking from life'. This state of mind can be most clearly seen in the use of the word simplification. There is a confusion here between the *validity* and *origin* of simplification. The validity of simplification is held to depend on its origin. If the simplification, such as that for example you get in Cézanne's treatment of trees, is derived from Nature and comes about as the result of an aim which is itself directed back to Nature, then it is held to be valid. I, on the other hand, should assert that the validity of the simplification lay in itself and in the use made of it and had nothing whatever to do with its descent, on its occupying a place in Nature's 'Burke'.

Take now the second prejudice – the idea that whatever he may do theoretically, at any rate practically, the artist must keep in continual contact with Nature – 'The individual relying on his imagination and his formula finds himself very limited, in comparison with the infinite variety of life. Brain ceases to act as it ceases to search out expression of Nature, its only true and healthy source.'

You see here again the ethical view of the matter – the idea of retribution. Get further and further away from dear old Mother Nature and see what happens to you: you fall into dead formulae.

My answer to this argument is: that while I admit it to be to a certain extent true, I deny the conclusion Mr Ginner draws from it.

I admit that the artist cannot work without contact with, and continual research into nature, but one must make a distinction between this and the conclusion drawn from it that the work of art itself must be an interpretation of nature. The artist obviously cannot spin things out of his head, he cannot work from imagination in that sense. The whole thing springs from misconception of the nature of artistic imagination. Two statements are confused: (1) that the source of imagination must be nature, and (2) the consequence illegitimately drawn from this, that the resulting work must be realistic, and based on natural forms. One can give an analogy in ordinary thought. The reasoning activity is quite different in character from any succession of images drawn from the senses, but yet thought itself would be impossible without this sensual stimulus.

There must be just as much contact with nature in an abstract art as in a realistic one; without that stimulus the artist could produce nothing. In Picasso, for example, there is much greater research into nature, as far as the relation of planes is concerned, than in any realist painting; he has isolated and emphasised relations previously not emphasised. All art may be said to be realism, then, in that it extracts from nature facts which have not been observed before. But in as far as the artist is creative, he is not bound down by the accidental relations of the elements actually found in nature, but extracts, distorts, and utilises them as a means of expression, and not as a means of interpreting nature.

It is true, then, that an artist can only keep his work alive by research into nature, but that does not prove that realism is the only legitimate form of art.

Both realism and abstraction, then, can only be *engendered* out of nature, but while the first's only idea of living seems to be that of hanging on to its progenitor, the second cuts its umbilical cord.

III: The London Group[1]

[*The New Age*, 14/21 (26 March 1914)]

This group has been formed by the amalgamation of the Camden Town Group and the Cubists. It thus claims to represent all the forward movements in English painting at the present moment. Judging from its first exhibition, it is probably destined, since the decline of the New English, to play a very important role in the next few years. Of the most realist section of the society I shall not say much here, as I intend to write about it at greater length later. Mr Spencer Gore's 'The Wood', and Mr Harold Gilman's 'Eating House' show in very different ways the same intimate research into problems of colour. Mr Charles Ginner's 'La Balayeuse' is the best picture of his that I have seen as yet. His peculiar method is here extraordinarily successful in conveying the sordid feeling of the subject. Mr Bevan exhibits a characteristic and interesting painting of horses. Although at the moment I am more in sympathy with the other section of the society, yet I am bound to say that the work of the painters I have just mentioned is better than that one finds at the New English, and infinitely better than the faked stuff produced by Mr Roger Fry and his friends. It is possible to point out, however, in looking at this kind of painting, the dissatisfaction which inclines one towards Cubism. These pictures are filled by contours which, when one is moved by the dissatisfaction I am speaking of, one can only describe as meaningless. They are full of detail which is entirely accidental in character, and only justified by the fact that these accidents did actually occur in the particular piece of nature which was being painted. One feels a repugnance to such accidents – and desires painting where nothing is accidental, where all the contours are closely knit together into definite structural shapes.

The Cubist section is particularly interesting, as it shows very clearly the unsettled state of the new movement. Though it has finally got clear away from its Post-Impressionistic beginnings, it cannot be said to have reached any final form. Two different tendencies can be distinguished. The main movement is that which, arising out of Cubism, is destined to create a new geometric and monumental art, making use of mechanical forms. It is possible, I think, to give an account of this movement, which will exhibit it as an understandable and coherent whole, closely allied to the general tendency of the period, and thus containing possibilities of development.

But this has now generated a second movement based simply on the idea that abstract form, i.e., form without any representative content, can be an adequate means of expression. In this, instead of hard, structural work like Picasso's you get the much more scattered use of abstractions of artists like Kandinsky.[2] It seems, judging by its development up to now, to be only a more or less amusing by-product of the first. Lacking the controlling sensibility, the feeling for mechanical structure, which makes use of abstractions a necessity, it seems rather dilettante. It so happens, however, that all explanations of the new movement as yet given, have been explanations of this second tendency only. In this way the real importance of the main tendency has been veiled. It has seemed rather in the air, rather causeless. The driving force behind it remained hidden.

What is really behind the main movement, what makes it important is the re-emergence of a sensibility akin to that behind geometrical arts of the past. At first, at its rather fumbling search for an appropriate means of expression, it naturally went back to these past arts. You thus got a period in which the work produced had a certain resemblance to Archaic, Byzantine and African art. But this state has already been left behind. The new sensibility is finding for itself a direct and modern means of expression, having very little resemblance to these past geometric arts. It is characterised, not by the simple geometric forms found in archaic art, but by the more complicated ones associated in our minds with machinery. Minor effects of this change of sensibility are very obvious in the pictures here. They do not shrink from forms which it is usual to describe as unrhythmical, and great use is made of shapes taken from machinery. The beauty of banal forms like teapot-handles, knuckledusters, saws, etc., seems to have been perceived for the first time. A whole picture is sometimes dominated by a composition based on hard mechanical shapes in a way which previous art would have shrunk from. It is not the emphasis on form which is the distinguishing characteristic of the new movement, then, but the emphasis on this particular kind of form.

But it is easy to see how this main movement, with its necessary use of abstraction of a particular kind for a particular purpose, has engendered on the side of it a minor movement which uses abstractions for their own sake in a much more scattered way. I do not think this minor movement is destined to survive. I look upon it rather as a kind of romantic heresy, which will, however, have a certain educative influence. It will lead to the discovery of conceptions of form, which will be extremely useful in the construction of the new geometrical art. But temporarily, at any rate, most of the painters in this exhibition seem to be very much influenced by an enthusiasm for this idea. One has here, then, a good opportunity for examining this heresy. Theoretically it is quite plausible. It seems quite conceivable that the directions of the forms in a picture, the subordination of the parts to the whole, the arresting of one form by the other, the relation of veiled to exposed shapes, might make up a understandable kind of music without the picture containing any representative element whatever. How does it work out in practice? Take Mr Wyndham Lewis's large canvases, which at first look like mere arbitrary arrangements of bright colours and abstract forms. Judged from this point of view, what can be said about them? They fail, in that they do not produce as a whole, the kind of coherent effect which, according to the theory, they ought to produce. The forms are not controlled enough. In the 'Eisteddfod', for example, long tranquil planes of colour sweeping up from the left encounter a realistically painted piece of ironwork, which, being very large in proportion to the planes, dwarfs any effect they might have produced. The second picture, 'Christopher Columbus', is hard and gay, contains many admirable inventions, but is best regarded as a field where certain qualities are displayed, rather than as a complete work of art. In Mr Lewis's work, there are always certain qualities of dash and decision, but it has the defects of these qualities. His sense of form seems to me to be sequent rather than integral, by which I mean that one form probably springs out of the preceding one as he works, instead of being conceived as part of a whole. His imagination being quick and never fumbling, very interesting relations are generated in this way, but the whole sometimes lacks cohesion and unity. The qualities of Mr Lewis's work are seen to better advantage in his quite remarkable drawing, 'The Enemy of the Stars'. Equally abstract is Mr Wadsworth's work.[3] In the most successful, 'Scherzo', a number of lively ascending forms are balanced by broad planes at the top. The painter whose work shows the greatest advance is Mr C.F. Hamilton. His 'Two Figures' shows a great sense of construction, and is one of the best paintings in this section. Mr F. Etchells' drawings are admirably firm and hard in character; but it would obviously be premature to form any sure judgment about this artist's work at a time when he almost seems to be holding himself back, in a search for a new method of expression. His fine 'Drawing of a Head' shows this state of hesitation and experiment very clearly. Mr Nevinson is much less abstract than the others. His best picture is 'The Chauffeur', which is very solid and develops an interesting contrast between round and angular shapes. I admire the ability of Mr Gaudier-Brzeska's sculpture; the tendencies it displays are sound though the abstractions used do not seem to me to be always thoroughly thought out.

In all painters I have mentioned so far abstract form has been used as the bearer of general emotions, but the real fanatics of form reject even this abstract use as savouring of literature and sentiment. Representation has already been excluded. They want to exclude even the general emotions conveyed by abstract form, and to confine us to the appreciation of form in itself *tout pur*. Some such intention must be behind the largest picture in the show, Mr Bomberg's 'In the Hold'[4]. Stated in more detail, the theory on which it is based seems to be this. In looking at a picture one never sees it as a whole, one's eye travels over it. In doing so, we continually find certain expectations fulfilled – a boot is followed by a leg, and even when there is no representation at all, certain abstract forms are naturally continued by other forms. Apparently this fulfilled expectation is an added non-aesthetic emotion, and must be excluded by those who wish to take an absolutely 'pure' pleasure in form itself. Mr Bomberg therefore cuts his picture up into sixty-four squares, and as each square is independent of its neighbours, the 'fulfilled expectation' I spoke of above is excluded, and whatever pleasure we take must be in the arrangement of shapes inside each square. The picture appears to have started off as a drawing of an actual subject, but that apparently was only because a purely mental invention of form would have inevitably produced those 'sequences' it was desired to avoid. The representation of the outside scene generates, in its passage through a square, an entirely accidental and 'unexpected' shape. The square I might call K.Kt.6, for example, makes an interesting pattern. That the picture as a whole is entirely empty is, I suppose, on the theory I have just put forward, no defect. All the general emotions produced by form have been excluded and we are reduced to purely intellectual interest in shape. This particular picture, then, is certainly the *reductio ad absurdum* of this heresy about form. I see no development along such lines, though such work may be an excellent discipline. I look forward, however, to Mr Bomberg's future work with interest; he is undoubtedly an artist of remarkable ability. For the present, I prefer his drawings. 'The Acrobats' breaks away from the sculptural treatment of his recent work and seems to me to be admirable.

Most of the work I have been talking about is experimental and is interesting because it is on the way to something else. Perhaps the only really satisfying and complete work in this section is that of Mr Epstein. He possesses that peculiar energy which distinguishes the creative from the merely intelligent artist, and is certainly the greatest sculptor of this generation; I have seen no work in Paris or Berlin which I can so unreservedly admire. At the present moment he has arrived at an interesting point in his development. Starting from a very efficient realism, he passed through a more or less archaic period; he seems now to have left that behind and, as far as one can judge from the drawings for sculpture he exhibits, to have arrived at an entirely personal and modern method of expression. The 'Carving in Flenite' comes at the end of the second period. Technically, it is admirable. The design is in no sense empty, but gives a most impressive and complete expression of a certain blind tragic aspect of its subject – something akin perhaps to what Plato meant by the vegetable soul. The archaic elements it contains are in no sense imitative. What has been taken from African or Polynesian work is the inevitable and permanent way of getting a certain effect. The only quite new work Mr Epstein exhibits, the 'Bird Pluming Itself' is in comparison with this profound work, quite light in character, but the few simple abstractions out of which it is built are used with great skill and discretion.

IV: Mr David Bomberg's Show

[*The New Age*, 15/10 (9 July 1914)]

Mr Bomberg stands somewhat apart from the other English Cubists. I noticed that in signing a collective protest, published a few weeks ago, he added in a footnote that he had nothing whatever to do with the Rebel Art Centre[1] – very wisely, in my opinion, for his work is certainly much more individual and less derivative than the work of the members of that group. The tendency to abstraction does seem in his case to have been a logical development of tendencies which were always present even in his earlier drawings, and not merely the result of a feverish hurry to copy the latest thing from Paris. The fact that his work shows these individual qualities justifies much more than is generally the case a one-man show, and separate consideration. But while I have great admiration for some of Mr Bomberg's work, that does not make it any easier for me to write an article about it. An article about one man's pictures is not a thing I should ever do naturally. The only absolutely honest and direct and straightforward word expression of what I think as I go round such an exhibition would be a monotonous repetition of the words 'This is good or fairly good. How much does that cost?' for I would certainly rather buy a picture than write about it. It seems a much more appropriate gesture. Any more rotund or fluent expression than these short sentences must, however admirable, be artificial. Only the expert art critic can prolong the gesture of admiration artificially by cliché – that, of course, is his métier. I wish I could do it myself. The fact that naturally one's expression is inadequate, springs entirely from a certain physical difference of *pace*. What you feel before a picture is long, slow, seems important. The rattle of sounds which expresses it is quick, short and unimpressive. The body as a tool of expression is obviously a failure, it is too light weight. Your sentence over, you feel that you have finished too soon; you feel uncomfortable and want to prolong the gesture. Hence is born the whole system of cliché; a system enabling you to 'last out' the feeling; hence also we might even say to the whole mechanism of literary expression. It all exists to cover the body's inefficiency. If only our arms were so heavy that an appreciative sweep lasted ten minutes we should be saved from literature. Opera, of course, can 'last out' by raising the sentence into aria. The American has his drawl, and consequently has no literature – not needing any. But I haven't these expedients; nor as an outsider in his business have I the necessary cliché at my command. I can only then write an article on one man's pictures by using the only form of incense natural to me; I can get up an argument about them – which I therefore proceed to do.

Mr Bomberg starts off by stating in the preface to his catalogue that his object in all his painting is the construction of 'pure form', and that he appeals constantly to a sense of form. We might all admit that this is true as a description of pure fact, at any rate. All the paintings are of the character he describes. They do appeal to very little else but a sense of form. Take, for example, one of the best of the drawings (No. 6) 'Ju Jitsu'. What strikes you first as excellent is the contrast between the bareness of certain parts as contrasted with the complex and intricate liveliness of others. Wherever it was felt to be necessary, representation has been sacrificed. The body line of one figure, which would be in reality hidden behind another figure in the foreground, is clearly shown. The realist would here urge that if that line was necessary in order to get a certain arrangement of form, it should have been continued by a line on the front figure, so that representation should not have been sacrificed. I will deal later with the validity of this kind of objection; I only mention the point here to show that the intention of the artist is clearly what he announces it to be. It is still clearer in the remarkable drawing, 'Zin' (No. 26), which contains hardly any representative element at all. In the upper part, which strikes me as best, there are no recognisable forms at all, but only an arrangement of abstract lines outlining no object. It is very difficult to state why one considers a drawing of this kind good when one hasn't it before one. Perhaps the best way of describing it would be to say that it looks like a peculiarly interesting kind of scaffolding. It is obvious, therefore,

that the only interest in it must be an interest in form. I should prob-
ably find it difficult to say what I found interesting in it if I had the
drawing here before me and could show it you. Its interest depends on
qualities peculiarly indescribable in words. Indescribable not for any
mysterious reason, but because forms are of their nature rather inde-
scribable, and even difficult, to point out. They depend, for example,
very often on a three dimensional relation between planes which is
very difficult to get at. The artist in front of a picture endeavouring to
explain it, by inexpressive motions of his hands, has often been
laughed at; but laughed at, I think, for a wrong reason. It is supposed
that he waves his hands, makes strange gestures with his thumbs,
peculiar twists with his wrists, because he lacks the power of
expressing himself in words; because he is a painter, in fact, and not a
literary man. This I believe to be a mistaken view of the phenomenon.
He is not using his hands through poverty of words, through lack of
the ability to express himself in the proper manner. He is trying to
describe the qualities of the picture in the only way they can be
described. But he is a figure for laughter because he is employing a
miserably inadequate tool. It is impossible to suppose that those
ancient prehensile implements, our hands, could ever be turned to this
new use – a description of the subtleties and intricacies of form. It
cannot be done, and surely the designer of the universe never intended
that it should be done. I think of designing a little brass instrument
which shall adequately perform the function which the hands now so
inefficiently perform. An arrangement of revolving graduated spheres
will enable you to indicate at once all the complicated twists and rela-
tions of form that you perceive in a picture. This invention would have
two advantages. It would do away with the art critic. On each picture
would be an indication as to how you must graduate your instrument,
in order to grasp the relations of forms the artist was after; this would
do away with any necessity for the confused and stuttering metaphors
by which the critic endeavours to express the inexpressible; one
painful scene the less in this world of trouble. Moreover, it would
please the conservatives in these matters, for the manufacture of my
instrument would soon fall into the hands of a trust, who, whenever a
new generation began to experiment with a new kind of form unpro-
vided for by the instrument, would see that the Press unanimously
denounced it.

To return, however, to Mr Bomberg's exhibition. Those who are curious as to the genesis of abstract form, as to the way in which it is actually constructed in the artist's mind, should find Nos. 23, II, I, which probably represent three stages in the development of the same idea, interesting. The first step towards the understanding of this process of genesis is to recognise that the mind cannot *create* form, it can only *edit* it. In this, as in other very different matters, existing here in this world, bound to this body, we have little spontaneity. Asked to fill a space with a *new* abstract design, and told at the same time to empty his mind of all recollection of the external world, an artist would produce nothing but a few arbitrary and uninteresting repetitions. The first suggestion must always come from some existing outside shape. This sets the mind going. Consider now the three things I mentioned above. No. 23 is the first drawing. The artist probably got the lines of his main design from some accidental material arrangement. The suggestions of form this contained were then probably continued and developed by thinking of them as parts of human figures. (This use of doll-like human figures is a characteristic of Mr Bomberg's work, as those who saw his drawings in *The New Age* will remember.) In the final stage, these figures are so abstract that they are not recognisable as such. In all this process what suggestions of real objects occur, are only as a means of getting the mind going, as fertiliser of the design. In themselves they are of no importance, the controlling interest all the time being the selection and production of abstract form. The first of these three works, No. 23, I do not think successful, taken by itself. One notes it as interesting, but it produces no definite effect. The two paintings developed from it, however, are much more interesting; No. I, 'The Mud Bath', being one of the best things Mr Bomberg has done; the colour in it being much more vigorous than in the earlier study, No. II of the drawings, which, while being abstract, at the same time contains recognisable representative elements. No. 5, 'Reading from Torah', seems to me to be the best. The abstract shapes here do reinforce a quite human and even dramatic effect, at the same time being interesting in themselves merely as a construction of shapes. They would probably be even more interesting carried out as three dimensional shapes in wood or something of that kind. Another extremely good drawing of an almost sculptural quality is 'Chinnereth', about which, however, I need say nothing, as it has already been reproduced in this paper.

So far I have only been concerned to show that on the assumption that an interest in pure form is a sufficient basis in itself Mr Bomberg's work is, as a matter of fact, good work. It may be worth while here to examine that assumption. Is pure form alone a sufficient basis for interest in art? The best answer is, of course, that certain people find it enough. They find that they are moved by, and interested in, the suggestions of abstract form they see about them, and do feel themselves prompted either to then organise these suggestions, or to look for them in art. When a man simply says: 'I do feel interested in abstract form, as another might in atmosphere and landscape', no objection can be made to his statement. But there is an erroneous way of transforming the statement into a theory, which makes it impossible for the layman to understand the motives of abstract art. For this reason I want to contradict it. The theory is that we contemplate *form* for its own sake – that it produces a particular emotion different from the ordinary everyday emotions – a specific *aesthetic* emotion. If this were a true account of the matter, it would be incomprehensible to the layman. 'Pictures with some dramatic or human interest I like, ... but this damned stylistic bunkum ...' And he would be right.

If form has no dramatic or human interest, then it is obviously stupid for a human to be interested in it.

But the theory is erroneous. There is no such thing as a specific aesthetic emotion, a peculiar kind of emotion produced by *form* alone, only of interest to aesthetes. I think it could be shown that the emotions produced by abstract form, are the ordinary everyday human emotions – they are produced in a different way, that is all.

What happens, then, is not

$$S_{(f)} \ldots \ldots F$$

where S is the spectator, F the outside form, and (f) the specific form emotion, but much more this –

$$S_{(de)} \ldots \ldots F_{(if)}$$

where (de) stands for quite ordinary *dramatic human emotions*, which occur in daily life, and not only in the contemplation of works of art. I do not say that in looking at pure form we are *conscious* of this emotion they produce. We are not fully conscious of it, but *project* it outside ourselves into the outside form F, and may only be conscious of it as (if) '*interesting form*'. But the (if) only exists because of the (de).

After all, this possibility of living our own emotions *into* outside shapes and colours is the basic fact on which the whole of plastic art rests. People admit it in the case of atmosphere, colour, and landscape, but they will not admit it in the case of abstract form. Very possibly the number of people who can thus be affected by form is much more limited, but the phenomena is the same. There is nothing mysterious in this process by which *form* becomes the *porter* or *carrier* of internal emotions. It admits of a simple, psychological explanation which I need not give here, however; all that concerns us for the moment is the *fact*. Bare abstract form can be dramatic; the mere shape of a tree as tragic has a long explicit history. As a rule, of course, much milder emotions of tension, balance, contrast, etc., are called up. But it remains possible to say all one wants about arrangements of pure form without ever once using the word beauty and employing always the vocabulary with which one would speak of a man's character, commonplace ... vigorous ... empty, etc.

It must be insisted that there is nothing esoteric or mysterious about this interest in abstract forms. Once he has awakened to it, once it has been emphasised and indicated to him by art, then just as in the case of colour perception and impression the layman will derive great pleasure from it, not only as it is presented to him organised in Cubism, but as he perceives it for himself in outside nature. He will feel, for example, probably for the first time, an interest in the extraordinary variety of the abstract forms suggested by bare trees in winter (an interest, I must repeat, which is really an interest in himself as these forms, by an obscure psychological process, become for him the bearers of certain emotions) or in the morning, he may contemplate with interest the shapes into which his shirt thrown over a chair has fallen.

Here comes a common objection. Admitting the existence of this special interest in form, it is asked, why cannot these forms, instead of being abstracted, be given *in* the objects in which they actually occurred, i.e., *in* a realistic setting? If an artist looking out of a high window on the street beneath is interested in the fish-like interweaving of the motor traffic, why cannot that interweaving be given in a representation of the motor? Why attempt to give the interweaving alone?

Why attempt to give the soul without the body – an impossible feat? Why could not Mr Bomberg have given the shape-design of his 'Men and Lads' or his 'Acrobats', embodied *in* a more realistic representation? For two reasons: First that the only element of the real scene which interests the artist is the abstract element; the others are for that interest irrelevant, and, if reproduced, would only damp down the vigour of the naked form itself. And secondly, the fact that the abstract element did occur as a matter of fact in external nature mixed up with other things is of no importance. The forms are either interesting in themselves, or not. They derive no justification from their occurrence. The only importance of nature in this connection is that it does suggest forms, which the artist can develop; the mind here, as elsewhere, having very little natural spontaneity.

The use of form is then constructive. The same may be said of Mr Bomberg's use of colour. The relations of colours used are not *right* because they are the kind of sets of colour that do, as a matter of fact, actually occur in nature. In some of his earlier work, however, this is the case. (No. 23) 'The Song of Songs', a very beautiful work, is an example of this older use of colour. The combination of greys, dead black and gold strikes one as distinguished, but at the same time the pleasure it gives may be partly the pleasures of association; it is the kind of colour that might occur in nature at times of the day which have a certain emotional accompaniment. In the 'Mud Bath', on the contrary, the colour is used in an entirely constructive way, and in no sense derivative from nature. Here I might deal with a quite reasonable objection which is frequently brought against this kind of art. I went round Mr Bomberg's show with a very intelligent painter of an older school. 'Although I find these abstract drawings extremely interesting,' he said, 'yet if I were buying I should get this' – pointing out No. 32, I think. 'I feel abstract work would become tiring when one continually saw it in a room.' Though this sounds plausible, yet I don't think that it would as a matter of fact turn out to be the case. Personally, I think I should find drawings in which your imagination was continually focused in one direction by a subject more fatiguing. The proportions of a room or the shape of a good window, though they exercise a definite effect on one, do not become tiresome. And the pleasure to be got from good abstract art is of the same kind, though infinitely more elaborate, as the pleasure you get from these other fixed elements of a room.

To turn now to Mr Bomberg's earlier work. Here I have a conve-
nient opportunity of dealing with an entirely fallacious argument
which I am now thoroughly tired of reading. The baffled art critic,
being entirely at sea in dealing with quite abstract work, and feeling
himself unable to pass any secure judgment on it, turns to the artist's
earlier and more conventional work, and says, 'This earlier work
which I *can* understand is commonplace, I can therefore legitimately
infer that this abstract work which I cannot understand is also entirely
commonplace.' Now this argument, although attractively simple, is a
non sequitur. Suppose that the qualities of a good naturalistic drawing
are A B C ... F where F is a sense of form. In any particular case (F)
might be good, but the man's attention and interest might be so
concentrated on (F) that A B C were comparatively uninteresting, so
that on the whole the drawing might be pronounced commonplace.
But when you came to the man's abstract work which entirely
depended on his sense of form, his work might be far from common-
place. I see, however, that one critic has already applied this faulty
criterion to Mr Bomberg's earlier work. 'This earlier work', he says,
'shows energy without patience... is very ordinary student's work ...
he has never had the patience to master form' and so on. These judg-
ments I consider to be entirely unjust. Bearing in mind what I said in
the last paragraph, I find it decidedly *not* commonplace, because all of
it shows emphasis on, and understanding of, that quality which, while
it may only be one element in the excellence of a naturalistic drawing,
is yet the whole of a more abstract one – a sense of form. That seems to
have been always excellent. He has all the time, and apparently quite
spontaneously, and without imitation, been more interested in form
than anything else. Take No. 46, a bedroom picture, for example. I
mention it because it shows the transitional period very clearly – the
bed and room quite in the Sickert tradition, quite realistic and with
Sickert's ideas about paint, but the figure of the girl in it treated quite
differently, very much simplified, getting on to abstraction, and
looking consequently very unreal in the midst of the other very solid
realistic things. All the early drawings show a preoccupation with form
– the heads, though, less than the figure studies. In all of them, there
is an insistency on shapes running through. You can see this most
clearly in the figure study in the first room. Done realistically the lines

of the deltoids in the two arms, and the line of the chest, would form three broken parts of one line. As he has done it, the three are joined to make one line running through. I am quite aware, of course, that this sort of thing has always been one element in good drawing, but I do think you find it emphasised here in a way which makes his later development very understandable. No. 32 is good, and gets a certain monumental effect.

That his work shows the impatience the critic regrets is only to be expected. People with any guts in them do not have catholic tastes. If they realise in a personal and vivid way the importance of *one* element, if they feel that they have anything fresh to say about that, they are naturally impatient with the other elements. Why, if you are only interested in form, should you be asked – once you have got down the elements of that form adequately – to add to it the alien elements which would make it into a solid realistic representation? The watercolour 'Rehoboam' (No. 21) admirably expresses the idea it is based on. Why should it be carried any further? Why not stop with the idea which started it – why artificially prolong it into something not present in that initial idea?

To sum up, then – in my notice of the London Group I said that I thought Mr Bomberg was an artist of remarkable ability. This show certainly confirms that impression. It also adds something. It convinces me that his work has always been personal and independent – much more independent than that of most Cubists – and never reminiscent. If I am to qualify this, I should add that as yet his use of form satisfies a too purely sensuous or intellectual interest. It is not often used to intensify a more general emotion. I do not feel, then, the same absolute certainty about his work that I do about Epstein's. In Mr Epstein's work the abstractions have been got at gradually, and always intensify, as abstractions, the general feeling of the whole work. But then Mr Epstein is in a class by himself. I think that in this merely intellectual use of abstraction Mr Bomberg is achieving exactly what he sets out to achieve. But at the same time it is quite legitimate for me to point out why I prefer another use of abstraction. In any case, I think he will develop remarkably, and he is probably by this kind of work acquiring an intimate knowledge of form, which he will utilise in a different way later.

256   *THE NEW AGE*   DECEMBER 25, 1913

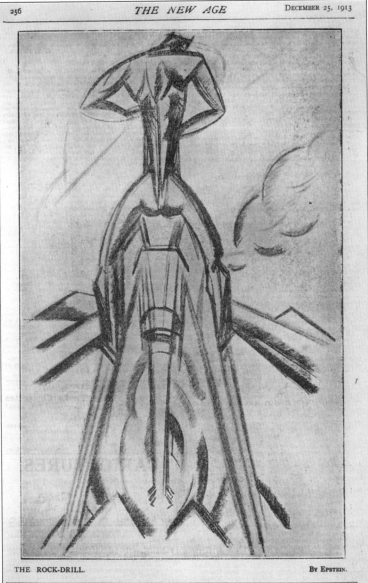

THE ROCK-DRILL.   BY EPSTEIN.

Published by the Proprietors, THE NEW AGE PRESS, LTD., 38, Cursitor Street, Chancery Lane, and Printed for them by BONNER & Co., The Chancery Lane Press, 1, 2, and 3, Rolls Passage, E.C. Agents for South Africa : Central News Agency, Ltd.

CHINNERETH.   BY DAVID BOMBERG.

APRIL 16, 1914. *THE NEW AGE* 753

STUDY by W. ROBERTS.

This drawing contains four figures. I could point out the position of these figures in more detail, but I think such detailed indication misleading. No artist can create abstract form spontaneously; it is always generated, or, at least, suggested, by the consideration of some outside concrete shapes. But such shapes are only interesting if you want to explain the psychology of the process of composition in the artist's mind. The interest of the drawing itself depends on the forms it contains. The fact that such forms were suggested by human figures is of no importance.

T. E. HULME.

THE CHAUFFEUR. By C. R. W. Nevinson.

THE FARMYARD. By EDWARD WADSWORTH.

CONTEMPORARY DRAWINGS—NO. 5.
EDITED BY T. E. HULME.

Contemporary Drawings

[*The New Age*, 2 April 1914]

This series will include drawings by David Bomberg, Jacob Epstein, F. Etchells, Gaudier-Brzeska, C.F. Hamilton, P. Wyndham Lewis, C.R.W. Nevinson, Roberts, and E. Wadsworth. Most of them are members of the London Group, which is now holding an exhibition in the Goupil Gallery. Some of the drawings are Cubist, some are not. Perhaps the only quality they possess in common is that they are all abstract in character. The series includes everyone in England who is doing interesting work of this character. In view of the amount of capable work continually being produced it is difficult to realise that the only part of this which is important, that which is preparing the art of the next generation, may be the work of a relatively quite small group of artists. I claim, however, that this series includes all those artists in England at the present moment who are working in the direction which alone contains possibilities of development.

Appended to each drawing will be a short note for the benefit of those who are baffled by the abstract character of the work. For this the editor, and not the artist, is alone responsible. You have before you a movement about which there is no crystallised opinion, and consequently have the fun of making your own judgments about the work. You will have, moreover, the advantage of comparing these drawings with the not very exhilarating work of the more traditional school – with those, shall I say, in the series Mr Sickert is editing?

Mr David Bomberg's drawing ['Chinnereth'] contains four upright figures in various attitudes. If you ask why the legs look like cylinders and are not realistically treated, the answer I should give would be this – the pleasure you are intended to take in such a drawing is a pleasure not in representation, but in the relations between certain abstract forms. Take, for example, the figure on the left of the drawing; consider particularly the line which runs up one leg, across the hips and down the other leg. If you take any interest in that form, just as a form, then you will see quite easily that it could not have been given with the same force and directness in a more realistic drawing. The accidental details of representation would have veiled or, better, 'damped down' this directness.

[*The New Age*, 16 April 1914]

This drawing ['Study', by William Roberts] contains four figures. I could point out the position of these figures in more detail, but I think such detailed indication misleading. No artist can create abstract form spontaneously; it is always generated or, at least, suggested by the consideration of some outside concrete shapes. But such shapes are only interesting if you want to explain the psychology of the process of composition in the artist's mind. The interest of the drawing itself depends on the forms it contains. The fact that such forms were suggested by human figures is of no importance.

[*The New Age*, 30 April 1914]

Mr Wadsworth's drawing this week ['Farmyard'] suffers somewhat by reproduction, as in the original it is coloured; the light background being yellow and grey, and the dark parts a very dark blue. The lighter parts of the drawing represent three farm buildings grouped round a pool. The space they enclose is concave to the spectator, the middle building being farther back than the two side ones. The darker parts represent the trunks and foliage of a tree standing on a slight mound.

It is interesting to compare this with the previous drawings in this series for it represents a much earlier stage in the process of abstraction. By considering this halfway stage, one can perhaps make this kind of art more comprehensible.

A school of painting is often interested in and emphasises one aspect of nature to the exclusion of others; but, though a painting may only pick out one of the hundred elements of which a natural scene consists, yet enough trace of the other ninety-nine remains in the picture for one to be able to recognise it as a representation. In impressionism, though the chief emphasis is on light and colour, yet the other elements – shape, outline, solidity, etc. – though not emphasised, do appear to an extent sufficient to make the picture a recognisable representation. (Though the first time the simple man sees an impressionist picture he finds it an incoherent chaos, he is as unable to synthesise its elements into a whole as he is those of a Cubist picture.) But a Cubist picture is in slightly different position to an impressionist one, for this reason: Like the impressionist picture, it emphasises one aspect out of many possible ones. But the nature of the element emphasised here – the relations between planes – is such, that emphasis on these relations disintegrates the thing as representation. In a drawing like Mr Wadsworth's this process has not gone far. It is a drawing made before an actual landscape, in which the planes which interested the artist are given in the objects in which they occurred. But it is easy to see how this emphasis on the relation between planes inevitably developed into later cubism, where the planes are given without any representation of the objects which suggested them.

Mr C.R.W. Nevinson's 'Chauffeur' is the study for the picture he exhibited in the London Group. I need not add much to what I said when I criticised it in my notice of that exhibition, except that the elongation of the right side of the face is an attempt to show the distortion produced by light.

A Tory Philosophy[1]

[Published in five instalments in *The Commentator*, 1912. Signed 'Thomas Grattan']

I. The Two Temperaments

It is my aim to explain in this article why I believe in original sin, why I can't stand romanticism, and why I am a certain kind of Tory. In regard to this last I ought to say exactly on what kind of level I am discussing the thing. I am not concerned with any facts or worked-out theories about it, but only with certain sentiments. In any piece of political argument use is made of certain catchwords and phrases, which stand for certain emotions to the believer. They provide the basis which the argument takes for granted; and though they may only appear in the peroration, yet they really provide the emotional background behind everything.

It is instructive in this connection to note the method by which the Boxers in the last Chinese rebellion made converts to their side. A messenger was sent to some remote inland village. Arrived there, he gathered round him all the inhabitants, and taught them to repeat after him certain phrases, which were called 'words of power'. He kept them repeating these phrases the whole of the evening until they had worked themselves up into a state of frenzy and excitement, which was sufficiently great to give them courage to dash out and kill the people they could not stand. Political parties in this country make use of similar 'words of power'.

Generally, these phrases are only 'alive' to one side. To the other they appear to be mere empty clichés. What I am trying to do in this article is to set out the kind of emotion which vivifies for me certain expressions which to you, if you are progressives, appear to be shrivelled up and empty, meaning nothing; and at the same time to pick out the sentiments on your side which appear to me to be loathsome and disgusting.

I think that I am justified in spending time over these sentiments, because they are the really important and deciding factors. Your theories in this subject are in the last resort merely the expression of your prejudices. To illustrate this by an analogy; if you wanted to investigate the cause of the peculiar route taken by a certain railway, it would be useless to go into the general principles which should govern the laying down of such railways. It would be a waste of time to seek for the cause, as it were, inside the subject itself. What you would have to do would be to find out what particular landlord refused to have railways on his property at any price, and what others consented, at a price. The shape of the railway would then, to a great extend, depend on the varying prejudices through which it had to pass. This, then, is the point of view I adopt in this paper. It can be put more academically in Renan's phrase, 'Philosophies and theories of politics are nothing in the last resort, when they are analysed out, but the affirmation of a temperament'; or in Nietzsche's more theatrical manner, 'Philosophy is autobiography.'

I am simply trying, then, to pick out certain contrasts in temperament. It might be urged that this is not a very hopeful attitude for any one to take who wants to 'convince' anybody. If one's theories in politics and in these other matters are simply the expression of one's fundamental prejudices, it would seem perfectly hopeless to argue with anyone about such things. But argument may have, however, one result. It is quite possible, under the influence of a certain environment, that a man may adopt a theory which is not at all the expression of his own prejudices; his own prejudices may even be hidden from him. By picking out these prejudices and showing that they have a natural expression in a completely worked-out attitude in all kinds of subjects, it is quite possible to convert a man.

You are in reality setting out to convert someone under the most promising circumstances. You do not propose to convert him, but only, to attempt to aid him, to change himself. You attempt solely to remove a certain veil which hides the man's own real position from himself. The influence of the present environment is so strong, its mere power of suggestion is so powerful, that a man may find himself advocating, with a certain enthusiasm, opinions which are in reality the exact contrary of those to which his own character would naturally take him. In more detail the method to be adopted in the removal of this veil is this. The type we are considering differs from other types in that a consistently worked-out theory has a strong attraction for it. It only finds at the present moment such a theoretical development on one side in politics. It does not suspect that the same consistency can be found on the other side. If you can present it with the developed theory of this other side, it will then be in the most favourable position for suddenly discovering its own inner sentiments. Previously its attraction for theories was such that, not finding one on this side, it was unable even to perceive its own prejudices. When you have led a man to perceive his own inside preferences in this way it is possible that you will produce not only a difference in his political view, but a series of reversals of judgment on a great variety of activities, for the detailed judgments in those other subjects being in reality only the manifestations of his prejudices, a change in prejudice will change the judgments everywhere.

I am trying to maintain, then, that behind the opposed attitudes, and one can take up a great many different subjects, from politics to art, lie two contrasted sets of prejudices and sentiments, two different points of view as to the nature of man, which I am calling the romantic and the classical.

It might be objected that I have no business to use words which have by now such an extraordinarily vague meaning. I justify myself in the first place by pointing out that it so happens that Lasserre, Maurras, etc., the people who have done most work on this particular aspect of political theory, have happened, as a matter of fact, to employ these two words, and it seems convenient for me to follow them, as I shall later on have frequent occasion to refer to them and to quote them. I could justify myself in the second place in this way. It seems to me that in the history of such words there are three stages. In the first and earliest stage a word has a definite and precise meaning. You are certainly justified in using it, then. After this there comes a period when the word has about a dozen meanings. At this stage it is dangerous, and should be left alone. But, finally, you get to the stage when it has three hundred meanings. It has then once again become useful and innocuous, for no one will have any preconceived notion of what it means, and will attentively wait to see exactly the shade of meaning, and the sense, which you yourself intend to give it. Their minds are in the receptive state; they are prepared to receive once again an accurate impression from a word. Now the words 'classic' and 'romantic' have, after their long history from their first use by Goethe, at last reached this stage; and as I am prepared to give precise and accurate definitions, I think that I am justified in using them.

I want to give first a kind of Euclidean demonstration of the difference between these two attitudes. It will sound rather artificial, but I want simply to show the connection between the sets of adjectives one uses to describe the difference when it becomes more concrete. It is a kind of criticism of categories; it is not meant at this stage to refer to anything real.

The 'classical' point of view I take to be this. Man is by his very nature essentially limited and incapable of anything extraordinary. He is incapable of attaining any kind of perfection, because, either by nature, as the result of original sin, or the result of evolution, he encloses within him certain antinomies. There is a war of instincts inside him, and it is part of his permanent characteristics that this must always be so. The future condition of man, then, will always be one of struggle and limitation. The best results can only be got out of man as the result of a certain discipline which introduces order into this internal anarchy. That is what Aristotle meant by saying that only a god or a beast could live outside the State. Nothing is bad in itself except disorder; all that is put in order in a hierarchy is good. Moreover, man being by nature constant, the kind of discipline which will get the best out of him, and which is necessary for him, remains much the same in every generation. The classical attitude, then, has a great respect for the past and for tradition, not from sentimental, but on purely rational grounds. It does not expect anything radically new, and does not believe in any real progress.

In art this spirit shows itself in the belief that there are certain rules which one must obey, which do not in themselves give us the capacity for producing anything, but in which the experience of several generations of artists has traced the limits outside which one can produce nothing solid or excellent. The idea of a personal inspiration jumping all complete from nature, capable of creating, by a kind of divine act, the whole organism of adaptable means of expression, is ridiculous to it. 'The root of classicism is this, that if the rules are of no value without genius, yet there is in them more of genius than there is in any great genius himself.'

I do not at this stage put this forward as anything more than a kind of game. I do not ask you to admit that it is a true account of anything. I merely say that, supposing it is true, it does join up together in some kind of logical sequence all the epithets that one naturally uses in expressing a certain attitude, such as 'order', 'discipline', 'tradition', and the rest of it.

Most people have been in the habit of associating these kinds of views with Nietzsche. It is true that they do occur in him, but he made them so frightfully vulgar that no classic would acknowledge them. In him you have the spectacle of a romantic seizing on the classic point of view because it attracted him purely as a theory, and who, being a romantic, in taking up this theory, passed his slimy fingers over every detail of it. Everything loses its value. The same idea of the necessary hierarchy of classes, with their varying capacities and duties, gets turned into the romantic nonsense of the two kinds of morality, the slave and the master morality, and every other element of the classic position gets transmuted in a similar way into something ridiculous.

The 'romantic' point of view is the exact opposite of this. It does not think that man is by nature bad, turned into something good by a certain order and discipline, but that, on the contrary, man is something rather wonderful, and that so far he has been prevented from exhibiting any wonderful qualities by these very restrictions of order and discipline that the classic praised. You get the most famous expression of it, of course, in Rousseau. I quote from one of his letters: 'The fundamental principle of all morality is that man is a being naturally loving justice. In *Emile* I have endeavoured to show how vice and error, foreign to the natural constitution of man, have been introduced from outside, and have insensibly altered him.'

When one has this conception of the infinite possibilities of man thus imprisoned, one is carried on to the conception that anything that increases man's freedom will be to his benefit. This attitude shows a certain impatience of tradition, for it thinks that tradition is only a hampering restriction which prevents the greater possibilities of man appearing. It gets a certain amount of generous emotion out of its destructive work. It has faith and ardour and awakes great hopes. In freeing mankind from tradition and discipline it imagines that it is preparing a new age. One can see most clearly its contrast with the classical point of view in literature. The romantic imagines everything is accomplished by the breaking of rules. The romantics of 1830 thought that they had, by freeing themselves from rules and traditions, attained liberty, that is to say, absolute spontaneity in artistic creation.

While the classic thinks that certain effects are got in certain fixed ways, the romantic persists in trying to get them in an absolutely new way. He is so compelled to search for interest in novelty, and in the pursuit of extraordinary subjects, of the exotic. It is in this way one can see how the definition of romantic I have given enables one by a process of deduction to pass from it to the more usual and derivative uses of the word. Take the matter to which it was first applied. The romantic movement in poetry started with the cult of Ossian and the old ballads, i.e., something exotic and strange to the eighteenth-century people. In them they found a different, a supernatural, and heightened conception of man, and it was that which makes any movement properly a romantic one.

In however many ways these two points of view differ, you can always in the end trace it back to this quite simple difference in their conception of the nature of man.

In order to avoid one misunderstanding in the use of the word classic, certain historical remarks should be made. What Taine called the classical spirit of the early eighteenth century was not classical, because it used the word 'reason' in a romantic way. Diderot and the encyclopaedists generally were romantics, in my sense of the word, because, like the modern political romantic, they despised tradition and thought that man in 'reason' possessed a kind of divine faculty which would enable him to alter his own nature into something better than had yet ever existed.

There is always at the back of any romanticism a certain characteristic sentiment, a certain kind of exhilaration. In fact, I should define a romantic as a person who was in a certain disordered state of mental health in which he can only remain sane by taking repeated doses of this kind of emotion. It is the kind of exhilaration you get from a sudden sense of release from weight, the sense of lightness and exhilaration you would get from rarer air. It is a necessity of your existence that you should go on believing that something wonderful and extraordinary can and is about to happen to man.

Just as in looking at the shading of a line drawing there is a certain distance at which the lines vanish and look like a wash, so in reading certain books there may come a point, if you are in this state, at which the definite contours of the ideas you are following melt away into this kind of exhilaration I have just been taking about. It betrays itself in certain clichés, 'breaking down barriers', freedom, emancipation, and the rest of it; but, above all, it betrays itself in the epithet NEW. One must believe that there is a NEW art, a NEW religion, even a NEW age.

To make the thing as concrete and as local as possible, however, I will quote a couple of sentences which seem to me to give you the whole secret of the psychology of romanticism: 'The spirit of man will go on its way with songs, and the burden of its most triumphant song will always be, "My soul is escaped like a bird out of the net of the fowler. The snare is broken, and we are delivered."' That's what the romantic is, somebody who is always just about to escape from something. Always 'escaping', that is it!

The important thing, for the purposes of getting at the exact emotion excited by romanticism, is to recognise that it isn't that it wants to escape from anything in particular, but just that it shall ESCAPE.

I am trying to define this emotion exactly, because it is only by doing so that I can avoid misunderstanding in getting at what I consider to be romanticism in politics. I have said that it is associated with the idea of progress, but the word progress can mean two quite different things. It can in the first case mean the metaphysical notion of automatic progress, the kind of thing you get in Hegel and Fourier. In that sense it is, of course, easily recognised as romanticism; but it is quite possible for anyone to retort that this has no necessary connection with what is generally known as the progressive side in politics. All that we believe they might say is that a certain progress can be achieved if we bring it about by definite effort. We don't believe that it is automatic. The answer to this is that, as a matter of actual fact, the real thing that does supply the enthusiasm which brings about certain changes, the emotion that you can actually observe at work, is the religious belief in absolute and inevitable progress. That, and not the more limited belief, is what you find in the propaganda of the side. I quote a typical example of the kind of thing I mean from Dr Clifford's address on New Year's Eve: 'The soul of the world aspires and yearns for the highest and the best.'

Having now defined this difference of temperament, I shall endeavour in the next article to show the exact difference that the change from one to the other would probably make in one's political views.

II. Programme

At the end of my last article I had roughly outlined the difference between the two temperaments that I considered were at the root of the pairs of contrasted attitudes and parties which one finds in a series of subjects ranging from politics to art. Let me recall for a moment my object in doing this, and the exact nature of the aim that I am pursuing in these articles. I am dealing with the question of 'conviction', and, more precisely, with that of 'conversion'. All that any argument can do, I urged, was to develop the consequences of some first position, which itself rests on nothing further, but which is an arbitrarily assumed basis. A dispute, then, between two persons, in which the reasoning is correct and logical, would always end in a definite result one way or the other; one of the parties to the dispute would find that he had been in the wrong. We know, as a matter of fact, that disputes do not have this logical conclusion; it is very seldom that any effect is produced by reasoning at all. What is the reason of this? Simply this, that the parties to the dispute start from different premises, the premises being the things which they take for granted as requiring no proof. If you started from the same premises and committed no errors of logic, you would infallibly finish by agreeing. The only employment for reasoning in these matters seems, then, to be in the extremely small field provided by those people who have mistakenly drawn the wrong conclusion from the same premises as you yourself start from. The number of people that you could convert from this cause is extremely small, and it is from not recognising this that most political polemic is so barren of result. Logical reasoning is simply a means of passing from a certain premise to certain conclusions. It has in itself no motive power at all. It is quite impotent to deal with those first premises. It is a kind of building art; it tells you how to construct a house on a given piece of ground, but it will not choose the ground where you build. That is decided by things outside its scope altogether. This enables me to fix the kind of purpose I have in mind in these articles. I am simply conducting an investigation of these 'premises'. Every man has inside himself a kind of rock on which he builds. I am concerned entirely with these rocks. I do believe that it is possible by getting down to the root of the matter in this way to conduct an attempt at political 'conversion', which shall not be entirely barren, but only in this way can it be done. I concluded the article which set out what I thought were the two contrasted temperaments and sets of prejudices on which political belief is ultimately based by saying that I would then endeavour to trace out the detailed consequences which would be produced in your beliefs as the result of the discovery that you did in reality start from a different base, and that your most fundamental prejudice was in reality different from what you had supposed it to be. (It would more accurately describe the process to say that you, for the first time, made the effort necessary to discover that you had such a basis, and then found that the development of that basis led you to the opposite side from that which you had formerly supposed yourself to be on.) What, then, would be the detailed consequences of a change from the romantic to the classical point of view? Following the natural slope down from your new starting- point, to what actual difference of opinion are you led? What different sets of catchwords do you respond to in political discussion? What phrases become alive to you, and what others which firmly moved you now turn into dead clichés?

I shall endeavour to answer this question by dealing in each article with that particular aspect of, and deduction from, the general contrast between the two attitudes which is embodied in each of the following pairs of contrasted epithets.

(1) 'Constancy and Progress'. – A history of the idea of progress, from the time of Turgot and Condorcet, through Saint Simon, down to its present use by the Socialists, tracking its pernicious and disastrous influence on political thought and action.

(2) 'Order, Authority, and Liberty'. – A discussion of the principles (as distinct from opportunist dodges) which ought to govern the action of the State during strike disturbances, etc.

(3) 'Equality and Hierarchy'. – A discussion of the Tory view of education, and an attack on the present disastrous democratic conception of it (together with an account of the French Syndicalist, Georges Sorel who, strangely enough, takes the Tory view).

(4) 'Nationalism and Universalism'. – An attack on universalism, not on the ground that nationalities do, as a matter of regrettable

though actual fact, still exist, but because it is desirable even on abstract grounds that they should.

Of this list two things can be said. All the contrasts in it can be shown to follow logically from the fundamental difference of attitude I started with. Also that the working out of the details does provide a set of Tory principles which are consistent with each other, and from which consistent judgments can be passed on the various matters which form the actual subject matter of modern political thinking. It is this kind of theoretical basis of conviction which is lacking to the average Conservative – at any rate, to the average Conservative leader. In his actions he opposes the progressives in that he wants to turn them out and obtain office for himself, but in his ideals he seems indistinguishable from them. He talks in many cases exactly as if he were a Socialist. He does so because he is not in reality a Tory at all. He has not the firm conviction which springs from a thought-out attitude, which enables one to judge matters of detail from the standpoint provided by certain principles.

We have been beaten, to a certain extent, because our enemies' theories have conquered us. We have played with those to our own undoing. Not until we are hardened again by conviction of the sort I have been talking about are we likely to do any good. In accepting the theories of the other side, we are merely repeating a well-known historical phenomenon. The Revolution in France came about, not so much because the forces which should have resisted were half-hearted in their resistance. They themselves had been conquered, intellectually, at any rate, by the theories of the revolutionary side. It was because the classes who were enthusiastic about Rousseau had not enough grip of reality to see that they were accepting ideas which would ultimately make for their own undoing that the Revolution was so successful. (Incidentally, one may note as typical of the curious ways in which these theories had penetrated the ruling classes, that the 'return to Nature', which was so popular in the form of shepherdesses' parties at the Court, and exemplified in the pictures of the time was merely Rousseauism – that is, the ideals which made against authority and for liberty – in another form.)

However, for the proper working out of my argument I must for the moment leave the detailed exposition of these principles. It is necessary if one is to be effective, so far as conversion goes, to get at, first of all, as accurately as possible, the exact contours of the prejudice from which one starts. So for the present let us leave this worked-out plan, to consider the sentiment which is at the root of the differences exhibited in that plan.

I stated that difference of prejudice is a difference in the conception one forms of the nature of man. Is it constant, or is man capable of development and progress into something much less limited and more perfect than at present? The Tory side, I asserted, depends on the conviction that the nature of man is absolutely fixed and unalterable, and that any scheme of social regeneration which presupposes that he can alter is doomed to bring about nothing but disaster. This conception of the constancy of man, which he may arrive at by way of induction from history, or by introspection and inner observation, which reveals what is and must be the characteristics of man's nature, is the basis of his whole belief. But the question may then be put, and must be answered before anything else can be done, 'What exactly do you mean by the constant nature of man? He appears, superficially at any rate, to change in every generation. In what sense do you conceive him to be constant?'

After that comes the further problem, which is really getting at the root of the matter as far as my argument is concerned: What is it which makes a man contemplate the idea of a constant world with such repugnance, so that he insists, in spite of all evidence, in believing that progress is continuous, and that man may and does change? At this stage I shall be getting at the sentiment which is at the root of all the evil.

To start with the first question. We must make the idea of constancy a little more precise. What is meant is not that man does not change at all, but that it is impossible that he should change in the remarkable way which would justify that particular kind of emotion I defined as 'romantic', the emotion of 'escaping'. I could get a crude kind of picture of the way I consider man is constant in this kind of way. Various instincts seem to me to be mixed up in him, as valuable metal might be in an ore. But the metaphor is inaccurate, because you can extract the ore. If you suppose an ore of such a kind of sticky nature that the whole thing held together and so was of fixed and unalterable composition, then you would get an accurate picture of what one intends. You are firmly convinced that nothing extraordinary in the way of change or improvement could happen to man, simply for this reason, that he is by nature made of this fixed composition. It is this kind of assurance of his nature that makes you impatient of the kind of enthusiasm that the romantic is always getting up about the 'future of man', and which makes it seem vulgar. I suppose it is all summed up in the profound truth that no man can be a hero to his valet. The modern romantic tends to put his heroes in the future, for, by the nature of things, no man can valet that.

Of course, man is capable of a certain kind of progress. He builds up sciences and civilisation, but the progress is here rather one of accumulation than of alteration in capacity. There is no necessary difference in mental capacity between a man driving a steam engine and a man driving a wooden plough, and progress in thought is exactly of the same kind; and though man has developed more complex mental conceptions and ways of dealing with things, the capacity which uses them remains the same. It is necessary in considering this question to make this division between intellectual 'capacity' and its 'content' – the number of conceptions which it can use. If you compare the intellect to a sponge, it is easy to see that the sponge can be empty or full of water, without its 'capacity' being altered. From the moment that the human species has been constituted, its intellectual possibilities were fixed at the same time. At the beginning of its career the white race was capable of genius in the same proportion as it is now, and the average intellectual capacity of a tribe in the Stone Age was probably exactly the same as any modern village at the present time.

This constancy is, of course, only true as far as capacity goes. As far as the content of the mind goes, the number of conceptions it can manipulate or is familiar with, there certainly is progress.

The important point to notice here is, so far as the point I am now trying to make is concerned, that this doesn't matter. In order that you shall be able to get the kind of emotion, either in politics associated with the kind of religious enthusiasm about progress, or that which in literature you call Romanticism, it is necessary that you should believe that man can change in a very different way to this. It is necessary to believe in a change of capacity.

I am, of course, only treating the question of intellectual constancy as an analogy for the case of moral constancy. Just the same holds good for that set of qualities, instincts, and prejudices which go to make up man's constitution as a member of society and a political unit. Any plan which supposes that his ethical standard can be raised, or that he can contain a less percentage of egoism, is building on sand.

The question might, by opponents, be forced out of the plane of sentiment and on to that of fact. They would triumphantly assert that man had evolved from the brute, and that there was no reason to suppose that the evolution had finished. There is no reason, they might say, why we should not suppose that selfishness will be gradually eliminated and a new kind of man, better fitted to live in the Socialist Utopia, be evolved. This is, of course, mere supposition; but the objection can be met on its own ground. It rests on an antiquated theory of evolution. There is hardly I suppose, one biologist left in Europe who could be described as an orthodox Darwinian. If you are a Darwinian, you suppose that each step in evolution has come gradually, by an accumulation of favourable small variations. If that were true, then it would be possible to conceive that man himself might, by the accumulation of such variations, gradually change into something better. But the theory of evolution which is now gradually accepted is that of De Vries. His Mutation theory gives quite a different account of the origin of species. It supposes that each new species came into existence in one big variation, as a kind of 'sport', and, that once constituted, a species remains absolutely constant. There would then be no hope at all of progress for man. Each race of man once having come into existence, is created with a certain mental and moral capacity, which is fixed from the moment of its creation, and never changes or increases.

There is another feature of De Vries' theory which might be noticed here, as it will be important later in considering the question of equality and hierarchy. 'Not only', he says, 'is the average level of each species absolutely constant, but the percentage of slight variations in different directions also remains constant.'

To pass from these biological suppositions to the consideration of the sentiment which prompts a man to escape from the acceptance of constancy at all costs. What is this hidden prejudice which insists that a man shall believe in progress? Here we are getting at the irreducible prejudice from which everything else springs.

This sentiment, then, putting it in the most abstract way possible, is this: the modern mind (if the expression may be permitted) is unable to support with equanimity the idea of an absolutely constant world, and any account of romanticism comes to nothing, in the end, but an examination of the various ways in which the mind wriggles away from constancy. To prove that this shrinking from the idea of constancy does exist, I give three quotations.

I may say that I quote from these people, not because I consider them of the slightest importance, but simply because other people seem to, that is, they represent a very widespread state of mind.

The first thing I have in mind is the opening chapter of Wells' *Modern Utopia*. It commences, as far as I remember, by satirising all previous Utopias, for this reason, that when they had attained their perfect state, they expected it to go on for ever in the same constant state of perfection, one generation following another, until the gods were sick of it. Any Utopia which would satisfy him would not have to be constant. You can see the man perfectly appalled at the idea of a constant state of society. At any rate, a constant state of society could not possibly be fitted in his mind with any ideal. His own Utopia would have to be dynamic. It is a very curious thing, the number of people who are obsessed by the word dynamic. Everything must be dynamic, even publishers' advertisements. Nobody knows exactly what it means, but that doesn't matter; it is your only epithet. There are other words of this kind. There was once a lady, the terror of my life, who used to take me aside in drawing-rooms, and whisper, 'Don't you think everything is vibration?' And now there is a whole set of people who live on the word 'rhythm'. They have a paper. If you look at rhythm in the dictionary, you find it means regular repetition. That doesn't seem particularly exciting in itself, but, in spite of that, every-thing must be rhythm, and so it will be, I suppose, for the next five years. It's all part of one phenomenon. There must be one word in the language spelt in capital letters. For a long time, and still for sane people, the word was God. Then one became bored with the letter 'G', and went on to 'R', and for a hundred years it was Reason, and now all the best people take off their hats and lower their voices when they speak of Life. The Deities' wanderings about the alphabet would make an interesting Odyssey.

However, to get back to the point. When you meet people who have got 'dynamic' on the brain in this way, you simply know that they are suffering from this modern disease, the horror of constancy.

I will take a more definite expression of the same feeling. In the *Hibbert Journal* a good many years ago Mr Lowes Dickinson published a paper on what he considered were the three necessary conditions for an optimist. It was necessary that the world should be progressing in a certain direction, that we personally should be able to help that purpose, and, finally, that we should be able to go on helping that purpose, that we should be in some way immortal. The childlike simplicity of this is almost pathetic. It is like a toy steam engine.

I just quote this, because it seems to me to show this same modern nervousness and horror of the idea of constancy. You must believe in progress if your mind is to maintain its equilibrium.

My third example, which is rather different, is from Mr Benn's book on 'Greek Philosophy'. He is describing Aristotle's views, and, by his manner of doing so, conveys an impression of the extraordinary way in which they surprised him.

He did not, like the Ionian physiologists, anticipate in outline our theories of evolution. He held that the cosmos had always been, by the strictest necessity, arranged in the same manner; the starry revolutions never changing, the four elements preserving a constant balance, the earth always solid, land and water always distributed according to their present proportions, living species transmitting the same unalterable type through an infinite series of generations, the human race enjoying an eternal duration, but from time to time losing all its conquests in some great physical catastrophe, and obliged to begin over again with the depressing consciousness that nothing could be devised that had not been thought of an infinite number of times already, and the existing distinctions between men and women grounded on the everlasting necessities of nature. He did not hope, like Plato, for the regeneration of the race by enlightened thought.

I am not concerned at all with the truth of this conception of the world. I am only concerned with its effects on Mr Benn's emotions. It is obvious that, like Mr Dickinson and Mr Wells, he couldn't stand the idea of a world of this kind. It appeared to him a kind of nightmare. In fact, he gets quite rhetorical and abusive about it. He comments: 'It seemed as if philosophy, abdicating her high function and obstructing the powers which she had first opened, were now content to systematise the forces of prejudice, blindness, immobility, and despair.'

This quotation brings to the sharpest focus the difference between the two attitudes. It is easy to see here that it is this repugnance to the idea of fixity which is at the bottom of a great many political ideals. But if you once face this repugnance in its nakedest form, you will find that it vanishes. Why should the idea of a constant, continuous, and endless progress be any more rational or satisfactory than the idea of constancy? Either the progress attains its end (when it is finished with), or it never attains its end, and then it is still more irrational; for progress towards an end which constantly recedes cannot be said to be a satisfactory view of the world-process. If you can only release yourself from this obsession by the words 'dynamic' and 'change', you will find that there is nothing absurd or repugnant in the notion of a constant world, in which there is no progress. But here the question verges on a philosophical one, which is outside the scope of this paper, and which I have treated elsewhere in book form.

It is quite as easy and natural for emotion and enthusiasm to crystallise round the idea of a constant world as round the idea of progress. An extraordinary solidarity is given to one's beliefs. There is great consolation in the idea that the same struggles have taken place in each generation, and that men have always thought as we think now. It gives to religion a great stability, for it exhibits it as a permanent part of man's nature, and the nature of man being constant, it places these beliefs beyond all change. All the pleasure that one takes in old literature comes from the fact that it gives us this strange emotion of solidarity, to find that our ancestors were of like nature with ourselves.

This concludes the abstract part of my argument. I have tried to show that an opposite sentiment to the one which provides the motive force of romanticism is possible. I have now to show the detailed consequences to which this leads in the shape of the four antitheses which I gave in a previous issue.

Translator's Preface to Georges Sorel's *Reflections on Violence*[1]

[Georges Sorel, *Reflections on Violence*, translated with an introduction by T.E. Hulme (London: George Allen and Unwin, 1916)]

> ... que si par impossible, la nature avait fait de l'homme un animal exclusivement industrieux et sociable, et point guerrier, il serait tombé, dès le premier jour, au niveau des bêtes dont l'association forme toute la destinée; il aurait perdu, avec l'orgueil de son héroïsme, sa faculté révolutionnaire, la plus merveilleuse de toutes, et la plus féconde. Vivant en communauté pure, notre civilization serait une étable... Philanthrope, vous parlez d'abolir la guerre, prenez garde de dégrader le genre humain... PROUDHON[2]

Nearly all the criticism of Sorel's work goes wrong, not so much in details as in its complete inability to understand its main motive; the sympathetic accounts being as irritating and as wide of the mark as the others.

What exactly is the nature of this general miscomprehension? In a movement like Socialism we can conveniently separate out two distinct elements, the working-class movement itself and the system of ideas which goes with it (though the word is ugly, it will be convenient to follow Sorel and call a system of ideas an *ideology*). If we call one (I) and the other (W), (I + W) will be the whole movement. The ideology is, as a matter of fact, *democracy*.[a] Now the enormous difficulty in Sorel comes in this – that he not only denies the essential connection between these two elements, but even asserts that the ideology will be fatal to the movement. The regeneration of society will never be brought by the pacifist *progressives*.

They may be pardoned then if they find this strange. This combi-

---

a. *Democracy* – the word is not used here either (1) as a general name for the working-class movement or (2) to indicate the true doctrine that all men are equal. It is not used then in its widest sense as indicating opposition to all aristocratic, oligarchic or class government, but in a narrower sense, to recall which I have always put the word in italics. Liberal might be a better word, were it not that the Socialists, while proclaiming their difference from liberalism in policy, at the same time adopt the whole liberal *ideology*; and though they do not acknowledge it to be liberal, they will recognise it under the label *democratic*.

nation of doctrines which they would probably call reactionary, with
revolutionary syndicalism, is certainly very disconcerting to liberal
Socialists. It is difficult for them to understand a revolutionary who is
anti-democratic, an absolutist in ethics, rejecting all rationalism and
relativism, who values the mystical element in religion 'which will
never disappear', speaks contemptuously of modernism and *progress,*
and uses a concept like *honour* with no sense of unreality.[b]

As a rule such sentiments, when the *democrat* meets with them, are
conveniently dismissed as springing from a disguised attempt to
defend the interest of wealth. But this obviously will not fit the case of
Sorel. There is then some danger of a foreign body lodging itself inside
the system of democratic thought. The latter deals with this irritant
very much as one would expect. It calls to its aid the righteous indig-
nation which every *real progressive* must feel at the slightest suspicion
of anything *reactionary*. Instead of considering the details of the actual
thesis, the *progressive* prefers to discredit it by an imagined origin.
Sorel's attitude is thus attributed to mysticism, to neo-royalism, or to
some confused and sentimental reaction against Reason. This
summary dismissal is accompanied by a distinct feeling of relief. 'You
see there is nothing in it. It is only our old adversaries in a new
disguise.' The people who make this kind of criticism are clearly inca-
pable of understanding the main thesis of the book. The misunder-
standing will be very stubborn. How can it be removed?

The first step is to note more exactly the feelings of the simple-
minded democrat towards this thesis. His behaviour may indicate the
source of his repugnance, and give some hints as to its removal. What
he mostly feels, I suppose, is a kind of exasperation. He cannot take the
anti-democratic view seriously. He feels just as if some one had denied
one of the laws of thought, or asserted that two and two are five. In his
natural state, of course, he never thinks of the movement as composed
of two elements (I + W). It is one undivided whole for him. When,
however, the denial of the connection between I and W forces the

---

b. An *ideology* naturally includes a system of sentiments. In this respect the book is even
more confusing to the democrat than in that of ideas. The divergence in sentiments is most
striking, however, in what Sorel says about the feelings of envy and retaliation as the basis of
liberal *democracy*. A careful analysis of this sentiment and its historical connection with
democracy can be found in Max Scheler's *Über Ressentiment u. Werttheorie.*

separate existence of (I) on his notice, he at once thinks of it, not as one possible ideology amongst others, but as an *inevitable* way of thinking, which must necessarily accompany (W) as it accompanies everything.

It is this notion of the *necessary*, the inevitable character of the *democratic* system of ideas, which is here the stumbling-block. It is this which makes him think Sorel's *anti-democratic* position and views *unnatural* or perverse. He has not yet thought of *democracy* as a system at all, but only as a natural and inevitable equipment of the emancipated and instructed man. The ideas which underlie it appear to him to have the *necessary* character of categories. In reality they are, of course, nothing of the kind. They depend on certain fundamental attitudes of the mind, on unexpressed major premises. If he could be made conscious of these premises, the character of inevitability would have been removed. The explanation of how these major premises get into the position of *pseudo-categories* goes a long way towards removing a man from their influence. They are unperceived because they have become so much part of the mind and lie so far back that we are never really conscious of them as ideas at all. We do not see them, but see other things *through* them, and consequently take what we see for the outlines of things themselves. Blue spectacles making a blue world can be pointed out, but not these pseudo-categories which lie, as it were, 'behind the eye'.

All effective propaganda depends then on getting these ideas away from their position 'behind the eye' and putting them facing one as *objects* which we can then consciously accept or reject. This is extremely difficult. Fortunately, however, all ideologies are of gradual growth, and that rare type of historical intelligence which investigates and analyses their origins can help us considerably. Just as a knowledge of the colours extended and separated in the spectrum enables us to distinguish the feebler colours confused together in shadows, so this type of history, by exhibiting certain ideas in a concreter form, existing as it were as objects in time, enables us to distinguish the same ideas, existing in us 'behind the eye' and to bring them to the surface of the mind. Their hidden influence on our opinions then at once disappears, for they have lost their status as categories. This is a violent operation, and the mind is never quite the same afterwards. It has lost a certain virginity. But there are so many of these systems in which we unwittingly 'live and move and have our being' that the process really forms

the major part of the education of the adult. Moreover the historical
method by exhibiting the intimate connection between such concep-
tions – that of *Progress* for example – and certain economical condi-
tions at the time of their invention in the eighteenth century, does
more than anything else to loosen their hold over the mind. It is this
method which Sorel has so successfully applied in *Les Illusions du
progrès* to the particular democratic ideology, with which we are here
concerned.

This *democratic* ideology[c] is about two centuries old. Its history can
be clearly followed, and its logical connection with a parallel move-
ment in literature. It is an essential element in the romantic move-
ment; it forms an organic body of middle-class thought dating from
the eighteenth century, and has consequently no necessary connection
whatever with the working-class or revolutionary movement. Liberal
Socialism is still living on the remains of middle-class thought of the
last century' and when vulgar thought of today is pacifist, rationalist,
and hedonist, and in being so believes itself to be expressing the
inevitable convictions of the instructed and emancipated man, it has all
the pathos of marionettes in a play, dead things gesticulating as though
they were alive. Our younger novelists, like those Roman fountains in
which water pours from the mouth of a human mask, gush as though
spontaneously from the depths of their own being, a muddy romanti-
cism that has in reality come through a very long pipe.

Democratic romanticism is then a body of doctrine with a recognis-
able and determinate history. What is the central attitude from which
it springs, and which gives it continued life? What is the unexpressed
major premiss here?

Putting the matter with the artificial simplicity of a diagram for the
sake of clearness, we might say that romanticism and classical
pessimism differ in their antithetical conception of the nature of man.
For the one, man is by nature good, and for the other, by nature bad.

---

c. The opposed ideology in Sorel can most conveniently be described by thinking of the
qualities of seventeenth as contrasted with eighteenth century literature in France, the
difference, for example, between Corneille and Diderot. Sorel often speaks of Cornelian
virtue. But the antithesis of Classical and Romantic is not enough to make the *Classical*
comprehensible to a *Romantic*; it is necessary to get down to fundamental attitudes from
which the difference really springs.

All romanticism springs from Rousseau,[d] and the key to it can be found even in the first sentence of the *Social Contract* – 'Man is born free, and he finds himself everywhere in chains.' In other words, man is by nature something wonderful, of unlimited powers, and if hitherto he has not appeared so, it is because of external obstacles and fetters, which it should be the main business of social politics to remove.

What is at the root of the contrasted system of ideas you find in Sorel, the classical, pessimistic, or, as its opponents would have it, the reactionary ideology? This system springs from the exactly contrary conception of man; the conviction that man is by nature bad or limited,[e] and can consequently only accomplish any thing of value by disciplines, ethical, heroic, or political. In other words, it believes in Original Sin. We may define Romantics, then, as all who do not believe in the Fall of Man. It is this opposition which in reality lies at the root of most of the other divisions in social and political thought.[f]

d. For a history of the romantic movement in French Literature from this point of view, see Pierre Lasserre's excellent *Le Romantisme français*.

e. This is by no means identical with materialism; rather it is characteristic of the religious attitude – cf. Pascal's *Pensées*. Romanticism confuses both human and divine things by not clearly separating them. The main thing with which it can be reproached is that it blurs the clear outlines of human relations – whether in political thought or in the treatment of sex in literature – by introducing into them the Perfection that properly belongs only to the non-human.

f. Not only here but in philosophy itself; this can be made clear by a parallel. The change of sensibility which has enabled us to appreciate Egyptian, Indian, Byzantine, Polynesian, and Negro work as *art* and not as archaeology or ethnology, has a double effect. While it demonstrates that what were taken for the necessary principles of aesthetics are merely a psychology of Classical and modern European art, it at the same time suddenly forces us to see the essential unity of this art. In spite of apparent variety, European art in reality forms a coherent body of work resting on certain presuppositions, of which we become conscious for the first time when we see them denied by other periods of art (cf. the work of Riegl on Byzantine art). One might say that in the same way, an understanding of the religious philosophy which subordinates man (regarded as part of nature) to certain absolute values – in other words, a realisation of the sense of this dogma – forces us to see that there is a much greater family resemblance between all philosophy since the Renaissance than is ever recognised. The philosophy rests, in reality, on the same presuppositions as the art, and forms a coherent system with it. It seems as if no sooner had Copernicus shown that man was not the centre of the universe, than the philosophers commenced for the first time to prove that he was. You get expressed explicitly, for the first time (in Pico della Mirandola), this idea of the sufficiency of natural man, and it has generally been assumed by all philosophers since. It may be expressed in very different languages and with very different degrees of profundity, but even

From the pessimistic conception of man comes naturally the view that the transformation of society is an heroic task requiring heroic qualities... virtues which are not likely to flourish on the soil of a rational and sceptical ethic. This regeneration can, on the contrary, only be brought about and only be maintained by actions springing from an ethic which from the narrow rationalist standpoint is irrational, being not *relative*, but absolute.[g] The transformation of society is not likely to be achieved as a result of peaceful and intelligent *readjustment* on the part of literary men and politicians. But on the optimistic and romantic view this is quite possible. For the optimistic conception of man leads naturally to the characteristic democratic doctrine of inevitable *Progress*.

An understanding of the classical side of this antithesis entirely removes the strangeness of Sorel's position. But though this tendency can be seen, even in his earlier work (the first book on Socrates maintaining that Socrates represents the decadence in Athens, having introduced expediency and calculation into ethics) – yet his final disillusionment with *democracy* came only after the bitter experience of political events which followed the Dreyfus case. A good part of the book consequently is concerned with people who are to us somewhat obscure. But it should be remembered that these obscure figures all have their counterparts here, and that the drama they figure in is a universal one.

The belief that pacifist democracy will lead to no regeneration of society, but rather to its decadence, and the reaction against romanti-

Hegel and Condorcet are one, from this point of view. Humanism thus really contains the germ of a disease that was bound to come to its full evil development in Romanticism.

It is promising to note signs of the break-up of this period in art, and there are some slight indications of a corresponding anti-humanistic movement in thought and ethics. (G.E. Moore, Duguit, Husserl and 'Phaenomenologie'.)

g. *Virtue* – Without too much exaggeration it might be said that the objective and absolute view of ethics to which Sorel adheres has at the present moment more chance of being understood. There has always been something rather unreal about ethics. In a library one's hand glided over books on that subject instinctively. That is, perhaps, because the only ethical questions that came before parasitical literary men were those of sex, in which (may I be forgiven, being here no disciple of Sorel) there seems very little but expediency, nothing that a man could honestly feel objective. But many sensualists lately have had to make an ethical decision for the first time, and uncomfortably recognise that as there is one one objective thing at least in ethics, so there may be many more.

cism in literature, are naturally common to many different schools. This is the secret, for example, of the sympathy between Sorel and the group of writers connected with *L'Action française* which is so eagerly fastened on by those anxious to discredit him. His *ideology* resembles theirs. Where he differs is in the application he finds for it. He expects a return of the classical spirit through the struggle of the classes.[h] This is the part of his thesis that is concerned with facts, and it would be impertinent on my part to offer any commentary on it. I have been only concerned with certain misapprehensions about the purely theoretical part of the argument.[i] One may note here, however, how he makes the two interact. Given the classical attitude, he tries to prove that its present manifestation may be hoped for in working-class violence, and at the same time the complementary notion that only under the influence of the classical ideal will the movement succeed in regenerating society.

Sorel is one of the most remarkable writers of the time, certainly the most remarkable socialist since Marx; and his influence is likely to increase, for, in spite of the apparently undisturbed supremacy of rationalist hedonism in popular thought, the *absolute* view of ethics which underlies his polemic, is gradually being re-established. A similar combination of the classical ideal with socialism is to be found, it is true, in Proudhon, but Sorel comes at a happier moment. The *ideology* attacked by Proudhon has now reached a fuller development, and its real consequences can be more easily perceived. There are many who begin to be disillusioned with liberal and pacifist *democracy*, while shrinking from the opposed *ideology* on account of its reactionary associations. To these people Sorel, a revolutionary in economics, but classical in ethics, may prove an emancipator.

h. It is this which differentiates Sorel's from other attacks on the democratic *ideology*. Some of these are merely dilettante, having little sense of reality, while others are really vicious, in that they play with the idea of inequality. No theory that is not fully moved by the conception of justice asserting the equality of men, and which cannot offer something to all men, deserves or is likely to have any future.

i. In doing this I have laid a disproportionate emphasis on one aspect of Sorel. I have not endeavoured, however, to give any general account of his work here, but only to remove the most probable cause of misunderstanding. Otherwise, I should have liked to have noted his relations to Marx, Proudhon, and to Vico, and also to have said something of his conception of history, of which Croce has written in the preface to the Italian translation.

A Notebook[1]

[Published in seven instalments in *The New Age*, December 1915 – February 1916]

RISK AND ETHICS. Behind the Liberal pacifists' incapacity to understand the importance of war lies probably this fundamental error. Certain historical accidents – security being the first – have made it difficult for them to grasp the nature of *Risk*; not of the incidental kind, but of Risk as an ultimate thing; they cannot take *certain entirely relative things for absolute*.

This explains two things: more proximately their incapacity to realise the consequences of defeat, and further back the source of the whole *ideology* from which this incapacity springs.

First, the proximate effect: They hypostatise their school atlases, and fail to realise that others do not regard Europe as fixed like arithmetic, but wish to change it; not temporarily and minutely, but permanently and on the large scale, justifying themselves by talk of *dynamic* as opposed to *static* justice. Moreover, regarding democracy, and all the other things for which they care, as grounded in the nature of things, they cannot understand that these can be seriously threatened by an arbitrary irrational cause like war. Their inane confidence rises above details, for they never realise that the best things are *constructions*, full of risk and not *inevitable*.

As for the *ideology*: It is based as a rule on a relativist utilitarian ethics. Why? Because taking relative things for absolute, it has no need of the real absolute. In the shadow of these mountains which are not really mountains, it lives securely and comfortably, finding a sufficient support in a sceptical rationalism. Individuals in a condition of danger, when these pseudo-absolutes melt away into a flux, require once more a real absolute, to enable them to live. While this may be admitted as a fact, it may be explained away by saying: 'This occasional and abnormal state requires a temporary but unreal consolation, as men when ill require medicine. It is natural that the sailor should be superstitious, that each ship in Pierre Loti's *Icelanders* should carry a Madonna. In a state of flux rafts are required, but not on dry land.' Or they might give as a parallel Pascal's advice to the sceptic on the remedy for unbelief: 'There are people who know the way ... follow the way by which they began ... by acting as if they believed ... taking the holy water, having masses said ... this will make you believe and *deaden your acuteness.*' But this is always misrepresented. It is *not pragmatism*, you are not to deaden your *natural acuteness*, but the false and artificial acuteness of an artificial condition. Living in a sceptical atmosphere, you are in an unnatural attitude which prevents you seeing objective truth. Taking the holy water, the attempt to assume another artificial attitude, will at least break up the first state, and, making your mind a *tabula rasa*, will enable you to see the truth as it is objectively, independent entirely, of your attitudes.

The same is true of security and ethics. It is not by way of *privation* that danger makes us believe in absolute ethics, but that danger *liberates* – by making us see the relativity of the things we took to be fixed.

THE EXIT. I put forward the contents of this note not as true but as a passage from a false to a true opinion. I at one time thought that the pragmatists, relativists, and humanists were right, and that all the 'ideal' sciences, logic, mathematics, ethics, etc., could all have meaning and validity only, in reference to the human mind; that the laws of thought were the ways in which the human mind *had* to think, that ethics was the way in which men must behave if they were to live together, etc. Moreover, since man is the result of a long evolution in which accident must have played a considerable part, there is nothing *inevitable* about these actual characteristics of the human mind. If the path of evolution had been different, the categories which govern our thinking would have been different.

I could now give any of the accepted refutations of the falsity of this position; in the matter of logic, for example, those in the first volume of Husserl's *Logische Untersuchungen*. But as I said at the beginning, that is not my object in this note. I am only concerned here with a very much smaller matter, the means by which I did actually grope my way out of this error. I began to put the matter to myself in this way – The human mind is not merely the mind of man, it is *mind* itself, as it must always be; not human mind but 'it'. Take the kind of example a relativist might give: life on a supposed planet of which chlorine formed the surrounding atmosphere. If life could exist under such conditions it would obviously be very different from life as we know it, but if it managed to produce the highest type, the mental characteristics of this type would exactly resemble those of men, for they would be the inevitable characteristics of all *mind*. Many would admit this in a matter like arithmetic. They would probably admit that if [in] the chlorine men thought arithmetically they would think that 'two and two were four', but I think it would also be true of almost every other side of the mind. It would be true of their ethics and even of their affections. There are certain statements about the difference, for example, between such apparently human and relative things as 'love' and 'sympathy' which would also be absolutely true of the affections of the imaginary men.

To turn back again for a moment to the picture of the 'lines' of evolution leading up to man; lines which might have had many different shapes. If you drop lead pellets down a funnel, the paths of each of the pellets will be different, but they all finish up in the same place, the tube to which the funnel narrows; for that is the only *exit*. In the same way one can say that whatever the lines of evolution that lead up to man might have been, the result would always have been the same, for *man is the only exit from the animal world*.

These very crude conceptions, constitute, at any rate, a first step away from subjectivism, though they still remain tainted with it. The fact asserted is true, but the explanation given 'for it is not human mind but mind itself' is false, having exactly the subjectivism of the Kantian philosophy.

MAN AS A FALLEN ANGEL. That philosopher was called the 'melancholy' who taught that all things are in a flux; and certainly nothing is so depressing as incapacity to arrive at a fixed opinion. 'If only', a philosopher might say, 'I could for once feel in my own subject, the absolute conviction that accompanies my belief that Free Trade principles are rubbish. The further away from the centre the subject lies, the solider my conviction seems; and I intensely dislike having a hard circumference and a fluid hub.' If one wishes to luxuriate in this feeling, to heighten it artificially, one cannot do better than read through the back numbers of a philosophical review. I remember one occasion, when failing to find an article I was looking for, and depressed by the museum dome, I let myself drift aimlessly through the controversies of three years. When the last ounce of solidity seemed thus to melt away in the universal deliquescence, the thing became a horror, and I had to rescue myself. I drew up a list of

antitheses, of perpetual subjects of dispute, on each of which I had
convictions, based on a *brutal* act of assertion, which no argument
could touch. These were solid rock, whatever might be the extent of
the flux elsewhere.

* * *

The first of these assertions was: 'There is an absolute difference
between men and animals. It is impossible to completely explain the
nature of man, as a complex development out of the animal world.'

This is perhaps best understood when it is taken as the crucial
instance of a number of parallel assertions of a similar type; assertions
which depend on the answer to this question: 'Can all the phenomena
we are accustomed to call "higher" be explained as *complexes* of
"lower" elements?' For the empirical philosophy this is so, and in
every subject it tends to pursue the same kind of explanation. All
'height' for it, then, is of the type of the pyramid, a more or less elabo-
rate *construction* of 'lower' elements. For another philosophy, however,
the 'higher' phenomena contain an irreducible element. As an
example, I give the following sentence which I happen to have read
today in Max Scheler's 'Phänomenologie der Sympathiegefühle': 'One
must entirely exclude all attempts to reduce love and hate to simpler
facts or to any complex of such facts.' The difference may be illus-
trated by a grotesque example. Some years ago, the Reichstag passed a
vote of censure on Bethmann-Hollweg, who took no notice of it what-
ever. This prompted a cartoon in which the Chancellor was repre-
sented with both his feet cut neatly off, but still upright, and smiling,
being supported by the Kaiser's hand stretched from a cloud. Is there
anything like this in reality? or is the world with which philosophy
deals entirely governed by the parliamentary system? (Perhaps the fact
that this system, and the empirical philosophy, grew up at the same
time has some significance.) For the present, I content myself here
with re-asserting that the contrast between men and animals is the
typical example of all these other antitheses. They all stand together.

* * *

I called the assertion I am discussing, a brutal assertion; in doing so, I

was thinking of two things – of the kind of conviction that attaches to
the assertion, and of the manner in which the assertion should be made
in face of all 'idealist' humbug.

First, as to the conviction – in comparison with the variable opinion
which we come to by argument, it seems to belong to another level of
certitude altogether. Psychologically, perhaps, for this reason. A man's
beliefs are made up of two strata, his opinions and what we call his
prejudices, so that his whole attitude can be labelled (O + P). Now, the
only men it is possible to convert are those in which the (O) is not
consonant with the (P). This disaccord is possible because most men
are ignorant of the more central (P), and mistake their accidental opin-
ions for their unchangeable prejudices. By a difficult, but not impos-
sible operation a man's own fundamental prejudices may be laid bare.
If he finds the opinions which he falsely took to be final, are not in
accord with these prejudices, he may change them. Now to this
conviction about the nature of man, no shadow of doubt is attached. It
consequently seems to seek out the phenomena which superficially
throw the greatest doubt on it, and so place it in the greatest danger. It
seeks out these things, precisely because the assertion of the absolute
difference between men and animals in the events which seem most to
obliterate that difference, manifests most definitely its own uncom-
promising nature. Take the two phenomena often chosen to illustrate
the animal nature of man – War and Sex. War is essentially human,
and the pacifists falsify its nature when they attempt to reduce it to a
development of animals' struggles for food. And just because man is
man, and not an animal, there is, in spite of many common elements, a
profound and radical difference between the sexual unions of mankind
and of animals.

Secondly, as to the manner in which the assertion should be made
in face of 'idealist' humbug. 'Idealism' in philosophy, is to a large
extent, merely a specious substitute for religion. Being neither reli-
gious nor materialist, it depends on a endeavour to combine incompat-
ible things under cover of a conveniently obscure terminology, thus
giving an unreal consolation to men. It is a bastard phenomena, and it
is time it was got rid of, and the only way to get rid of it, is to face its
plausible rhetoric, by the brutal question, 'Is man an extra-natural
phenomena or not? Does he differ absolutely from the animal world or
not?'

A METHOD. – One of the main achievements of the nineteenth century was the elaboration and universal application of the principle of *continuity*. The destruction of this conception is, on the contrary, a pressing necessity of the present.

Originally urged only by the few, it has spread – implicit in the popular conception of evolution – till it has attained the status of a category. We now absorb it unconsciously from an environment already completely soaked in it; so that we regard it not as a principle in the light of which certain regions of fact can be conveniently ordered, but as an inevitable constituent of reality itself. When any fact seems to contradict this principle, we are inclined to deny that the fact really exists. We constantly tend to think that the discontinuities in nature are only *apparent*, and that a fuller investigation would reveal the underlying continuity. This shrinking from a *gap* or jump in nature has developed to a degree which paralyses any objective perception and prejudices our seeing things as they really are. For an objective view of reality we must make use both of the categories of continuity and discontinuity. Our principal concern then at the present moment should be the re-establishment of the temper or disposition of mind which can look at a *gap* or chasm without shuddering.

I am not concerned in these notes, however, with gaps in nature, in the narrow sense of the word. I am thinking rather of general theories about the nature of reality. One of the results of the temper of mind I have just discussed is that any general theories of this kind which assert the existence of absolute gaps between one region of reality and another, are at once almost instinctively felt to be inadmissible. Now the method of criticism I wish to employ here is based on the fact that most of the errors in certain subjects spring from an almost instinctive attempt on our part to gloze over and disguise a particular *discontinuity* in the nature of reality. It was then necessary first of all to deal with the source of this instinctive behaviour, by pointing out the arbitrary character of the principle of continuity.

* * *

What is this Method? It is only possible here to describe it quite abstractly, leaving the details till later. Certain regions of reality differ not relatively but absolutely. There exists between them a real discontinuity. As the mind looks on discontinuity with horror it has attempted to exhibit these opposed things, as differing only in degree, as if there is in reality a continuous scale leading from one to the other. From this springs a whole mass of confused thinking in religion and ethics. If we first of all form a clear conception of the nature of a discontinuity, of a chasm, and form in ourselves the temper of mind which can support this opposition without irritation, we shall then have in our hands an instrument which may shatter all this confused thinking, and enable us to form accurate ideas on these subjects. In this way a flood of light may be thrown on old controversies.

A necessary preliminary to this however must be some account of the nature of the particular absolute discontinuity, that I want to use.

In order to simplify matters, it may be useful here to give the exposition a kind of geometrical character. Let us assume that reality is divided into three regions separated from one another by absolute divisions, by real discontinuities. (1) The inorganic world, of mathematical and physical science, (2) the organic world, dealt with by biology, psychology and history, and (3) the world of ethical and religious values. Imagine these three regions as the three zones marked out on a flat surface by two concentric circles. The outer zone is the world of physics, the inner that of religion and ethics, the intermediate one that of life. The outer and inner regions have certain characteristics in common. They have both an absolute character, and knowledge about them can legitimately be called *absolute* knowledge. The intermediate region of life is, on the other hand, essentially relative; it is dealt with by *loose* sciences like biology, psychology and history. A muddy mixed zone then lies between the two absolutes. To make the image a more faithful representation one would have to imagine the extreme zones partaking of the perfection of geometrical figures, while the middle zone was covered with some confused muddy substance.

* * *

I am afraid I shall have to abandon this model, for to make it represent faithfully what I want, I shall have to add a further complication. There must be an *absolute* division between each of the three regions, a kind of *chasm*. There must be no continuous leading gradually from one to the other. It is these *discontinuities* that I want to discuss here.

A convenient way of realising the nature of these divisions is to consider the movement away from materialism, at the end of the nineteenth century. In the middle period of the century, the predominant popular view entirely ignored the division between the inner and outer zones, and tended to treat them as one. There was no separating chasm and the two were muddled together. Vital phenomena were only extremely complicated forms of mechanical change (cf. Spencer's Biology and the entirely mechanical view involved in the definition of life as adaptation to environment). Then you get the movement represented in very different ways by Nietzsche, Dilthey, and Bergson, which clearly recognised the chasm between the two worlds of life and matter. Vital events are not completely *determined* and mechanical. It will always be impossible to completely describe them in terms of the laws of physics. This was not merely a local reaction against a local false doctrine. It contained an original element. This movement made the immense step forward involved in treating life, almost for the first time, as a unity, as something positive, a kind of stream overflowing, or at any rate not entirely enclosed, in the boundaries of the physical and spatial world. 'In Dein Auge schaute ich O Leben',[2] etc.

So far so good. But the same movement that recognises the existence of the first absolute chasm (between the physical and the vital), proceeds to ignore the second, that between the biology, and the ethical, religious values. Having made this immense step away from materialism, it believes itself adequately equipped for a statement of all the *ideal* values. It does not distinguish different levels of the non-material. All that is non-material, must it thinks be *vital*. The momentum of its escape from mechanism carries it on to the attempt to restate the whole of religion in terms of vitalism. This is ridiculous. Biology is not theology, nor can God be defined in terms of 'life' or 'progress'. Modernism entirely misunderstands the nature of religion. But the last twenty years has produced masses of writing on this basis, and in as far as thought today is not materialistic, it tends to be exclusively of this kind.

It is easy to understand why the absolute division between the inorganic and the organic is so much more easily recognised than the second division. For the first falls easily into line with humanism, while the second breaks the whole Renascence tradition.

It is necessary, however, that this second *absolute* difference should also be understood. It is necessary to realise that there is an absolute, and not a relative, difference between humanism (which we can take to be the highest expression of the vital), and the religious spirit. The *divine* is not *life* at its intensest. It contains in a way an almost *anti-vital* element; quite different of course from the non-vital character of the outside physical region. The questions of Original Sin, of chastity, of the motives behind Buddhism, etc., all part of the very essence of the religious spirit, are quite incomprehensible for humanism. The difference is seen perhaps most obviously in art. At the Renascence, there were many pictures with religious subjects, but no religious art in the proper sense of the word. All the emotions expressed are perfectly human ones. Those who choose to think that religious emotion is only the highest form of the emotions that fall inside the humanist ideology, may call this religious art, but they will be wrong. When the intensity of the religious attitude finds proper expression in art, then you get a very different result. Such expression springs not from a delight in life but from a feeling for certain absolute values, which are entirely independent of vital things. The disgust with the trivial and accidental characteristics of living shapes, the searching after an austerity, a monumental stability and permanence, a perfection and rigidity, which vital things can never have, leads to the use of forms which can almost be called *geometrical*. (Cf. Byzantine, Egyptian and early Greek art.) If we think of physical science as represented by geometry, then instead of saying that the modern progress away from materialism has been from physics through vitalism to the absolute values of religion, we might say that it is from *geometry through life and back to geometry*. It certainly seems as if the extreme regions had resemblances not shared by the middle region. This is because they are both, in different ways, absolute.

We can repeat this in a more summary form. Two sets of errors spring from the attempt to treat different regions of reality as if they were alike. (1) The attempt to introduce the *absolute* of mathematical physics into the essentially relative middle zone of life leads to the mechanistic view of the world. (2) The attempt to explain the *absolute* of religious and ethical values in terms of the categories appropriate to the essentially relative and *non-absolute* vital zone, leads to the entire misunderstanding of these values, and to the creation of a series of mixed or bastard phenomena, which will be the subject of these notes. Cf. Romanticism in literature, Relativism in ethics, Idealism in philosophy, and Modernism in religion.

To say that these bastard phenomena are the result of the shrinking from discontinuity would be an entirely inadequate account of the matter. They spring from a more positive cause, the inability of the prevailing ideology to understand the nature of this absolute. But they are certainly shaped by this instinctive effort to dig away at the edges of the precipice, which really separates two regions of reality, until it is transformed into a slope leading gradually from one to the other.

Romanticism for example confuses both human and divine things, but not clearly separating them. The main thing with which it can be reproached is that it blurs the clear outlines of human relations – whether in political thought or in the literary treatment of sex, by introducing in them, the *Perfection* that properly belongs to the non-human.

The *method* I wish to pursue then is this. In dealing with these confused phenomena, to hold the real nature of the *absolute disconti-nuity* between vital and religious things constantly before the mind; and thus to clearly separate those things, which are in reality separate. I believe this to be a very fertile method, and that it is possible by using it, not only to destroy all these bastard phenomena, but also to recover the real significance of many things which it seems absolutely impossible for the 'modern' mind to understand.

A CRITIQUE OF SATISFACTION: In a previous Note, I made this assertion, 'In spite of its extreme diversity, all philosophy since the Renascence is at bottom the *same* philosophy. The family resemblance is much greater than is generally supposed. The obvious diversity is only that of the various species of the same genus.' It is very difficult to see this when one is *inside* this philosophy; but if one looks at it from the standpoint of another philosophy it at once becomes obvious. A parallel may make this clearer. The change of sensibility which has enabled us to regard Egyptian, Polynesian and Negro work, as *art* and not as archaeology has had a double effect. It has made us realise that what we took to be the necessary principles of aesthetic, constitute in reality only a psychology of Renascence and Classical Art. At the same time, it has made us realise the essential *unity* of these latter arts. For we see that they both rest on certain common pre-suppositions, of which we only become conscious when we see them *denied* by other arts. (Cf. the work of Riegl on Byzantine art.) In the same way an understanding of the religious philosophy which preceded the Renascence makes the essential unity of all philosophy since seem at once obvious. It all rests on the same conception of the nature of man, and exhibits the same inability to realise the meaning of the dogma of Original Sin. Our difficulty now, of course, is that we are really incapable of understanding how any other view but the humanistic, could be seriously held by intelligent and emancipated men. To get over this difficulty I intend in later Notes, to say a good deal about those comparatively unknown philosophers at the beginning of the Renascence, who are exceptionally interesting from this point of view, because they exhibit clearly the transition from one ideology to the other. They at least were capable of understanding that an intelligent man might not be a humanist.

* * *

But we can leave this on one side. In order to explain this family likeness between all philosophers since the Renascence, it is not necessary to state *specifically*, what the likeness consists in. The fact can perhaps be made comprehensible by the *manner* of its occurrence; by stating the aspect or *department* of philosophy in which the resemblance occurs, without stating in detail what it is.

Philosophy is a surprising subject to the layman. It has all the appearance of an impersonal and exact science. It makes use of a terminology as abstruse as that of mathematics, and its method is so technical that he cannot follow it; yet he can see for himself that it is not a science, or it would have the same solid growth as the other sciences. It ought surely to have arrived by now at results valid for everyone. But the scandal in philosophy of the contrast between apparently *impersonal*, scientific method, and its results – which are often so *personal*, that no one but their author accepts them – is obvious to everyone.

This scandal is so evident, that certain philosophers have endeavoured to end it, by *acknowledging* it. They say that the subject should renounce its claim to be a science, and should acknowledge itself to be, what it clearly is, a *weltanschauung*, or expression of an attitude

towards the world. The personal element in it would then be legiti-
mate.

This I now believe to be a false solution.

What is the right solution? To recognise that actual Philosophy is
not a pure but a *mixed* subject. It results from a confusion between two
subjects which stand in no essential or necessary relation to each other,
though they may be combined together for a certain practical end. One
of these subjects is a science, the other not. The scientific element in
philosophy is a difficult investigation into the relations between
certain very abstract categories. Though the subject matter is abstract,
the method employed should be as purely scientific and impersonal as
that of mathematics.

Mixed up with this is the function which philosophy has assumed
of acting as a pale *substitute* for religion. It is concerned here with
matters like the nature and destiny of man, his place in the universe,
etc., all matters which would, as treated, fit very well into a personal
Weltanschauung. Here the word 'standpoint' may legitimately be used,
though it is quite illegitimate in the scientific part of philosophy.

The two elements are mixed after this fashion. The machinery
elaborated by the first element in philosophy is used to further the
aims of the second. Put very crudely these aims make it first of all
necessary that the world should be shown to be in *reality* very different
from what it *appears* to be. It must be moulded 'nearer to the heart's
desire'. By the aid of his technical equipment – the result of the first
element – the philosopher is able to disintegrate the solid structure of
the world as it appears to common sense. In the last chapter in his
'conclusions' he presents us with his reconstructed world; with the
world as it is *in reality*. Consider the nature of this second feature for a
moment. The philosopher undertakes to show that the world is other
than it appears to me; and as he takes the trouble to prove this, we
should expect to find, that consciously or unconsciously, the *final*
picture he presents, will to some degree or other *satisfy* him.

* * *

It is in these final pictures that it was true to say that there was a family
resemblance between all philosophers since the Renascence. Though
the pictures are as different as can be, yet curiously enough they are all

satisfactory for approximately the same reasons. The *final* pictures they present of man's relation to the world all conform to the same probably unconscious *standards* or *canons* of what is *satisfying*. It would be more accurate to say that it is the similarity of these *canons* that constitutes the unity of modern philosophy. If we think, then, of philosophy as divided into a *scientific*, and a more *personal* part, we may say that the various systems agree where they might have been expected to differ – and disagree where they ought to have been impersonal; they vary where no variation should have been possible – in the scientific part.

It should be noticed that these canons of *satisfaction* are quite unconscious. The philosophers share a view of what would be a *satisfying* destiny for man, which they take over from the Renascence. They are all satisfied with certain conceptions of the relation of man to the world. These *conclusions* are never questioned in this respect. Their truth may be questioned, but never their *satisfactoriness*. This ought to be questioned. This is what I mean by a *critique of satisfaction*. When Croce, for example finishes up with the final world picture of the 'legitimate' *mystery of infinite progress and the infinite perfectibility of man* – I at once want to point out that not only is this not true, but what is even more important, if true such a shallow conception would be quite unworthy of the emotion he feels towards it.[3]

These *canons of satisfaction*, which are the results of an entirely uncritical humanism, should be subject to a *critique*. This is a special subject, having no connection with philosophy. I hope to be able to show that it is a real and complicated subject inside the limits of which detailed investigation is possible, by the aid of a refined and subtle analysis.

This is a very rough account of the matter. To make it convincing, it is first of all necessary to examine in more detail, the nature of the alleged confusion in actual philosophy. In pointing out that the scientific part of the subject was actually used to serve very human ends, I did not want to imply any scepticism as to the possibility of a really scientific philosophy. I do not mean what Nietzsche meant when he said, 'Do not speculate as to whether what a philosopher says is true, but ask how he came to think it true'. This form of scepticism I hold to be just fashionable rubbish. Pure philosophy ought to be, and may be, entirely objective and scientific.

* * *

The best account I know of the sense in which Philosophy may be a science is that given by Husserl in *Logos*, 1911 – 'Philosophie als strenge Wissenschaft'. One definition would be that of philosophy as the science of *what is possible* as contrasted with the *science of what is* – something similar to what Meinong means by *Gegenstandstheorie*.[4] I have no space here to explain what is meant by these definitions. All that it is necessary to keep in mind here is that Philosophy may be a patient investigation into entities, which although they are abstract, may yet be investigated by methods as objective as those of physical science. There are then two distinct subjects.

(P.) Pure Philosophy.

(H.) This should be the critique of satisfaction; but instead it is, as a matter of fact, an entirely uncritical acceptance of Humanist views of man's nature, and destiny.

These two ought to be clearly separated. What you actually do get in philosophy, is a presentment of these humanist ideas, with a tremendous and overwhelming appearance of being *impersonal objective* science. You get something perfectly human and arbitrary cloaked in a scientific vocabulary. Instead of H or L, you get L(h) where the (h) is the really important factor. H moves in the stiff armour of L. Something quite *human* but with quite *inhumanly* sharpened weapons.

I remember being completely overawed by the vocabulary and scientific method of the various philosophers of the Marburg School, and in particular by Hermann Cohen's 'Logik der reinen Erkenntniss'. But one day, hearing Cohen lecture on religion, where his views are, as is well known, entirely sectarian, I realised very easily that the overwhelming and elaborate method only served to express a perfectly simple and fallible human attitude.

This was very exhilarating and enlightening. One could at last stand free, disentangled from the influence of their paralysing and elaborate method. For what was true of their work in religion was also true elsewhere. It becomes possible to see a good deal of Cohen's work as the rigid, scientific expression of an attitude that is neither rigid nor scientific, but sometimes romantic, and always humanist. One can illustrate the effect of such work on the mind by this parallel. A man might be clothed in armour so complicated and elaborate, that to an inhabitant of another planet who had never seen armour before, he might seem like some entirely impersonal and omnipotent mechanical force. But if he saw the armour running after a lady or eating tarts in the pantry, he would realise at once, that it was not a godlike or mechanical force, but an ordinary human being extraordinarily armed. In the pantry, the essence of the phenomena is *arms, and not the man.*

When you have recovered from the precision and refinement of the *method* in such philosophers, you will be able to recognise the frequent vulgarity of their *conclusions.* It is possible to combine extreme subtlety in the one, with exceeding commonplaceness in the other.

If you ask what corresponds to the pantry which betrayed the man in armour, I should answer that it was the *last* chapters of the philosophers in which they express their conception of the world as it really is, and so incidentally expose the things with which they are satisfied. How magnificently they may have been clad before, they come out naked here!

* * *

This emancipation is however only a secondary matter. What I wish to emphasise here is the corrective, the *complexity* of this supposed '*Critique of Satisfaction*'. By the complexity of this subject, I mean amongst other things, the many possible different ideals, or *canons of satisfaction.* It is difficult to make the people I am attacking realise this, because they always assume automatically, that all *ideals* must be *one* ideal, and that everything that is not sceptical materialism, must be some form of *humanism.* One of the causes of this assumption can be easily dealt with. The difficulty is exactly parallel to the difficulty the scientific materialists of the last century used to experience, in realising that metaphysics was a real region of knowledge.

One can put the parallel clearly.

(1) The *Naturalists* refused to recognise metaphysical knowledge because

(2) They themselves were under the influence of an *unconscious metaphysic* which consisted in

(3) Taking physical science as the only possible *type* of real knowledge.

The parallel is:

(1) The *Humanists* would refuse to recognise the existence of a subject, like the critique of satisfaction because

(2) They themselves are under the influence of an *unconscious critique* of this kind of which consists in

(3) Taking the satisfaction and consolation which can be obtained from humanist idealism, and its view of man, as the only possible *type* of satisfaction.

This removes an *a priori* objection to the subject. What then finally is the nature of the subject?

* * *

I feel grave doubts about this last Note. I have no space to give any account that will be full enough to be *comprehensible*, and yet I don't like to leave the argument of the article hanging in mid-air.

What actually would be the subject matter of a *Critique of Satisfaction*?

Very roughly, the *Sphere of Religion*. But to say this at once calls up a different conception, than the one I am driving at.

It is on the whole correct to say that while Ethics is concerned with certain absolute values, and has nothing to do with questions of existence, that Religion fills in this gap by its assertion of what Höffding calls the characteristic axiom of religion: the '*conservation* of values'. It gives us the assurance that values are in some way permanent.

This is in a sense correct, in that it gives us so to speak the *boundaries* of the subject. But it is entirely empty. To get at the motive forces one would have to start in an entirely different way. I should say that the starting point for the religious attitude was always the kind of discussion you find in *Pascal, fragment* 139 (*Brunschvig edition*); and that is exactly what I mean by a *Critique of Satisfaction*. You get exactly similar discussion in the Buddhist books (entirely misunderstood of course by their translators and editors). My point is that this is a *separate* subject. It is *not* philosophy, *nor* is it *psychology*. Always the subject is the '*Vanity of desire*' but it is not desire merely as a psychological entity. And it is this special region of knowledge, marked out from all other spheres of knowledge, and absolutely and entirely *misunderstood* by the moderns, that I have baptised for the purpose of this Note only with the somewhat grotesque title of the *Critique of Satisfaction*.

In attempting, in my notes of last week, to state the whole sequence of an argument, I left parts of it rather obscure. I want to remedy this here, by treating these parts in more detail. The subject of the Notes was the mixed nature of Philosophy, and the necessity of analysing it with *Scientific* philosophy and *weltanschauung*. What I have to say here bears upon (1) a more detailed account of the *existence* of these two elements; and (2) a discussion of the consequences of this separation.

* * *

(1) A *weltanschauung* is by no means necessarily connected with a philosophy. The effort to find some 'interpretation of life', to solve what it feels to be in the riddle of existence, is obviously a permanent characteristic of the human mind. It may find expression not only in philosophy, however, but in literature; where in a relatively formless way attempts may be made to deal with the relation of man to the world, and with all those questions, the answers to which used to be designated as *Wisdom*.

But though it can thus exist quite independently of philosophy, yet a *weltanschauung*, a particular view of the relation of man to existence, always tends to lose its independent status for this reason – the people who are under its influence want to fix it, to make it seem not so much a particular *attitude* as a *necessary* fact. They then endeavour, by expressing it in the elaborately worked out categories of a metaphysic, to give it a universal validity. Philosophy in this way provides a conceptual clothing for the interpretation of life current in any partic- ular period. But the interpretation of life should always be distin- guished from the refined organisation of concepts by which it has been expressed.

This process can be illustrated more concretely by taking a definite period. Consider the most obvious example of the emergence of a new *weltanschauung* – the Renascence. You get at that time the appearance of a new attitude which can be most broadly described as an attitude of acceptance to life, as opposed to an attitude of renunciation. As a consequence of this, there emerges a new interest in man and his rela- tionship to his environment. With this goes an increasing interest in character and *personality* for its own sake, which makes *autobiographies* such as that of Cellini possible for the first time. An autobiography for its own sake would have been inconceivable before.

(Though these are platitudes, yet their real significance is entirely missed by people who do not see this change as a change from one *possible* attitude to another, but as a kind of discovery, like that of gravitation. The thus fail to realise the possibility of a change in the contrary direction, and also to understand the real nature of such *attitudes*.)

When this new *attitude* became firmly established, men sought to make it seem *objective* and *necessary* by giving it a philosophical setting, exactly as in the case of the religious attitude which had preceded it. This was a need actually felt by many men of the Renascence. One has only to read of the reception given to the philosophers who attempted to ground the new attitude on a theory of the nature of things ... of the travels of *Bruno*, and the recorded eagerness of the men to whom he talked at a banquet in Westminster.

To make this clear, I shall later on attempt to describe the working out of the process in the sixteenth and seventeenth centuries. It is interesting to see how the conceptual expression of the new attitude was affected by the influence of the physics of Galileo, and the revived knowledge of Stoicism, to name only two things. It becomes possible to see the whole period as very much more of a unity than it appears superficially, when the existence of the new *attitude* as the driving force behind very diverse phenomena has once been realised. This is, of course, a process which is repeated whenever the general 'interpretation of life' changes. At the end of such periods you get a constant phenomenon, the unsystematic philosopher. When the *weltanschauung*, the interpretation of life, changes, the values expressed by the elaborate and subtle conceptual form of a developed philosophy no longer fit the changed conditions. You then get philosophers of the type of Marcus Aurelius, who express the new attitude in a more personal, literary, and unsystematic way. Perhaps Marcus Aurelius is not a good example of this type, for behind his unsystematic expression lay a certain remnant of the Stoic principles. A more perfect example of the type is Montaigne, coming after the decay of the scholastic system. There are people at the present day who look for a philosophy of this character, who desire an 'interpretation of life' without the elaborate conceptual system of the older philosophy. 'Their eyes are directed with great earnestness on the Riddle of Life, but they despair of solving it by a universally valid metaphysic.' The fact that philosophy has always contained this element of *weltan-schauung* can be illustrated by some examples of the use of the word. *Justin* called Christianity a philosophy, for he claimed that it had solved all the riddles with which philosophy had busied itself. Minucius Felix spoke of philosophy as perfected in Christianity... eternal truths about God, human responsibility and immortality, which are grounded on Reason and can be proved through it... For Porphyrios the motive and end of philosophy was the salvation of the soul... and even Böhme called his own life-work, a holy philosophy.

Such has been, in fact, the relation between *weltanschauung* and Pure Philosophy. What *ought* to be the character of this relation?

* * *

(2) As typical of the demand for a truly scientific philosophy, we can take the article by Edmund Husserl I cited last week, and in England various lectures and essays of Bertrand Russell.[5] These two writers have most clearly insisted on the necessity for an absolute separation between *Pure* Philosophy and *Weltanschauung*.

RUSSELL: 'It is from science rather than from religion and ethics that philosophy ought to draw its inspiration.' He cites Spinoza as a philosopher whose value lies almost entirely in the second element. 'We do not go to him for any metaphysical theory as to the nature of the world. What is valuable in him is the indication of a new way of feeling towards the world.' His conclusion is 'the adoption of the scientific method in philosophy compels us to abandon the hope of solving the more ambitious and humanly interesting problems of traditional philosophy.'

HUSSERL: 'Es treten also scharf auseinander: Weltanschauungs philosophie und wissenschaftliche Philosophie als zwei in gewisser Weise auf einander bezogene aber nicht zu *vermengende* Ideen...'[6] The first is not the imperfect anticipation of the second... Any combination or *compromise* between these two subjects must be rejected... *Weltanschauung* philosophy must give up all pretence to be scientific.

While I entirely agree with what they say as to the possibility of a purely *scientific* philosophy and the necessity for a clear separation between that and a *weltanschauung*, yet for the purpose of my argument in this Notebook I must lay emphasis on a different aspect of this separation. They insist on a clear separation, because they wish to free the scientific element in philosophy from the bad influence of the other. They want the *weltanschauung* separated from philosophy because they think it has often injuriously affected the scientific part of the subject. I, on the contrary, want it separated because I think it also forms part of a *separate* subject, which has in reality no connection with philosophy.

My interest, then, is a different one, and I examine what they have to say on the separation from a different point of view. I find that while what they say is satisfactory in its description of the nature of a purely scientific philosophy, it is extremely unsatisfactory in what it has to say about the nature of a *weltanschauung*. After the remarkably clear exposition of the scientific element, one expects but does not find a similarly clear explanation of the other element.

What Mr Russell has to say on the subject in 'A Free Man's Worship' is so extremely commonplace, and is expressed in such a painful piece of false and sickly rhetoric, that I have not patience to deal with it here.

HUSSERL, though he is better than this, is not very satisfactory. 'A *weltanschauung* should be the highest possible exaltation of the life and culture of the period. The word "Wisdom" taken in its widest sense comes to mean the most perfect possible development of the idea of Humanity. Personality is to be developed, to the greatest intensity in a many-sided activity – the result will be a *philosopher* in the original sense of the word… while science is impersonal… a *weltanschauung* can only spring from the highest possible development of personality.'

The emphasis laid on the word *personality* at once shows us that instead of the complicated subject it really is, *weltanschauung* philosophy is for Husserl, as it is for most moderns, merely an uncritical humanism.

* * *

How does it come about that the writers who show such subtlety in the scientific part of the subject, exhibit when they come to the subjects, which I propose to deal with by a Critique of Satisfaction, such entirely uncritical and naïve crudity; what is the reason for this commonplace, unquestioning acceptance of humanist ideas?

In general perhaps for some reason of this kind. The ordinary citizen reasons correctly, without necessarily being aware that the cogency of a chain of reasoning depends on the fact that it approximates to certain standards or *canons* of implication. The philosophers, in their *conclusions* in the region of *weltanschauung* are exactly in the position of the citizen in regard to logic. They are moved by certain unconscious *canons* of satisfaction. But while this was legitimate in the case of logic, it is not legitimate here, for the *canons* of satisfaction are not inevitable norms, like those of logic. The humanist *canons* are, I think, demonstrably false. But it is difficult to make these people realise that the canons are *false*, for they do not yet recognise that they exist. Now we only become conscious of such hidden presuppositions when they are denied: just as we become conscious of the existence of air, when we breathe something that is not air. It is possible to destroy this *naïveté* about the subject, by an historical investigation of the varied ideals of a *satisfactory* position of man that have as a matter of fact been held. I shall deal with this matter later. For the moment, I want to try to get at the *critique of satisfaction*, by the *direct method*.

* * *

My notes here will necessarily be rather disjointed; but I only intend to suggest the kind of subject matter to be dealt with by such a Critique.

This subject matter was, I asserted in my last Notes, that of religion; but in a very radical sense. Most explanations of the religious attitude deal with the *consequences* of that attitude rather than with the attitude itself; they are concerned more than they ought to be with the statements about the ultimate nature of things, which it, as it were, projects out from itself. The only fertile method is to start at the real root of the subject, with reflections on the nature of the 'satisfying'. You then get at a unique subject, with a special structure; of such a nature, that the reasonings it employs have real cogency and real effect on action.

You get thus to the actual source of religion. Moreover, it might be pointed out here, that the difficulty about religion at the present day, is not so much the difficulty of believing the statements it makes about the nature of the world, as the difficulty of understanding *how if true* these statements can be satisfactory. (Cf. Original Sin.)

Put very crudely, the question from which everything here springs is then 'what is finally *satisfying?*'

For the purpose of this discussion, I assume the truth of the statement I made in an earlier note: 'The whole subject has been confused, by the failure to recognise the *gap* between the regions of vital and human things, and that of the *absolute* values of ethics and religion. We introduce into human things the *Perfection* that properly belongs only to the divine, and thus confuse both human and divine things by not clearly separating them.' To illustrate the position, imagine a man situated at a point in a plane, from which roads radiate in various directions. Let this be the plane of actual existence. We place *Perfection* where it should not be – on this human plane. As we are painfully aware that nothing *actual* can be *perfect*, we imagine the perfection to be not where we are, but some distance along one of the roads. This is the essence of all Romanticism. Most frequently, in literature, at any rate, we imagine an impossible *perfection* along the road of sex; but anyone can name the other roads for himself. The abolition of some discipline and restriction would enable us, we imagine, to progress along one of these roads. The fundamental error is that of placing Perfection in *humanity*, thus giving rise to that bastard thing Personality, and all the bunkum that follows from it.

For the moment, however, I am not concerned with the errors introduced into *human* things by this confusion of regions which should be separated, but with the falsification of the *divine*.

If we continue to look with satisfaction along these roads, we shall always be unable to understand the religious attitude. The necessary preliminary *preparation* for such an understanding is a realisation that satisfaction is to be found along none of these roads.

I am not thinking here of actual experience, but of an *understanding* of religious experience. It is only when the 'conclusions' of the philosophers are seen to be even if true, *unsatisfactory*, that a beginning has been made towards an understanding of religion.

This realisation, that there is nothing wonderful in man, will not lead necessarily to this. It is only the necessary preparation. By itself, it leads only to a rejection of Romanticism, and the adoption of the classical attitude. But to those who have a certain conception of Perfection, a further step is taken.

The effect of this necessary *preparation* is to force the mind back on the centre, by the closing of all the roads *on* the plane. No 'meaning' can be given to the existing world, such as philosophers are accustomed to give in their last chapters. To each conclusion one asks, 'In what way is that *satisfying?*' The mind is forced back along every line in the plane, back on the centre. What is the result? To continue the rather comic metaphor, we may say the result is that which follows the snake eating its own tail, an *infinite* straight line *perpendicular* to the plane.

In other words, you get the religious attitude; where things are separated which ought to be separated, and Perfection is not illegitimately introduced on the plane of human things.

It is the closing of all the roads, this realisation of the *tragic* significance of life, which makes it legitimate to call all other attitudes shallow. Such a realisation has formed the basis of all the great religions, and is most conveniently remembered by the symbol of the *wheel*. This symbol of the futility of existence is absolutely lost to the modern world, nor can it be recovered without great difficulty.

One modern method of disguising the issue should be noticed. In November 1829, a tragic date for those who see with regret the establishment of a lasting and devastating stupidity, Goethe – in answer to Eckermann's remark that human thought and action seemed to repeat itself, going round in a circle, – said '*No, it is not a circle, it is a spiral.*' You disguise the wheel by tilting it up a bit; it then becomes 'Progress', which is the modern substitute for religion.

I ought here to point out that these crude conceptions are designed only to *suggest* the subject-matter, which properly developed has no connection with philosophy. And just as exceeding refinement and subtlety in pure philosophy may, we have seen, have been combined with exceeding commonplaceness in the subject, so the reverse of this is also true. It may and has happened that a cobbler may on this subject exhibit a refined sensibility, and yet be incapable of thought in philosophy at all.

This crude discussion about the wheel must sound entirely unreal to the humanist. The direct method of approval will not do for propaganda purposes. Fortunately a more indirect method is open to us. We can make a preliminary attempt to shake the humanist *naïveté* by the historical method.

HISTORY. – The greater part of these Notes will be taken up by an analysis of the history of ideas at the *Renascence*. A proper understanding of the Renascence seems to me to be the most pressing necessity of the subjects of these Notes, without continual use of the historical method. I entirely agree then with Savigny that 'history is the only true way to attain a knowledge of our own condition'. When I say I agree with Savigny's phrase, I am however attributing an entirely different meaning to the words. As actually used in 1815, they were an incident in the dispute as to the nature of the ideal sciences – economics, law, ethics, etc. Are they capable of a theoretical foundation like geometry, or are the principles they involve merely expressions of the conditions at a given moment in history? While the eighteenth century had attempted to change legal institutions in accordance with the Rights of Man deduced from theoretical principles, Savigny was opposing to these the entirely historical foundation of jurisprudence. This historical scepticism has now been vanquished in every subject. I approve of this victory; in what sense then do I think Savigny's words true?

I think that history is necessary in order to *emancipate* the individual from the influence of certain *pseudo-categories*. We are all of us under the influence of a number of abstract ideas, of which we are as a matter of fact unconscious. We do not see them, but see other things *through* them. In order that the kind of discussion about 'satisfaction' which I want, could be carried on, it is first of all necessary to rob certain ideas of their status of categories. This is a difficult operation. Fortunately, however, all such 'attitudes' and ideologies have a gradual growth. The rare type of historical intelligence which investigates their origins can help us considerably. Just as a knowledge of the colours extended and separated in the spectrum enables us to distinguish the feebler colours confused together in shadows, so a knowledge of these ideas, as it were *objectified*, and *extended* in history enables us to perceive them hidden in our own minds. Once they have been brought to the surface of the mind, they lose their *inevitable* character. They are no longer categories. We have lost our *naïveté*. Provided that we have a great enough length of history at our disposal, we then thus always vaccinate ourselves against the possibility of harbouring false categories. For in a couple of thousand years the confused human mind works itself out clearly into all the separate attitudes it is possible for it to assume. Humanity ought then always to carry with it a library of a thousand years as a balancing pole.

The application of this to the present subject is this: It is possible by examining the history of the Renascence, to destroy in the mind of the humanist, the conviction that his own attitude is the *inevitable* attitude of the emancipated and instructed man.

We may not be able to convince him that the religious attitude is the right one, but we can at least destroy the *naïveté* of his canons of *satisfaction*.

NEO-REALISM – Having lived at Cambridge at various times during the last ten years, I have naturally always known that the only philosophical movement of any importance in England is that which is derived from the writings of Mr G.E. Moore.[7] I now find these writings extremely lucid and persuasive, yet for years was entirely unable to understand in what lay their value. It was not so much that I did not agree with what was said, as that I was entirely unable to see how any meaning could be attached to some of its main contentions. I give examples of these contentions later on.

A few years ago I came across similar views differently expressed in the work of Husserl and his followers. I then began for the first time, if not to agree with these views, at least to understand how they came to be held. It is not that the Germans are better or more lucid than Mr Moore – that is very far from being the case. The reason is entirely personal; but it seems to me worth while explaining, for my difficulties are at least the *typical* difficulties of the dilettante. It would be no exaggeration, I think, to assert that all English amateurs in philosophy are, as it were, *racially* empiric and nominalist; there is their hereditary endowment. And so long as their interest in the subject is a dilettante one they are unlikely to find much meaning in philosophers who are intellectualist and *realist*. For the reading of the dilettante in philosophy, though it may be extensive and enthusiastic, always proceeds along easy slopes. As he only reads what he finds interesting, the only arguments he is likely to come into close contact with – or, at any rate, into that extremely close contact which is necessary for the understanding of disputed points in this subject – will be those which approximate to his own position. If his own mental make-up, at a given moment be A, his only chance of understanding an opposed position B will be in the case when the detailed exposition of B as b_1, b_2, b_3, a, contains one element (a) which he can lay hold of. This is the only way in which he will ever obtain a foothold. From that he may gradually proceed to understand the rest. But without that he would never exhibit the concentration of mind necessary to grasp the meaning of an argument which he rejects. There is, you perceive, nothing very admirable about this type of mind. In the end it probably gets everywhere, though as it always shrinks from precipices, and proceeds along easy slopes, through a hundred graduations of a_1, a_2, a_3, before it gets from A to B – it will always require an unlimited time. As its interests change, it may read many different parts of the same book, at long intervals, until finally as the result of many enthusiasms, it has read the whole. This blind following of interest along long and intricate paths may indirectly approximate to the results which concentration achieves directly. At any rate, I prefer people who feel a *resistance* to opinion. Except for the gifted few, this may be the best method to pursue in philosophy up to forty. It might be argued that a concentrated direct study of such matters should be postponed to this time, when a man really has prejudices to be moulded. There is, perhaps, more chance of getting *shape* out of stone than out of undergraduate plasticine. That this is a fair analysis of that very wide-spread phenomenon 'Superficial thinking', we can verify by examining our own procedure in these matters. It, at any rate, enables me to explain my own difficulties. When, with entirely empirical and nominalist prejudices, I read Moore and Russell, there was no foothold for me; they dealt with logic and ethics, and holding, as I did, entirely relativist views about both, I naturally found nothing familiar from which I might have started to understand the rest. The Germans I mentioned were useful in this way; they made the intellectualist, non-empirical method comprehensible to me, by enlarging its scope – applying it not only to logic and ethics, but to things which at the time did interest me. This provided me with the required foothold. When I had seen in these further subjects the possibility of the *rationalist, non-empirical* method, I began to see that it was this method which formed the basis of the writing on logic and ethics which I had before found incomprehensible.

This will be then the order of my argument here. I give certain views of the Realists, which I at one time found incomprehensible.

When I began to see for the first time the possibility of a non-empirical type of knowledge, the incomprehensibility of these views disappeared. In this Note I am, however, not concerned with their realism, but with the attitude (the assumption of this type of knowledge) from which the realism and its attendant difficulties spring.

In this kind of knowledge, the same type of non-empirical reasoning is possible as in geometry; and its subject-matter stands in much the same relation to the concepts we generally, but falsely, call mental, that geometry does to physical matter. When the only admitted kind of knowledge is empirical, the only type of explanation considered legitimately is that which reduces all the 'higher' concepts to combinations of more elementary ones. It is for this reason that I deal here with a subject that does not seem to have much relation to the general argument of this Notebook. For this false conception of the nature of 'explanation' prejudices the understanding of the 'critique of satisfaction'. It is first of all necessary before entering on this subject to destroy prejudices springing from empiricism, which tend to make us think certain concepts unreal.

* * *

The first difficulty was that Moore's only book was about Ethics. To anyone taking a thoroughly sceptical and relativist view of this subject, the whole discussion would quite wrongly appear almost entirely verbal. The only solution to this difficulty is the gradual realisation of the fact that there are objective things in Ethics, and this seems to me the only solution. I do not think any argument on the matter would have any effect unless a man had by some change in himself come to see that ethics was a real subject.

* * *

The principal difficulty, however, is the importance the Neo-Realists seem to attach to *language*. Mr Russell says, 'That all sound philosophy should begin with an analysis of propositions is a truth too evident perhaps to demand a proof'. 'The question whether all propositions are reducible to the subject predicate form is one of fundamental importance to all philosophy.'

'Even amongst philosophers, we may say, broadly, that only those universals which are named by adjectives or substantives have been much or often recognised, while those named by verbs and propositions have been usually overlooked... This omission has had a very great effect upon philosophy, it is hardly too much to say, that most metaphysics, since Spinoza, has been largely determined by it.'

Mr G.E. Moore in an article on the 'Nature of Judgment', 'It seems necessary, then, to regard the world as formed of concepts... which cannot be regarded as abstractions either for things or ideas... since both alike can, if anything be true of them, be comprised of nothing but concepts... an existent is seen to be nothing but a concept or complex of concepts standing in a unique relation to the concept of existence.'

Such assertions must seem meaningless to the nominalist and empiricist. The whole thing seems to him to be a new kind of scholasticism. He cannot understand how the study of such an apparently relative and trivial thing as the nature of propositions, the study of the accidental characteristics of human speech should be an indispensable preliminary to philosophy.

The first step towards making the matter intelligible is to note the use of the word *human*. A proposition in the sense used in the above quotation is not something relative to the *human*. 'A proposition... does not itself contain words... it contains the entities indicated by words.' One recalls Bolzano's 'Sentences in themselves'. Logic, then, does not deal with the laws of human thought but with these quite objective sentences. In this way the anthropomorphism which underlies certain views of logic is got rid of. Similarly, ethics can be exhibited as an objective science, and is also purified from anthropomorphism.

All these subjects are thus placed on a entirely objective basis, and do not in the least depend on the human mind. The entities which form the subject-matter of these sciences are neither physical nor mental, they 'subsist'. They are dealt with by an investigation that is *not* empirical. Statements can be made about them whose truth does not depend on experience. When the empirical prejudice has been got rid of, it becomes possible to think of certain 'higher' concepts, that of the good, of love, etc., as, at the same time, *simple*, and not necessarily to be analysed into more *elementary* (generally sensual) elements.

To make this intelligible, two things must be further discussed: (1) the possibility of this non-empirical knowledge; (2) what is meant by saying that these entities are neither physical nor mental, but *subsist*?

A PROGRAMME. – It has been suggested that I might make these rambling notes a good deal more intelligible if I gave first a kind of programme, a general summary of the conclusions I imagine myself able to establish.

* * *

The main argument of these notes is of an *abstract* character; it is concerned with certain ideas which lie so much in the centre of our minds, that we quite falsely regard them as having the nature of categories. More particularly, I am concerned with two opposed conceptions of the nature of man, which in reality lie at the root of our more concrete beliefs – the Religious and the Humanist.

It would perhaps have been better to have avoided the word religious, as that to the 'emancipated' man at once suggests something exotic, or mystical, or some sentimental reaction. I am not, however, concerned so much with religion, as with the attitude, the 'way of thinking', the categories, from which a religion springs, and which often survive it. While this attitude tends to find expression in myth, it is independent of myth; it is, however, much more intimately connected with dogma. For the purposes of this discussion, the bare minimum without any expression in religion is sufficient, the abstract categories alone. I want to emphasise that this attitude is a possible one for the 'emancipated' and 'reasonable' man at this moment. I use the word religious, because as in the past the attitude has been the source of most religions, the word remains convenient.

A. – The Religious attitude: (1) Its first postulate is the impossibility, I discussed earlier, of expressing the absolute values of religion and ethics in terms of the essentially relative categories of life... Ethical values are *not* relative to human desires and feelings, but absolute and objective... Religion supplements this... by its conception of *Perfection*.

(2) In the light of these absolute values, man himself is judged to be essentially limited and imperfect. He is endowed with Original Sin.

While he can occasionally accomplish acts which partake of perfection, he can never himself *be* perfect. Certain secondary results in regard to ordinary human action in society follow from this. As man is essentially bad, he can only accomplish anything of value by discipline – ethical and political. Order is thus not merely negative, but creative and liberating. Institutions are necessary.

B. – The Humanist attitude: When a sense of the reality of these absolute values is lacking, you get a refusal to believe any longer in the radical imperfection of either Man or Nature. This develops logically into the belief that life is the source and measure of all values, and that man is fundamentally good. Instead, then of

Man (radically imperfect) . . . apprehending . . . Perfection,

you get the second term (now entirely misunderstood) illegitimately introduced inside the first. This leads to a complete change in all values. The problem of evil disappears, the conception of sin loses all meaning. Man may be that bastard thing, 'a harmonious character'. Under ideal conditions, everything of value will spring spontaneously from free 'personalities'. If nothing good seems to appear spontaneously now, that is because of external restrictions and obstacles. Our political ideal should be the removal of everything that checks the 'spontaneous growth of personality'. Progress is thus possible, and order is a merely negative conception.

* * *

The errors which follow from this confusion of things which ought to be kept separate are of two kinds. The true nature both of the human and the divine is falsified.

(1) The error in human things; the confusion blurs the clear outlines of human relations by introducing into them the Perfection that properly belongs to the non-human. It thus creates the bastard conception of *Personality*. In literature it leads to romanticism... but I deal with the nature of these errors later.

(2) The confusion created in the absolute values of religion and ethics is even greater. It distorts the real nature of ethical values by deriving them out of essentially subjective things, like human desires and feelings; and all attempts to 'explain' religion, on a humanist basis,

whether it be Christianity, or an alien religion like Buddhism, must always be futile. As a minor example of this, take the question of immortality. It seems paradoxical at first sight, that the Middle Ages, which lacked entirely the conception of personality, had a real belief in immortality; while thought since the Renascence, which has been dominated by the belief in personality, has not had the same conviction. You might have expected that it would be the people who thought they really had something worth preserving who would have thought they were immortal, but the contrary is the case. Moreover, those thinkers since the Renascence who have believed in immortality and who have attempted to give explanation of it, have, in my opinion, gone wrong, because they have dealt with it in terms of the category of individuality. The problem can only be profitably dealt with by being entirely re-stated. This is just one instance of the way in which thought about these things in terms of categories appropriate only to human and vital things distort them.

THE TWO PERIODS. – The importance of this difference between the two conceptions of the nature of man becomes much more evident when it is given an historical setting. When this somewhat abstract antithesis is seen to be at the root of the difference between two historical periods, it begins to seem much more solid; in this way one gives it body.

The first of these historical periods is that of the Middle Ages in Europe – from Augustine, say, to the Renascence; the second from the Renascence to now. The ideology of the first period is religious; of the second, humanist. The difference between them is fundamentally nothing but the difference between these two conceptions of man.

Everyone would assent to the statement that on the whole the first period believed in the dogma of original sin, and the second did not. But this is not enough. It is necessary to realise the immense importance of this difference in belief, to realise that in reality almost everything else springs from it. In order to understand a period it is necessary not so much to be acquainted with its more defined opinions as with the doctrines which are thought of not as doctrines but as FACTS. (The moderns, for example, do not look for their belief in *Progress* as an opinion, but merely as a recognition of fact.) There are certain doctrines which for a particular period seem not doctrines, but inevitable categories of the human mind. Men do not look on them merely as correct opinion, for they have become so much a part of the mind, and lie so far back, that they are never really conscious of them at all. They do not see them, but other things *through* them. It is these abstract ideas at the centre, the things which they take for granted, which characterise a period. There are in each period certain doctrines, a denial of which is looked on by the men of that period just as we might look on the assertion that two and two make five. It is these abstract things at the centre, these *doctrines* felt as *facts*, which are the source of all the other more material characteristics of a period. For the Middle Ages these 'facts' were the belief in the subordination of man to certain absolute values, the radical imperfection of man, the doctrine of original sin. Everyone would assent to the assertion that these beliefs were held by the men of the Middle Ages. But that is not enough. It is necessary to realise that *these beliefs were the centre of their whole civilisation, and that even the character of their economic life was regulated by them* – in particular by the kind of ethics which springs from the acceptance of sin as a fact. It is only lately that the importance of the relation has been recognised, and a good deal of interesting work has been carried out on these lines in investigating the connection between the ideology of St Thomas Aquinas and the economic life of his time.

Turn now to the second period. This does not seem to form a coherent period like the first. But it is possible to show, I think, that all thought since the Renascence, in spite of its apparent variety, in reality forms one coherent whole. It all rests on the same presuppositions which were denied by the previous period. It all rests on the same conception of the nature of man, and all exhibits the same complete inability to realise the meaning of the dogma of Original Sin. In this period not only has its philosophy, its literature, and ethics been based on this new conception of man as fundamentally good, as sufficient, as the measure of things, but a good case can even be made out for regarding many of its characteristic economic features as springing entirely from this central abstract conception.

Not only that, but I believe that the real source of the immense change at the Renascence should be sought not so much in some material cause, but in the gradual change of attitude about this seemingly abstract matter. Men's categories changed; the things they took for granted changed. Everything followed from that.

There are economists now who believe that this period has been capitalist because it *desired*, it had the will, to be so. An essential preliminary to the growth of capitalism for them is, then, the growth of the capitalist 'spirit'. Other ages have not been industrial, not because they lacked the capacity, the scientific intelligence, but because on the whole they did not *desire* to be industrial, because they lacked this particular 'spirit'. We may note that Max Weber, one of the most remarkable economists of this school, sees in 'the spontaneous change in religious experience (at the Renascence), and the corresponding new ethical ideals by which life was regulated – one of the strongest roots of the capitalist spirit'.

The thoroughness with which these two conceptions of man penetrate the life of their respective periods can be illustrated by the difference between their arts. What is the difference between modern art since the Renascence, and Byzantine mosaic, which we may take as most typical of the other period? Renascence art we may call a 'vital' art in that it depends on pleasure in the reproduction of human and natural forms. Byzantine art is the exact contrary of this. There is nothing vital in it; the emotion you get from it is not a pleasure in the reproduction of natural or human life. The disgust with the trivial and accidental characteristics of living shapes, the searching after an austerity, a perfection and rigidity which vital things can never have, leads here to the use of forms which can almost be called geometrical. Man is subordinate to certain absolute values; there is no delight in the human form, leading to its natural reproduction; it is always distorted to fit into the more abstract forms which convey an intense religious emotion.

These two arts thus correspond exactly to the thought of their respective periods. Byzantine art to the ideology which looks on man and all existing things as imperfect and sinful in comparison with certain abstract values and *perfections*. The other art corresponds to the humanist ideology, which looks on man and life as good, and which is thus in a relation of harmony with existence. Take Goethe as typical of the period. 'Human nature knows itself one with the world, and consequently feels the outer world not as something foreign to it, but recognises it as the answering counterpart to the sensations of its own inner world.'

Such a humanism in all its varying forms of pantheism, rationalism and idealism, really constitutes a complete anthropomorphisation of the world, and leads naturally to art which is founded on the pleasure to be derived from vital forms.

THE END OF HUMANISM. – Now it should be noted that the coherent attitude and art of these two periods have occurred many times before in history. The Renascence period corresponds very nearly both in its conception of man and in its art to the classical. The Byzantine art corresponds to many other geometric arts in the past, to Egyptian and Indian, for example, both, also, civilisations with a similar religious, non-humanistic conception of man. In the same way, then, it may be possible that the humanist period we live in, may also come to an end, to be followed by a revival of the anti-humanist attitude. In saying this I do not in the least wish to imply any mechanical view of history as an inevitable alternation of such periods; I am so far from such scepticism about the matter, that I regard difference between the two attitudes as simply the difference between true and false. The great obstacle which prevents people seeing the possibility of such a change is the apparently *necessary* character of the humanist conception. But the same situation formerly existed in aesthetics. One result of the fact that both classical and modern art, springing from a similar attitude to the world, is that we tend to look on these arts, as *Art* itself; the art of other periods we have regarded as archaeology or ethnology. We neglected Byzantine art, for example, just as we neglected scholastic philosophy... May it not, then, be significant that it is only just lately that we have begun to understand these other arts... May not the change of sensibility, in a region like aesthetics, a by-path in which we are, as it were, off our guard, be some indication that the *humanist tradition is breaking up* – for individuals here and there, at any rate.

* * *

When I say that it may be breaking up for individuals, I ought to correct a little this picture of the two contrasted periods. While such periods are on the whole coherent, they are never absolutely so. You always get people who really belong to the other period. At the beginning of a period you have the people who continue the tradition of the preceding period, and at the end those who prepare the change to that which follows. At the beginning of the Christian period you have many of the Fathers continuing the classical conception of man. At the same time as St Augustine, you get Pelagius, who has many resemblances to Rousseau, and might easily be applauded at a meeting of *progressives*. It is, as a rule, on such people that the men like Pico, who come at the end of a period, and prepare the change to the next, base themselves.

There is a similar overlapping of the religious period into the humanist one. It was this overlapping which was in reality responsible for the virtues which we often find in the earlier humanists, and which disappeared so completely when humanity attained its full development in romanticism. Compare for example, the early Protestants and the Puritans with the sloppy thought of their descendants today.

Moreover, you may get, at any stage in the history of such a period, isolated individuals, whose whole attitude and ideology really belong to the opposed period. The greatest example of such an individual is, of course, Pascal. Everything that I shall say later in these notes is to be regarded merely as a prolegomena to the reading of Pascal, as an attempt to remove the difficulties of comprehension engendered in us by the humanism of our period.

* * *

When I say that I think that humanism is breaking up, and that a new period is commencing, I should like to guard against exaggeration by two reservations.

(1) I do not in the least imagine that humanism is breaking up merely to make place for a new mediaevalism. The only thing the new period will have in common with mediaevalism will be the subordination of man to certain absolute values. The analogy of art may again help us here. Both Byzantine and Egyptian art spring from an attitude towards life which made it impossible to use the accidental shapes of living things as symbols of the divine. Both consequently are geometrical in character; but with this very general quality the resemblance ends. Compare a Byzantine relief of the best period with the design on a Greek vase, and an Egyptian relief. The abstract geometrical char-

acter of the Byzantine relief makes it much nearer to the Egyptian than to the Greek work; yet a certain elegance in the line-ornament shows that it has developed out of the Greek. If the Greek had never existed it could not have the character it has. In the same way, a new anti-humanist ideology could not be a mere revival of mediaevalism. The humanist period has developed an honesty in science and a certain conception of freedom of thought and action which will remain.

(2) I do not imagine that men themselves will change in any way. Men differ very little in every period. It is only our categories that change. Whatever we may think of sin, we shall always be sensual. Men of different sorts exist in constant proportion in different generations. But different circumstances, different prevailing ideologies, bring different types to the top. Exactly the same type existed in the Middle Ages as now. This constancy of man thus provides perhaps the greatest hope of the possibility of a radical transformation of society.

THE RENASCENCE. – For an understanding of the way in which everything really depends on these abstract conceptions of the nature of man a study of the Renascence is important.

The best-known work on the Renascence, while valuable historically, seems to me to miss the whole point, for this reason: It describes the emergence of the new attitude towards life, of the new conception of man, as it might describe the gradual discovery of the conception of gravitation – that is, as the gradual emergence of something which once established would remain always, the period before being characterised thus as a *privation* of the new thing. The whole point of the thing is missed if we do not recognise that the new attitude towards man at the Renascence was thus just an *attitude*, one attitude amongst other possible ones, deliberately chosen. It is better to describe it as a heresy, a mistaken adoption of false conceptions.

* * *

In an account of the Renascence three things should be noticed:

(1) The changed conception itself, the putting of the Perfection into man, man no longer endowed with original sin, but by nature good. In Machiavelli you get the conception of human nature as a natural power, a living energy. Mankind is not by nature bad, but subject to

passions. The absolute standards in comparison with which man was sinful disappear, and life itself, is *accepted* as the measure of all values. You get Lorenzo Valla (1407) in his *De Voluptate*, daring to assert for the first time that pleasure was the highest good. A secondary consequence of this acceptance of life is the development of the conception of personality. The stages in this emphasis on the individual from Petrarch (1304) to Montaigne can be easily followed. Michelet writes, 'To the discovery of the outward world the Renascence added a still greater achievement by bringing to light the full, the whole nature of man.' This is ridiculous. The proper way to put the matter is to say that the decay into a false conception of values did in this way bring certain compensations with it.

(2) So with the establishment of the new conception of man as good, with the conception of personality comes an increased interest in the actual characteristics of man. This is at first merely manifested directly in literature. You get autobiographies for the first time – those of Cellini and Cardano, for example. It leads later, however, to more direct study of man's emotions and character, of what we should call psychology. You get works like Vives, *De Anima*, and Telesio, *De Rerum Natura*.

(3) This new study of man, this new psychology, or anthropology, has considerable influence on the philosophers who provided a conceptual clothing for the new attitude, and worked out its consequences in ethics and politics... on Descartes, Hobbes, and Spinoza, for example.

This process is worth while following in considerable detail for the following reason: It is necessary to emphasise how very coherent in thought such periods are, everything being in them really dependent on certain instinctive ways of judging, which, for the period, have the status of natural categories of the mind. The moderns, whether philosophers or reformers, make constant appeals to certain ideals, which they assume everybody will admit as natural and inevitable for the emancipated man. What these are you may discover from peroration of speeches – even from scrap books. 'To thine own true self, etc... Over the portal of the new world, *Be Thyself* shall be written... Culture is not satisfied till we all come to a perfect man... the free growth of personality' – and so on. We think these things not because they are inevitable ways of thinking, but because we absorb them unconsciously from the humanist tradition which moulds the actual apparatus of our thought. They can all be traced back to the Stoics, Epicureans, and Pantheists of the Renascence. The detailed exposition of the process by which this attitude was gradually embodied in the conceptional apparatus we inherit may do more than anything else to convince us how very far it is from being an inevitable attitude.

PARTIAL REACTIONS. – It is important to distinguish two stages inside the modern period – *humanism* properly so called, and *romanticism*. The new conception of man as fundamentally good manifests itself at first in a more heroic form. In art, Donatello, Michael Angelo, or Marlowe might stand for this period. I do not deny that humanism of this kind has a certain attraction. But it deserves no admiration, for it bears in itself the seed which is bound inevitably later to develop into sentimental, utilitarian romanticism. Such humanism could have no permanence; however heroic at the start, it was bound sooner or later to end in Rousseau. There is the parallel development in art. Just as humanism leads to Rousseau so Michael Angelo leads to Greuze.

There are people who, disgusted with romanticism, wish for us to go back to the classical period, or who, like Nietzsche, wish us to admire the Renascence. But such partial reactions will always fail, for they are only half measures – it is no good returning to humanism, for that will itself degenerate into romanticism.

* * *

This is one type of an *inadequate reaction* against humanism. There are at the present many indications of other *partial* reactions. In philosophy and ethics, for example, the work of Moore and Husserl, which is often attacked as a kind of scholasticism. A complete reaction from the subjectivism and relativism of humanist ethics should contain two elements: (1) the establishment of the *objective* character of ethical values, (2) a satisfactory ethic not only looks on values as *objective*, but establishes an order or *hierarchy* among such values, which it also regards as absolute and objective.

Now while the school of Moore and Husserl break the humanist tradition in the first matter, they seem to continue it quite uncritically in the second. In as far, then, as they free ethical values from the anthropomorphism involved in their dependence on human desires and feeling, they have created the machinery of an anti-humanist reaction which will proceed much further than they ever intended.

THE RELIGIOUS ATTITUDE. – In discussing the religious as contrasted with the humanist attitude, in my last notes, I said, 'While it tends to find expression in myth it is independent of myth; it is, however, much more intimately connected with dogma.' I want to make this clearer by a more detailed account of what I mean by 'an attitude' in this context.

* * *

The main purpose of these notes is a practical one. I want to show that certain generally held 'principles' are false. But the only method of controversy in any such fundamental matter of dispute is an 'abstract' one; a method which deals with the abstract conceptions on which opinions really rest.

You think A is true; I ask why. You reply, that it follows from B. But why is B true, because it follows from C, and so on. You get finally to some very abstract attitude (h) which you assume to be self-evidently true. This is the central conception from which more detailed opinion about political principles, for example, proceeds. Now if your opponent reasons correctly, and you are unable to show that he has falsely deduced A from B, then you are driven to the abstract plane of (h), for it is here that the difference between you really has its root. And it is only on this abstract plane that a discussion on any fundamental divergence of opinion can usefully be carried on.

* * *

Any attempt to change (h), however, should be prefaced by some account of the nature of such abstract attitudes, and the process by which we come to adopt them.

It is possible to trace, in every man's mind, then, trains leading in various directions, from his detailed ethical and political opinions, back to a few of these central attitudes.

A. . . . B. . . . . c. . . . . g. . . . . (h)

Instead, of the first concrete statement 'A is true', we might have 'A is good'; in which case (h) would be an ultimate *value*; the process, however, is the same. Another metaphor, by which we may describe the place of (h) in our thought, is to compare it to the axes, to which we refer the position of a moving point, or the framework, on which A and B are based. This is, perhaps, a better description, for the framework, inside which we live, is something *we take for granted*; and in ordinary life we are very seldom conscious of (h). We are only led up to it by this dialectical questioning, described above. All our 'principles' are based on some unconscious 'framework' of this kind. As a rule, then, we are quite unconscious of (h), we are only conscious of the detailed principles A and B, derived from it. Now while we probably acquire the opinions A and B consciously, the same is not true of (h). How do we come to hold it, then? For we did not produce it ourselves, but derived it ready made from society. It came to be an essential part of our mind without our being conscious of it, because it was already implicit, in all the more detailed opinions, A and B, society forced upon us. It was embedded in the actual matter of our thought, and as natural to us as the air; in fact, it is the air that all these more concrete beliefs breathe. We thus have forced upon us, unconsciously, the whole apparatus of categories, in terms of which all our thinking must be done. The result of (h) having in this way the character of a category, is that it makes us see (A) not as an opinion, but as a fact. We never see (h) for we see all things *through* (h).

In this way these abstract categories, of course, *limit* our thinking; our thought is compelled to move inside certain limits. We find, then, in people whose mental apparatus is based on (h) while ours is not, a certain obstinacy of intellect, a radical opposition, and incapacity to see things which, to us, are simple.

Now the limitation imposed on our thinking by such categories is sometimes quite legitimate. Some categories are objective. We cannot think of things outside of space and time, and it is quite right that we are subject to this limitation.

But (h) often belongs to the large class of pseudo-categories – categories which are not objective, and it is these that I wish to deal with here. They are exceedingly important, for the difference between the mentality of one great period of history and another really depends on the different pseudo-categories of this kind, which were imposed on every individual of the period, and in terms of which his thinking was consequently done. It is not difficult to find examples of this.

(1) A Brazilian Indian told a missionary that he was a red parrot. The missionary endeavoured to give some explanation of this statement. You mean, he said, that when you die you will *become* a red parrot, or that you are in some way related to this bird. The Indian rejected both these plausible attempts to explain away a perfectly simple fact, and repeated quite *coldly* that he *was* a red parrot. There would seem to be an impasse here then; the missionary was *baffled* in the same way as the humanist is, by the conception of sin. The explanation given by Lévy Bruhl, who quotes the story, is that the Indian, has imposed on him by his group a conception of the nature of an object, which differs radically from ours. For him an object can be something else without at the same time ceasing to be itself. The accuracy of this explanation need not detain us. The point is that it serves as an illustration of the way in which minds dominated by *different* pseudo-categories, may have a very *different* perception of fact.

(2) Greek. It has been recently argued that the only way to understand early Greek philosophy is to realise that it continued on the plane of speculation the categories, the ways of thinking that had earlier created Greek religion, … the conception of *Moira*, to which even the gods submitted, … etc. The difference between the religious attitude and myth is here quite clear.

The more intimate connection with dogmas I referred to, depends on the fact that dogma is often a fairly intellectual way of expressing these fundamental categories – the dogma of Original Sin, for example. At the Renascence, in spite of opinion to the contrary, the philosophy did not express the categories, the ways of thinking which had earlier been expressed in the Christian religion; it reversed them.

* * *

It is these categories, these abstract conceptions, which all the individuals of a period have in common, which really serve best to characterise the period. For most of the characteristics of such a period, not only in thought, but in ethics, and through ethics in economics, really depend on these central abstract attitudes. But while people will readily acknowledge that this is true of the Greeks, or of Brazilian Indians, they have considerable difficulty in realising that it is also true of the modern humanist period from the Renascence to now. The way in which we instinctively judge things we take to be the inevitable way of judging things. The pseudo-categories of the humanist attitude are thought to be on the same footing as the objective categories of space and time. It is thought to be impossible for an emancipated man to think sincerely in the categories of the religious attitude.

The reason for this is to be found in the fact noticed earlier in the 'Note' that we are, as a rule, unconscious of the very abstract conceptions which underlie our more concrete opinions. What Ferrier says of real categories, 'Categories may be operative when their existence is not consciously recognised. First principles of every kind have their influence, and, indeed, operate largely and profoundly long before they come to the surface of human thought, and are articulately expounded,' is true also of these pseudo-categories. We are only conscious of A, B,... and very seldom of (h). We do not see that, but other things *through* it; and, consequently, take what we see for facts, and not for what they are – opinions based on a particular abstract valuation. This is certainly true of the *progressive* ideology founded on the conception of man as fundamentally good.

* * *

It is this unconsciousness of these central abstract conceptions, leading us to suppose that the judgments of value founded on them are *natural* and *inevitable*, which makes it so difficult for anyone in the humanist tradition to look at the religious attitude as anything but a sentimental survival.

But I want to emphasise as clearly as I can, that I attach very little value indeed to the *sentiments* attaching to the religious attitude. I hold, quite coldly and intellectually as it were, that the way of thinking about the world and man, the conception of sin, and the categories which ultimately make up the religious attitude, are the *true* categories and the *right* way of thinking.

I might incidentally note here, that the way in which I have explained the action of the central abstract attitudes and ways of thinking, and the use of the word *pseudo*-categories, might suggest that I hold relativist views about their validity. But I don't. I hold the religious conception of ultimate values to be right, the humanist wrong. From the nature of things, these categories are not inevitable, like the categories of time and space, but are *equally objective*. In speaking of religion, it is to this level of abstraction that I wish to refer. I have none of the feelings of *nostalgie*, the reverence for tradition, the desire to recapture the sentiment of Fra Angelico, which seems to animate most modern defenders of religion. All that seems to me to be bosh. What is important, is what nobody seems to realise – the dogmas like that of Original Sin, which are the closest expression of the categories of the religious attitude. That man is in no sense perfect, but a wretched creature, who can yet apprehend perfection. It is not, then, that I put up with the dogma for the sake of the sentiment, but that I may possibly swallow the sentiment for the sake of the dogma. Very few since the Renascence have really understood the dogma, certainly very few inside the Churches of recent years. If they appear occasionally even fanatical about the very word of the dogma, that is only a secondary result of belief really grounded on sentiment. Certainly no humanist could understand the dogma. They all chatter about matters which are in comparison with this, quite secondary notions – God, Freedom, and Immortality.

* * *

The important thing about all this – which I hope to make clearer when I come to deal with its effect on literature – is that this attitude is not merely a *contrasted* attitude, which I am interested in, as it were, for purpose of *symmetry* in historical exposition, but a real attitude, perfectly possible for us today. To see this is a kind of conversion. It radically alters our physical perception almost; so that the world takes on an entirely different aspect.

Notes

Poems and Fragments

1. Hulme published six poems in his lifetime. 'A City Sunset' and 'Autumn' appeared in January 1909 in *For Christmas MDCCCCVIII*, published by the Poets' Club. 'The Embankment' and 'Conversion' appeared in the Poets' Club's second volume, *The Book of the Poets' Club* in December of that year. *The New Age* published 'Autumn', 'The Embankment' and 'Conversion' on 25 January 1912, along with two further poems, 'Mana Aboda' and 'Above the Dock', under the title 'The Complete Poetical Works of T.E. Hulme'. Ezra Pound published them later that year in his collection *Ripostes*, writing in his prefatory note: 'In publishing his *Complete Poetical Works* at thirty, Mr Hulme has set an enviable example to many of his contemporaries who have had less to say.' These versions are based on those published by Alun R. Jones in *The Life and Opinions of T.E. Hulme*, for which Jones uses Hulme's manuscripts and the 'Fragments' published after his death. I have stayed with Jones's titles, but have added one poem from the 'Fragments': 'Now though the skirt be fallen'.
2. This poem occurs in Ezra Pound's *Catholic Anthology* (1915), and is reprinted in Jones, p. 182.
3. These appeared in *The New Age*, 29 (6 October, 1921) beneath the heading 'Fragments (From the Notebooks of T.E. Hulme, who was killed in the war)'.

Belated Romanticism

1. F.S. Flint (1885–1960), English poet and critic, Imagist and colleague of Pound and Eliot. Flint was greatly responsible for introducing modern French poetry to English readers. His substantial article, 'Contemporary French Poets', appeared in *Poetry and Drama* in 1912. Despite their unpropitious first encounter, Hulme and Flint became friends, and it was Flint who helped Hulme translate Sorel's *Réflexions sur la violence*.

Cinders

1. These notes, in which Hulme intended to set out his 'personal philosophy, cast into an allegorical form' (Herbert Read), were begun in 1906–7. The title is Hulme's own. Read edited a slightly different version in four instalments in *The New Age* in 1922 (19, 26 January; 9, 16 February), entitled 'The Note-Books of T.E. Hulme'. The protagonist of Hulme's 'allegorical' philosophical writing was probably the figure of 'Aphra', who emerges later in the notes.
2. Hulme's 'Preface' appears in the fourth instalment of the abovementioned version. Read prints it at the beginning of *Speculations* as 'A Preface by the Author'.

Notes on Language and Style

1. These notes were probably written around 1907. Herbert Read published about half of them in the *Criterion* in July 1925, and again in the Washington Chapbook series in 1929.
2. Hulme illustrates this by a little sketch of a curve rising above a fixed horizontal line (the level of *meaning*) and falling again. [Roberts's note]
3. The Greek, as used by Aristotle, for 'matter' or 'material': *hule energes*, meaning the active or productive 'raw material'.
4. Hulme has two little sketches, one a small central squiggle with half a dozen radiating strokes, the other a small rectangle like a frame. [Roberts's note]
5. Hulme has a small sketch of one circle rolling inside another. [Roberts's note]

A Lecture on Modern Poetry

1. This lecture was probably given to the Poets' Club in 1908, and was not published during Hulme's lifetime.
2. The French 'Parnassian' poets preceded the Symbolists. Their verse is characteristically impassive and formal, and often classical in subject-matter. Major poets of this *école* include Gautier and Leconte de Lisle, though Verlaine and Mallarmé also appeared in Parnassian anthologies during the late 1860s. Hulme expands on the limitations of 'Parnassian' poetry, and the development of Symbolist and post-Symbolist poetry, in his review of Tancrède de Visan's *L'Attitude du lyrisme contemporain*.
3. Gustave Kahn (1859–1936), French Symbolist poet, critic and promoter of *vers libre*.
4. *Poiema*: Poem.
5. James Abbott MacNeill Whistler (1834–1903), American painter who settled in Europe and became associated both with the Pre-Raphaelites and with the Symbolists. It is probable, given the way Hulme continues, that he had Whistler's *Nocturnes* in mind.
6. *Hule [energes]*.

Romanticism and Classicism

1. One of Hulme's most anthologised pieces, this was probably prepared as a lecture and written around 1911 or early 1912. It is dateable from the reference to René Fauchois's lectures on Racine, which took place in Paris in autumn 1910.
2. The distinction between Imagination and Fancy was made by Coleridge in *Biographia Litteraria* (1817).
3. Charles Maurras (1868–1952) and Pierre Lasserre (1867–1930) were leading figures in the French reactionary political movement l'Action française, founded in the wake of the Dreyfus case. Lasserre's influential *Le Romantisme français* appeared in 1907, and deeply impressed Hulme, who refers to it on numerous occasions. Lasserre contends that Rousseau and Romanticism were responsible for the intellectual and political decadence of the late nineteenth century, and advocates, as Hulme was to do, a 'Classical' antidote. Hulme met Lasserre in 1911, and gives an account of their meeting in *The New Age* of 9 November 1911

('Mr Balfour, Bergson and Politics'), during which Lasserre 'endeavoured to prove to me that Bergsonism was nothing but the last disguise of romanticism'.

4. Hulme misquotes Shakespeare, and the lines should read: 'Golden lads and girls all must,/ As chimney-sweepers, come to dust' (*Cymbeline*, 4.2.263).

5. Hulme is misquoting Bosola's song in Webster's *The Duchess of Malfi*, IV, 2. The line should read: 'End your groan and come away.'

6. John Ruskin (1819–1900), the Victorian art and social critic, published *Modern Painters* from 1843 to 1860.

7. Robert Herrick (1591–1674); the phrase is from his poem 'Delight in Disorder'.

8. John Donne, 'Elegie: To his Mistris Going to Bed'.

Review of Tancrède de Visan's L'Attitude du lyrisme contemporain

1. Tancrède de Visan, French poet and critic, published *L'Attitude du lyrisme contemporain* in 1911. Visan's book is both a history and a theory of Symbolism, based on the adaptation and extension of Bergson's philosophy to the poetic process.

German Chronicle

1. Brooke's poem 'The Old Vicarage, Granchester' has as its date-line 'Café des Westens, Berlin, May 1912'.

2. '[To get] away from Naturalism'.

3. 'Snootiness'

4. 'Sunset', by Ernst Blass (1890–1939): 'I still dream of lands where red/ Palace façades stare like faces./ The moon hangs, full of itself,/ Does it know of the dead?/ I walk along the soft beach/ sidelong among acquaintances. (Did lions not scream once?)/ From the coffee garden music comes, / The large sun rides with silken seagulls/ Over the sea.'

5. 'An Old Tibetan Carpet', by Else Laske-Schüler (1869–1945): 'Your soul in love with mine/ is entwined with it in the Tibetan carpet,// Strand in strand, colours in love, / Stars which wooed each other across the skies. // Our feet rest on that preciousness/ Thousands and thousands of stitches wide.// Sweet llama's son on your musk-plant throne, / For how long has your mouth been kissing mine, / And cheek by cheek, the ages joined together in colour?'

6. Georg Heym (1887–1912): 'Pitched barrels rolled from the thresholds of dark store-houses onto the high barges./ The tugs pulled in. The smoke's mane/ Hung sootily down onto the oily waves.// Two steamers came with music bands./ They cut off their chimney on the arch of the bridge./ Smoke, soot, stink lay on the dirty waves/ Of the tanneries with the brown skins.// On every bridge, beneath us the barge/ Was driven through, the signals sounded/ like drumbeats, growing in the quietness.// We set off and slowly went along the canals/ Past the gardens. In the idyll/ we saw the dark funnel of the huge chimneys.'

7. From 'Cloister', by Arthur Drey: 'And walls stand without moving/ Like grey fists that freeze in the wind'.

8. 'On Friedrichstrasse at Sunset', by René Schickele (1883–1940): 'On the corner stands a man/ His face transfigured./ You push him/ He does not notice.// Stares upwards with a pale look/ Arms limp at his side./ His fate becomes more deeply formed/ And the sky more colourful.'

Modern Art and Its Philosophy

1. Given as a lecture to the Quest Society in London on 22 January 1914.
2. Jacob Epstein (1880–1959), British sculptor. Hulme included 'Rock-Drill' in his 'Contemporary Drawings' series for *The New Age*.
3. Paul Ernst (1866–1933), German writer and critic, advocate of neo-classicism.
4. Alois Riegl (1858–1905), Austrian art historian.
5. Wilhelm Worringer, author of *Abstraktion und Einfühlung* (*Abstraction and Empathy*), which appeared in 1908.
6. Jean Metzinger (1883–1956), French artist and co-author of *Du Cubisme* (1912).
7. Percy Wyndham Lewis (1884–1957), English artist and writer, founder of the 'Rebel Art Centre', *Blast*, and founding member of the 'Vorticists'.

Mr Epstein and the Critics

1. Epstein was exhibiting at the Twenty-One gallery in London. The review by Anthony Ludovici to which Hulme responds appeared in *The New Age* in December 1913.
2. The 'New English Art Club' was founded in 1886, and included Steer, John and Sickert, to whom Hulme refers.

Modern Art I: The Grafton Group

1. The Grafton Group, an amalgamation of Roger Fry's Friday Club and Sickert's Camden Town Group, exhibited at the Alpine Gallery in London. Wyndham Lewis was a member of the Camden Town Group, but broke away in 1913 to form the London Group.
2. Frederick Etchells (1886–1973), English artist. He took part in the 1915 Vorticist exhibition.
3. Christopher Nevinson (1889–1946), English artist. Hulme included one of his drawings in 'Contemporary Drawings'.
4. William Roberts (1895–1980), English artist. Roberts became a member of the Vorticist movement and painted the famous picture 'The Vorticists in the Eiffel Tower Restaurant'. Hulme included one of his drawings in 'Contemporary Drawings'.
5. Henri Gaudier-Brzeska (1891–1915), French sculptor, was killed in action in Neuville St. Vaast. His 'Vortex Gaudier Brzeska (Written from the Trenches)' appeared in *Blast* (No. 2, July 1915). Hulme included one of his drawings in 'Contemporary Drawings'.

Modern Art II: A Preface Note and Neo-Realism

1. Hulme's article refers to a piece by the English painter Charles Ginner (1879–1952) entitled 'Neo-Realism', which appeared in *The New Age* in January 1914.

Modern Art III: The London Group

1. This eclectic exhibition included such diverse artists as Wyndham Lewis and Spencer Gore.
2. Wassily Kandinsky (1866–1944), Russian painter and author of *Concerning the Spiritual in Art* (*Über das Geistige in der Kunst*), written in 1910.
3. Edward Wadsworth (1881–1949), English artist. Hulme included 'Farmyard' in 'Contemporary Drawings'.
4. David Bomberg (1890–1957), English painter. Hulme included 'Chinnereth' in Contemporary Drawings'.

Modern Art IV: Mr David Bomberg's Show

1. The Rebel Art Centre, organised by Wyndham Lewis in 1914, closed a few months after opening, but was a focal-point for the activities which later centred around *Blast* and Vorticism.

A Tory Philosophy

1. The article is also published in Alun R. Jones, *The Life and Opinions of T.E. Hulme*.

Preface to Reflections on Violence

1. Georges Sorel (1847–1922), French Syndicalist and former socialist. Hulme's introduction was first published in slightly diferent form in *The New Age* 17/24 (14 October 1915).
2. Pierre Joseph Proudhon (1808–65), French anarchist thinker. The French translates as follows: 'If, by mistake, nature had made man into an exclusively industrious and sociable animal, and not at all belligerent, he would have fallen, from the first day, to the level of the beasts, whose association forms all destiny; he would have lost, along with the pride of his heroism, his revolutionary faculty, the most marvellous of all faculties and the richest. If we lived in pure community, our society would be a stable... Philanthropist, you talk about abolishing war, be careful of degrading the human species...'. Both Sorel and Proudhon attack Romanticism, but from positions that, though reactionary, cannot be construed as right-wing.

A Notebook

1. An abridged version of this series was published by Herbert Read in *Speculations* with the title 'Humanism and the Religious Attitude'.
2. 'Into your eyes I gaze, O Life'
3. Benedetto Croce (1866–1952), Italian philosopher, historian and critic. His aesthetic theory cultivated the idea of art as 'lyrical intuition'.
4. Alexius Meinong (1853–1920), Austrian philosopher.
5. Bertrand Russell (1872–1970), English philosopher, who wrote on aesthetics, politics, religion, economics and education. Between January and March 1914 Hulme, writing under the *nom de plume* 'North Staffs', entered into a dispute with Russell over pacifism in *The Cambridge Magazine* and *The New Age*.
6. Edmund Husserl (1859–1938), German philosopher who developed phenomenology into a non-empirical science. The German translates as: 'They thus separate clearly from each other: *Weltanschauung* philosophy and scientific philosophy are two ideas which are in a certain way associated, but which are not to be combined.'
7. G.E. Moore (1873–1958), English moral philosopher and Cambridge professor.

Index

Fyfield*Books*

Two millennia of essential classics

The extensive Fyfield*Books* list includes

Djuna Barnes *The Book of Repulsive Women and other poems*
edited by Rebecca Loncraine

Elizabeth Barrett Browning *Selected Poems* edited by Malcolm Hicks

Charles Baudelaire *Complete Poems in French and English*
translated by Walter Martin

Thomas Lovell Beddoes *Death's Jest-Book* edited by Michael Bradshaw

Aphra Behn *Selected Poems*
edited by Malcolm Hicks

Border Ballads: A Selection
edited by James Reed

The Brontë Sisters *Selected Poems*
edited by Stevie Davies

Sir Thomas Browne *Selected Writings*
edited by Claire Preston

Lewis Carroll *Selected Poems*
edited by Keith Silver

Paul Celan *Collected Prose*
translated by Rosmarie Waldrop

Thomas Chatterton *Selected Poems*
edited by Grevel Lindop

John Clare *By Himself*
edited by Eric Robinson and David Powell

Arthur Hugh Clough *Selected Poems*
edited by Shirley Chew

Samuel Taylor Coleridge *Selected Poetry* edited by William Empson and David Pirie

Tristan Corbière *The Centenary Corbière in French and English*
translated by Val Warner

William Cowper *Selected Poems*
edited by Nick Rhodes

Gabriele d'Annunzio *Halcyon*
translated by J.G. Nichols

John Donne *Selected Letters*
edited by P.M. Oliver

William Dunbar *Selected Poems*
edited by Harriet Harvey Wood

Anne Finch, Countess of Winchilsea *Selected Poems*
edited by Denys Thompson

Ford Madox Ford *Selected Poems*
edited by Max Saunders

John Gay *Selected Poems*
edited by Marcus Walsh

Oliver Goldsmith *Selected Writings*
edited by John Lucas

Robert Herrick *Selected Poems*
edited by David Jesson-Dibley

Victor Hugo *Selected Poetry in French and English*
translated by Steven Monte

T.E. Hulme *Selected Writings*
edited by Patrick McGuinness

Leigh Hunt *Selected Writings*
edited by David Jesson Dibley

Wyndham Lewis *Collected Poems and Plays* edited by Alan Munton

Charles Lamb *Selected Writings*
edited by J.E. Morpurgo

Lucretius *De Rerum Natura: The Poem on Nature*
translated by C.H. Sisson

For more information, including a full list of Fyfield*Books* and a contents list for each title, and details of how to order the books in the UK, visit the Fyfield website at www.fyfieldbooks.co.uk or email info@fyfieldbooks.co.uk. For information about Fyfield*Books* available in the United States and Canada, visit the Routledge website at www.routledge-ny.com.